Perspective in Whitehead's Metaphysics

SUNY Series in Systematic Philosophy
Robert C. Neville, EDITOR

Whether systematic philosophies are intended as true pictures of the world, as hypotheses, as the dialectic of history, or as heuristic devices for relating rationally to a multitude of things, they each constitute articulated ways by which experience can be ordered, and as such they are contributions to culture. One does not have to choose between Plato and Aristotle to appreciate that Western civilization is enriched by the Platonic as well as Aristotelian ways of seeing things.

The term "systematic philosophy" can be applied to any philosophical enterprise that functions with a perspective from which everything can be addressed. Sometimes this takes the form of an attempt to spell out the basic features of things in a system. Other times it means the examination of a limited subject from the many angles of a context formed by a systematic perspective. In either case systematic philosophy takes explicit or implicit responsibility for the assessment of its unifying perspective and for what is seen from it. The styles of philosophy according to which systematic philosophy can be practiced are as diverse as the achievements of the great philosophers in history, and doubtless new styles are needed for our time.

Yet systematic philosophy has not been a popular approach during this century of philosophical professionalism. It is the purpose of this series to stimulate and publish new systematic works employing the techniques and advances in philosophical reflection made during this century. The series is committed to no philosophical school or doctrine, nor to any limited style of systematic thinking. Whether the systematic achievements of previous centuries can be equalled in the twentieth depends on the emergence of forms of systematic philosophy appropriate to our times. The current resurgence of interest in the project deserves the cultivation it may receive from the SUNY Series in Systematic Philosophy.

Perspective In
Whitehead's Metaphysics

Stephen David Ross

PROFESSOR OF PHILOSOPHY
STATE UNIVERSITY OF NEW YORK AT BINGHAMTON

State University of New York Press   •   Albany

Acknowledgments

Excerpts from the following books by Alfred North Whitehead are reprinted with permission of Macmillan Publishing Co., Inc.:

Process and Reality, Corrected Edition. Edited by David Ray Griffin and Donald W. Sherburne. Copyright © 1978 by The Free Press, a Division of Macmillan Publishing Co., Inc. Copyright 1929 by Macmillan Publishing Co., Inc., renewed 1957 by Evelyn Whitehead.

Adventures of Ideas (Copyright 1933 by Macmillan Publishing Co., Inc., renewed 1961 by Evelyn Whitehead)

Modes of Thought (Copyright 1938 by Macmillan Publishing Co., Inc., renewed 1966 by T. North Whitehead)

Science and the Modern World (Copyright 1925 by Macmillan Publishing Co., Inc., renewed 1953 by Evelyn Whitehead)

Symbolism (Copyright 1927 by Macmillan Publishing Co., Inc., renewed 1955 by Evelyn Whitehead)

Published by State University of New York Press, Albany

© 1983 State University of New York

For information, address State University of New York Press, State University Plaza, Albany, N.Y., 12246

Library of Congress Cataloging in Publication Data

Ross, Stephen David.
Perspective in Whitehead's metaphysics.

Includes bibliographical references and index.
1. Whitehead, Alfred North, 1861–1947—Metaphysics.
2. Metaphysics—History—20th century.   I. Title.
B1674.W354R65   1982   110   82-8332
ISBN 0-87395-657-5   AACR2
ISBN 0-87395-658-3 (pbk.)

10 9 8 7 6 5 4 3 2 1

CONTENTS

v

PREFACE

In his remarkable description of *speculative philosophy*, in the first chapter of *Process and Reality*, Whitehead makes no mention of the quality in which his own work excels: that of vision or wonder.[1] In a philosophy indebted so heavily to Plato, this is an unfortunate omission. No one willing to submit to the rigors of a system of novel metaphysical categories can remain untouched by the power of Whitehead's vision. Yet few works of philosophy place such extraordinary demands upon their readers. Few philosophers demand that their readers so completely re-evaluate their prior commitments and preconceptions.

Process and Reality is particularly overwhelming in what Whitehead calls its *coherence* and *adequacy*. Its principles are profoundly interconnected. Remarkably diverse issues are grounded in common principles. Among these principles is one which I believe to be the key to Whitehead's philosophy—the *principle of perspective*: being as perspective. It represents an important and novel approach to metaphysics, and has been acknowledged incompletely by many of Whitehead's commentators.[2] I will argue, however, that it must be carried much further than Whitehead's recent commentators have taken it; that it is fundamental to most of Whitehead's thought, an interpretive principle that establishes a coherent and intelligible thread throughout his system, and that it constitutes a basis for criticizing his entire cosmological vision, for he does not in fact carry the principle of being in perspective far enough.[3]

The issue, here, is one of cosmology. A central strain in Whitehead's thought is that of the oneness of the world, consummated in God's primordial conception of all forms of definiteness in one comprehensive valuation and in his consequent synthesis of all actualities in his complete satisfaction.

There is finitude—unless this were true, infinity would have no meaning. The contrast of finitude and infinity arises from the fundamental metaphysical truth that every entity involves an indefinite array of perspectives, each perspective expressing a finite characteristic of that entity. But any one finite perspective does not enable an entity to shake off its essential connection with totality. The infinite background always remains as the unanalyzed reason why that finite perspective of that entity has the special characteristic that it does have. (Whitehead 1951a, p. 682)

There is, I will argue, a continual tension between these two fundamental strains in Whitehead's thought: the perspectivity of being and the unity of the world. Indeed, I will argue further that perspectivity and cosmology are incompatible, that perspectives are always limited and conditioned (though not *finite*) while cosmology, even without monism, is wedded to totality, unlimitedness and unconditionedness. Nevertheless, no philosopher has been more successful than Whitehead in mating plurality of beings (in perspectives) with a comprehensive cosmological synthesis. Whitehead here is the major synthetic philosopher of the twentieth century, the culmination of all that has gone before. Yet the difficulties for his thought that are engendered by the cosmological principle that there is a totality or unity to the world suggest that a very different, but perhaps more effective, theory may be established on the basis of his other fundamental principle: that being is perspective.[4]

The following chapters represent a unified interpretation of Whitehead's mature thought, largely in terms of *Process and Reality*, based fundamentally on the principle of being-in-perspective and its pervasive tension with the cosmological principle. The primary aim of this study is to define a systematic interpretation of Whitehead's metaphysics. I will argue that the enduring contribution Whitehead has made to the future of metaphysics lies in his principle of perspective, which he was the first to employ in a systematic theory, and that his reputation has suffered to the extent that this principle has not been fully acknowledged at an adequate level of generality.

It will be both necessary and natural, in this context, to explore the limitations and difficulties Whitehead faces in trying to mate the principle of perspective with the cosmological principle, and to show how the principle of perspective may be carried even further than he carries it, to a very different metaphysical point of view, devoid of cosmological commitments. Yet this point of view—I call it "ordinal"—could not have been developed without Whitehead's understanding of perspectival being. In this respect, I intend above all too pay homage to one of the giants of philosophic thought.

Notes to Preface

1. Alfred North Whitehead, *Process and Reality*, ed. D. R. Griffin and D. W. Sherburne, corr. ed. (New York: Free Press) (hereafter cited as PR).

2. See Elizabeth Kraus (1979):

> When a volume is an object of conscious experience, it possesses a unity of structure of a different sort—not the sort of structure which would be grasped by a privileged observer in his view from no viewpoint, but a structure unique to each possible perspective within the volume.
>
> Furthermore, each position *is* the perspective which it takes on the other included subvolumes. In other words, the structure of the volume from the perspective constitutes the perspective.... The aspect *from* the perspective enters into the constitution *of* the perspective. Therefore, it is equally true that the togetherness of the perspectival aspects constitutes the perspective and that the perspective "decides" the aspects. Each is what the other makes it to be. (Pp. 18–19)
>
> The multiplicity of aspects which is the world from a possible perspective is woven together in the determinate structure which constitutes the perspective as real.... An actual entity is a realized perspectival harmonization of the world. (Pp. 21–22)

An approach to Whitehead's theory somewhat similar to mine can be found in *Whitehead's Ontology*, by John Lango: "I maintain ... that the types of entity in Whitehead's ontology are defined by a principle of being.... his types of entity are defined by the principle that entities have being for one another" (1972, p. 1). This principle of *being-for-another* Lango calls "synonty." There is some similarity between synonty and the principle of perspective, but it is minimal, since perspectivity is intensely plural as synonty cannot be. Perspectivity is always being for many others and being through many others, but includes reciprocity and inexhaustibility of identity. The closest Lango comes to perspectivity is his recognition that multiadic relations are essential to synonty and perspective. "Substance ... has inspired the use of the logic of (monadic) properties; conversely, Whitehead's view that process is fundamental ... motivates the use of the logic of (dyadic) relations" (1972, p. 11). Perspectivity is, however, far more complex, technically and metaphysically, than is synonty. It is a fusion of limits, conditions, and inexhaustible uniqueness.

3. A remarkable awareness of the principle of perspective can be found in the writings of George Herbert Mead and Arthur A. Murphy of over fifty years ago. Perspectives, here, are "objective" and "real": "there in nature." "What I wish to pick out of Professor Whitehead's philosophy of nature is this conception of nature as an organization of perspectives, which are there in nature" (Mead 1959, p. 163). Lovejoy's criticisms of "objective relativism," in *The Revolt*

Agaisnt Dualism (1930, chs. 3, 4), would have been far less effective against Dewey's, Whitehead's, and Mead's "objective perspectivism" if Lovejoy had fully understood the nature of perspectival relativity.

Mead understood the richness and power of perspectivity for Whitehead's organic and social theory: "It is only in so far as the individual acts not only in his own perspective but also in the perspective of others, especially in the common perspective of a group, that a society arises. . . . The individual enters into the perspectives of others, in so far as he is able to take their attitudes, or occupy their points of view" (1959, p, 165). "It is the relation of the individual perspective to the common perspective that is of importance" (P. 167). Perspectivity absorbs within it as species of a genus Whitehead's generalized principle of experience. The "process, in which a perspective ceases to be objective, becomes if you like subjective, and in which new common minds and new common perspectives arise, is an instance of the origination of perspectives in nature, of the creative advance of nature" (P. 172).

By far the most sweeping and penetrating account of Whitehead's perspectivism prior to my treatment here is to be found in Arthur A. Murphy. Murphy apparently coined the phrase "objective relativism," which

> attempts to unite two propositions which have uniformly been taken to be incompatible. (a) The objective facts of the world of nature and of reality are the very "apparent" and relative happenings directly observed by us in perception. (b) In spite (or because) of such objectivity such happenings remain ultimately and inescapably relative. Such relativity is hence an ultimate fact about the objective world. (Murphy 1927a, p. 122)

> Whitehead has recurrently been led to express the same fact in terms of "prehension" or perspective. The world of events is a world of perspectives, because each event is a center, an existence here and now, and this aspect is not to be transcended. (P. 131)

> The world of reality is the very system of events disclosed in direct experience; there is no other. And all character belongs to that world of events in one relation or another. Hamlet and the phoenix of McTaggart's famous argument belong there. But none of these constitute it. . . . The alternative is to recognize that neither is constitutive but that each is real in its context. (P. 139)

Murphy's penetrating insight is that a radical metaphysical point of view is to be found in Whitehead and Dewey, but that it is weakened by incompleteness and by competition with other features of their writings.

> We have spoken of "objective relativism" as a completed doctrine, yet it is not to be found in that state in Dewey, nor even in Whitehead. . . . This is particularly true of Dewey, and the reason is fairly evident. While recognizing the relativity of meaning to a context, he has personally made it relevant to a *human* context. (1927a, p. 141)

> Whitehead started with a marked preference for sense objects. . . . But the world can no more be built up from those meanings immediately disclosed to sense than from those of social relations. (P. 143)

A similar emphasis on *human* perspectives and experience can be found in Evander McGilvary's otherwise general treatment of perspective, in *Toward a Perspective Realism* (1959).

Murphy's powerful understanding of what was most important in Dewey and Whitehead was matched by his equally penetrating but tragic understanding of what was misleading, for later commentators appear to have valued Dewey's humanity and Whitehead's empiricism and cosmology far more than they valued perspectivity. My study here is an attempt to return objective perspectivism to where it should have been fifty years ago, supplemented by some far-reaching developments which neither Dewey nor Whitehead could have anticipated and of which they might well have disapproved (see Justus Buchler [1966], and Ross [1980 and 1981].

Nevertheless, Murphy's description is still apt, though it is a description waiting for a theory.

> I conclude therefore that there is rather less than more reason than heretofore to interpret all events in anthropocentric terms. . . .
>
> (a) Modern science has held that the terms of physical analysis are both pervasive and exclusive. We now deny that they are exclusive but have no good reason for denying that they are pervasive and literally true *of the aspect of events with which they deal.* . . .
>
> (b) The irrelevance of human experience in its more special features to a scientific description of natural interactions can not be made the basis for their exclusion from nature. . . . But the fact remains that they *are* irrelevant to many physical processes.
> . . .
>
> (c) That relative human perspectives are objectively real is true, and a false absoluteness was in error in denying that fact. But it is just as true that if the relative is objectively real it is also really and objectively relative. Human experience is a natural occurrence just where, when, and as it has been found to occur. As such it is found to be an effective though limited factor in many types of interaction. (1927b, p. 299)

Perspectives here are real and all being is perspectival, including perspectives themselves. An extremely rich and complex notion of perspective is involved permitting us to say that being is both *in* perspective and *a* perspective, that there is nothing but perspectives, but to deny the damaging force of "mere" perspectivity. The conclusion, as Murphy notes, is that all being is relational and conditioned, including perspectives themselves, but that identity and reality are included in every perspectival being. Perspectivity is an inexhaustible fusion of identity and relationality, similarity and difference, determinateness and indeterminateness.

4. I am referring here to Buchler's *Metaphysics of Natural Complexes* (1966) and to my *Transition to an Ordinal Metaphysics* (1980) and *Philosophical Mysteries* (1981).

My view of metaphysics must be distinguished from that of Hartshorne, for whom metaphysics is clearly cosmological in the sense I take the cosmological principle to have, although he defines cosmology very differently.

By "metaphysics" I mean the study of the necessary, eternal, completely universal aspects of reality; by "cosmology," the attempt, combining metaphysics and scientific knowledge, to discern the large, comparatively universal features of nature as now constituted. . . . Whitehead was a metaphysician as well as a cosmologist. (Hartshorne 1972, p. 9)

These "necessary, eternal, completely universal aspects" are unconditioned, therefore nonperspectival. Hartshorne's drive toward totality is greater by far than Whitehead's:

If individuals have no parts then either the universe is the only individual . . . or it is not an individual at all. But the latter alternative is little better than a refusal to consider the problem of the cosmic totality; and is not that problem precisely the characteristic and central one for philosophy? (Hartshorne 1972, p. 43)

Hartshorne offers a recurrent cosmological argument, a very strong version of which is as follows:

To stand outside the occasion and say, "it exists," is to refer it to a *common measure or register of existence* by reference to which other things also exist. This measure cannot be the thing's own solipsistic or private self-awareness; for then existence would have no common or public meaning. . . . To refer to "existence" as a public meaning is to refer to a register on which, with infinite exactitude, everything is recorded just as it "really is." (1972, p. 81)

A clear example of the sacrifices Hartshorne is willing to make in the self-determination of actual entities to assign a cosmological role to God is the following:

If all individuals make their own decisions, act with a certain spontaneity, what prevents universal conflict and confusion? Can all things freely conspire together to make an orderly world? . . . The supreme agent decides the outline of the world order, this decision the lesser agents accept; what is still left for them to decide is by comparison trivial. (1972, p. 133)

See particularly Hartshorne's defense of metaphysics: "The denial of metaphysics consists simply in the assertion that everything so far as knowable (or even conceivable?) is relative, contingent, finite, imperfect, and less than strictly universal." Metaphysics is "the study which seeks to clarify our conception of the absolute, necessary, strictly universal, infinite, or perfect" (Hartshorne 1961, p. 107). A perspectival metaphysics is then what Hartshorne takes to be a *denial* of metaphysics. Victor Lowe has an interesting comment to make on this subject, though he intends it to very different ends.

It would be unrealistic to suppose that any human being can produce a substantial work of metaphysics which is motivated simply and solely by desire to frame a general characterization of the universe around us. . . . Being an emotional animal and a civilized animal, he is bound to desire one kind of characterization more than another. Lowe 1961, p. 206)

I think fruitful and insightful generality is a supreme philosophical value and that it can be attained without arbitrary and unjustifiable presuppositions defining metaphysical adequacy. A perspectival metaphysics is a general characterization of our experience and its surroundings, a theory in which limitation and context are at the forefront and in which no regulative principles of metaphysical adequacy are taken to be absolute.

CHAPTER ONE

PERSPECTIVE

The concept of perspective is referred to several times in *Process and Reality*, in a variety of different contexts. Yet Whitehead never explicitly assigns it the general and pervasive categorial role it plays in his system. The closest he comes is in *Modes of Thought*[1]:

> Let us ... assume that each entity, of whatever type, essentially involves its own connection with the universe of other things. This connection can be viewed as being what the universe is for that entity either in the way of accomplishment or in the way of potentiality. It can be termed the perspective of the universe for that entity. For example, there are the perspectives of the universe for the number three, and for the colour blue, and for any one definite occasion of realized fact.
>
> Each perspective for any one qualitative abstraction such as a number, or a colour, involves an infinitude of alternative potentialities. On the other hand, the perspective for a factual occasion involves the elimination of alternatives in respect to the matter-of-fact realization involved in that present occasion, and the reduction of alternatives as to the future; since that occasion, as a member of its own contemporary world, is one of the factors conditioning the future beyond itself. (MT 91)

Even here, however, Whitehead appears to regard an entity as *taking* a perspective more than *being* a perspective. The reason may well be that he does not regard perspective as a technical category, so he does not develop its precise characteristics and pervasiveness. One of the purposes of this book is to develop the concept of perspective as a metaphysical category and to show its strength and scope throughout Whitehead's metaphysical system.[2] I will argue that being *is* perspectivity, that Whitehead affirms this principle but incompletely, and that this incompleteness is a pervasive source of difficulties in his theory.

Nevertheless, the variety of references to perspective in *Process and Reality* and Whitehead's later works does indicate without reservation that perspective plays both an important and a divided role. The two most prominent references are to the perspectives provided by the extensive continuum and the perspectives upon the past defined by every actual entity:

> Our direct perception of the contemporary world is thus reduced to extension, defining (i) our own geometrical perspectives, and (ii) possibilities of mutual perspectives for other contemporary entities *inter se*, and (iii) possibilities of division. (PR 61–62)

> Objectification is an operation of mutually adjusted abstraction, or elimination, whereby the many occasions of the actual world become one complex datum. This fact of the elimination by reason of synthesis is sometimes termed the perspective of the actual world from the standpoint of that concrescence. (PR 210)

The former passage expresses the natural and traditional meaning of perspective, defined in perceptual and geometrical terms. The latter defines the unique and fundamental meaning it is given in Whitehead's system, essential to every concrescence, every actual entity. The two meanings are bridged by Whitehead in a passage that makes eminently clear the primacy of the becoming of actual entities as perspectival standpoints:

> An act of experience has an objective scheme of extensive order by reason of the double fact that its own perspective standpoint has extensive content, and that the other actual entities are objectified with the retention of their extensive relationships. (PR 67)[3]

A natural conclusion, based on the primacy of concrescence in defining perspectival standpoints, is that perspectives are a direct manifestation, an equivalent of, the experiential nature of Whitehead's theory.[4] "Actual entities are drops of experience, complex and interdependent" (PR 18). Whitehead's *principle of experience* is evident here, that reality is experience. "Apart from the experiences of subjects, there is nothing, nothing, nothing, bare nothingness" (PR 167). The functioning of an actual entity as a subject prehending other actual entities and eternal objects defines a perspective upon those other entities from a particular point of view, that of the prehending occasion. Here the parallel with perception is very strong, and the perspectival prehensive standpoint of each actual occasion is closely analogous to the perceptual standpoint defined by a human organism, subject to the qualifications differentiating a drop of experience from an enduring experiencing subject. The emphasis is on a focal standpoint whereby many are integrated into one experience by selection and exclusion. There is a double emphasis on multiplicity: a multiplicity of data prehended from a particular point of view and a multiplicity of points of view that may be taken toward the same data. The second of these is fundamental within the system, since it is the basis of the plurality of occasions which balances off the strong cosmological impulses in Whitehead's system toward unification in God. Equally important, however, and closely related to the latter sense of multiplicity, is the coordination provided by each occasion of its multiplicity of data into one experience. Perspective here is a solution to the problem of the one and many, grounded in the notion of experience and looking back to Kant's synthetic unity of apperception. Experience is the synthetic unification of many data into one experience from the standpoint of an experiencing subject, defining a unifying perspective on the many data. This perspective, then, is the individuating criterion for actual entities, as well as the relational expression of their togetherness.

All of this is but another expression of Creativity:

> ... the universals of universals characterizing ultimate matter of fact. It is that ultimate principle by which the many, which are the universe disjunctively, become the one actual occasion, which is the universe conjunctively. It lies in the nature of things that the many enter into complex unity. (PR 21)

> The ultimate metaphysical principle is the advance from disjunction to conjunction, creating a novel entity other than the entities given in disjunction. The novel entity is at once the togetherness of the "many" which it finds, and also it is one among the disjunctive "many" which it synthesizes. The many become one, and are increased by one. (PR 21)

Actual entities are related to each other *constitutively* in that past occasions enter into the constitution of later occasions by being prehended by them, elements in their final satisfaction. Whitehead's reformulation of the subjectivist principle is precisely a rejection of the view that past occasions are prehended "only" through the mediation of universals: they are prehended *as past occasions* entering into the constitution of later occasions. There is an essential equivalence, then, between the categorial expression of Creativity and the perspective each occasion defines on its past—a perspective that is constitutive of, as well as equivalent with, the actual world of the occasion's concrescence. From this point of view, in which perspective is fundamental to the conception of an actual entity, the past actual world is a natural corollary and expresses no additional principles in Whitehead's thought.[5]

Equally fundamental here is the concept of prehension, that mode of relation whereby an actual entity is related to anything outside itself.[6]

A prehension reproduces in itself the general characteristics of an actual entity: it is referent to an external world, and in this sense will be said to have a "vector character"; it involves emotion, and purpose, and valuation, and causation. (PR 19)

The emphasis on emotion, purpose, and valuation repeats the experiential theme of Whitehead's theory and may be postponed for future consideration. The paradigm of experience as the ground of unification is essential to Whitehead's theory, but it may be interpreted here as no more than the foundation of the principle of perspective.[7] More important for our immediate purposes is the *vectoral* nature of prehension, for example:

In a simple feeling there is a vector character which transfers the cause into the effect. It is a feeling *from* the cause which acquires the subjectivity of the new effect without loss of its original subjectivity in the cause. (PR 237–38)

This vectoral nature of prehensions, *from* a datum (whether it be a past occasion or an eternal object) *to* a subject, embodies within it the perspectival standpoint of the prehending occasion.

A feeling is the appropriation of some elements in the universe to be components in the real internal constitution of its subject. The elements are the initial data; they are what the feeling feels. But they are felt under an abstraction. The process of the feeling involves negative prehensions which effect elimination. Thus the initial data are felt under a "perspective" which is the objective datum of the feeling. (PR 231)

Indeed, Whitehead's relatively infrequent references in *Process and Reality* to internal relations among actual entities are misleading precisely to the extent that they suggest a view of internal relations like F. H. Bradley's where the identity of what is related is diminished by internal relations.[8] Prehensions define a solution to Bradley's criticism of internal or constitutive relations by emphasizing the focal identity of the prehending occasion in every prehension.[9] Prehensions constitute an occasion because they are *its* prehensions. Put another way, however, prehensions define the basis of a perspectival theory of relatedness: a relation that is constitutive of an occasion *from its point of view*.[10]

> This mutual determination of the elements involved in a feeling is one expression of the truth that the subject of the feeling is *causa sui*. The partial nature of a feeling, other than the complete satisfaction, is manifest by the impossibility of understanding its generation without recourse to the whole subject. (PR 221)

The analogy between prehension and perception, conjoined with Whitehead's generalization of experience, manifests quite clearly his generalization of Berkeley's principle, *esse ist percipi*, into the principle of perspective: "to be is to be in perspective." In Whitehead's theory, to be is to be prehended by an actual entity; to be is to be a constitutive element of a perspective. I have emphasized up to this point the prehensive or subjective side of the constituting perspective. The power of the concept of perspective lies equally on the other side, defining the elements of constitution.

> The philosophy of organism holds that, in order to understand "power," we must have a correct notion of how each individual actual entity contributes to the datum *from which* its successors arise and *to which* they must conform. (PR 56)

Only this understanding of perspective can enable us to understand Whitehead's principle of relativity: "It belongs to the nature of a 'being' that it is a potential for every 'becoming' " (PR 22). To be is to be a constituent of some becoming and to be a potential for other becomings. The postulate that being is potential for *every* becoming is cosmological and is not essential to the nature of perspective.[11] More important here is the principle that all being is qualified, from some point of view. Perspectivity thus has two essential elements. First, being is always from some point of view—*many* points of view—in Whitehead's theory, entering into some particular concrescence. This may be regarded as a simple restatement of the ontological principle.

> Every condition to which the process of becoming conforms in any particular instance has its reason *either* in the character of some actual entity in the actual world of that concrescence, *or* in the character of the subject which is

in process of concrescence. . . . This ontological principle means that actual entities are the only *reasons*. (PR 24)

There are cosmological elements in this principle to the extent that actual entities are the *only* reasons.[12] Yet the grounding of being in a standpoint is essential to the principle of perspective. As formulated here, in terms of the ontological principle, the principle of perspective is closely related to the principle of experience. Generalized, however, the principle asserts that every being is to be regarded as a focal center of relations which constitute it on the one hand, and yet which it constitutes, on the other, by its focal presence. This double constitution is essential to the meaning of perspective. Every perspective—every being—is at once constitutive of its relations, from *its* point of view, thereby defining a vectoral relation, and constituted *by* its relations. This conjunction of reciprocal constitution, inclusive of each being's identity, is what is meant by calling every being a perspective.

The second element of the principle of perspective is that every perspective is located in, constitutive of and constituted by, other perspectives. The property or relation of being constituted by a term is itself perspectival—for all being is perspectival. Thus, both perspectives and their constituents are what they are—perspectives and constituents—perspectivally, relative to some other perspectives, and there is no absolute, total, all-encompassing perspective, for it could not then be perspectival itself: it could be relative to no other perspective. A corollary here is that being is always qualified, from a point of view. There is no self-sufficient, independent, unconditioned mode of being. "No actual entity can rise beyond what the actual world as a datum from its standpoint—*its* actual world—allows it to be" (PR 83). A striking expression of this principle can be found in Whitehead's criticism, in his essay "Mathematics and the Good," of the philosophical tradition in which the world is made dependent on God, but God is not dependent on the world (1951b, p. 678). Whitehead's own acknowledgment of this principle is limited, for the primordial nature of God is unconditioned although God as an actual entity is not. Yet there are passages which strongly imply perspectival conditions: "No entity is merely characterized by its individual characteristics, or merely by its relationships. Each entity possesses essentially an individual character, and also is essentially a termini of relationships, potential or actual." [13]

We naturally simplify the complexity of the Universe by considering it in the guise of two abstractions—namely, the World of multiple Activities and the World of coalesced Value. The prime characteristic of one world is change, and of the other world is immortality. But the understanding of the Universe requires that each World exhibits the impress of the Other. (Whitehead 1951a, p. 693) [14]

Each is a function of the other, and the universe then is a perspective comprised of them together, irreducibly. The reference to the universe, however, is cosmological; moreover, perspectival limitation and totality are incompatible.

Particularly important here is Whitehead's argument that universals and particulars are not different modes of being but different *functions* of eternal objects and actual occasions.

An actual entity cannot be described, even inadequately, by universals; because other actual entities do enter into the description of any one actual entity. Thus every so-called "universal" is particular in the sense of being just what it is, diverse from everything else; and every so-called "particular" is universal in the sense of entering into the constitutions of other actual entities. (PR 48)

Nevertheless, he does not consider the possibility that actual entities and eternal objects might themselves be only functionally distinct, perspectival and relative, rather than nonoverlapping modes of existence.

The philosophy of organism ... admits two ultimate classes of entities, mutually exclusive. One class consists of "actual entities," which in the philosophical tradition are mis-described as "particulars" ; and the other class consists of forms of definiteness, here named "eternal objects." (PR 158)

Incompleteness with respect to the principle of perspective is the source of many of Whitehead's difficulties—for example with respect to God's primordial nature and the unconditioned multiplicity of eternal objects, but also with respect to the self-causation of actual entities. I will argue that this principle is incompatible with the cosmological elements in Whitehead's theory, and that carried through consistently, it leads to a theory very different from Whitehead's but immensely indebted to him for the principle of perspective.[15]

Virtually Whitehead's entire theory, with the exception of its cosmological elements, may be regarded as an expression and development of the principle of perspective. It may be worth tracing some of these expressions here in anticipation of later extended discussions. The place to begin is with the categoreal scheme.

Categories of Existence. There are, according to Whitehead, *eight* categories of existence, eight kinds of existence or modes of being: actual entities, prehensions, nexūs, subjective forms, eternal objects, propositions, multiplicities, and contrasts (PR 22). Many difficulties found by commentators in Whitehead's theory rest on their failure to understand that he means these eight to be genuine modes of existence.[16] They exist because they are constituent elements of perspectives, constitutive of actual entities. Nevertheless, Whitehead also claims that " 'actual entities' . . . are the final real things of which the world is made up" (PR 18). And he says as well, in the context of defining the categories of existence, that "among these eight categories of existence, actual entities and eternal objects stand out with a certain extreme finality" (PR 22). These latter remarks, I will argue, are a consequence of Whitehead's cosmological principle. From the standpoint of the principle of perspective, whatever is required for, constitutive of, contributes to, a perspectival standpoint is real, a mode of being. Whitehead here is listing the general ways in which perspectives are constituted.

There are two notable exceptions: Whitehead does not include the extensive continuum or God among his categories of existence. The reason in both cases, I will argue, is that these are included within other categories. Nevertheless, the ontological status of both God and the extensive continuum is problematic, and for cosmological reasons. By the principle of perspective, both are real, for they contribute to and constitute actual occasions. In the case of God, he *is* an actual entity. Yet there are important cosmological considerations inherent in both notions, defining a condition for unifying all occasions under a common set of properties, and this all-encompassing unifying function creates fundamental difficulties. I will put God aside for later discussion with the note that his totality and perfection, in both his primordial and consequent natures, threatens the viability of all individual perspectives in Whitehead's system, as if they were but incomplete, partial moments of a total world order. In Whitehead's theory, the viability of individual perspectives, individual occasions, and of an inexhaustible variety of such perspectives, is central to the principle of perspective and an important source of its tension with cosmological principles.

The extensive continuum is more directly relevant to perspectivity, and we should note its general function in Whitehead's theory and its role in the mode of prehension he calls "presentational immediacy": "the perceptive mode in which there is clear, distinct consciousness of the 'extensive' relations of the world. . . . In this 'mode' the contemporary world is consciously prehended as a continuum of extensive relations"

(PR 61). Two modes of prehension or "perception" are fundamental in Whitehead's theory: causal objectification and presentational immediacy. Both express perspectival relations: one to the past, the other to extended regions and locations relative to contemporary events. Both of these are essential to Whitehead's notion of standpoint. In this sense, actual occasions are located by causal prehension in an order of succession in which each location is a perspectival standpoint upon past occasions, and in addition, actual occasions are located together in one world under extensive patterns. The extensive continuum here is necessary if there is to be a perspectival standpoint at all:

> The real potentialities relative to all standpoints are coordinated as diverse determinations of one extensive continuum. This extensive continuum is one relational complex in which all potential objectifications find their niche.
>
> This extensive continuum is "real," because it expresses a fact derived from the actual world and concerning the contemporary actual world. All actual entities are related according to the determinations of this continuum; and all possible actual entities in the future must exemplify these determinations in their relations with the already actual world. (PR 66)

The reality of the extensive continuum here is unquestionable, for that continuum is required for the totality of standpoints and the uniqueness of each standpoint. The totality of standpoints is cosmological; the uniqueness of each standpoint is essential to perspectivity. We may regard Whitehead's entire theory of extension as an answer to the question of what minimal conditions are necessary to the definition of both unique standpoints (locations) for each concrescence and a totality of all standpoints. The function of space and time—or of a more general sense of extension—has traditionally been to define a homogeneous totality of standpoints, locations in which events transpire, a relational scheme within which natural laws may be said to be intelligible. In this sense, the extensive continuum is real as a perspectival constituent, a potential for every concrescence, but also as a basis for every standpoint. The question of its invariance with time and distance is a question concerning the primordial nature of God and will be considered in later discussions.

Closely related to Whitehead's theory of perspective is his distinction between actuality and potentiality, for example, with respect to extensive location and divisibility, for these are potential and not actual in his theory, though both are perfectly real. Potentiality functions perspectively in Whitehead's theory to the extent that potentials are as genuine and efficacious constituents of occasions as are other occasions. I will argue that eternal objects are not only constituents of standpoints (potentials) but themselves comprise standpoints and require a generalized theory of perspective if we are to understand both their relational and individual essences. Indeed, to have *both* essences is to be a perspective—constituted by relations to other eternal objects and defining a unique point of view upon or among them. Similarly, extensiveness is a perspectival function of both the geometrical or temporal patterns in the primordial nature of God and social conditions in past actual worlds, a complex sphere of relations that is fundamentally perspectival in nature, if not prehensive like actual occasions.

We may return to the eight categories of existence. Actual entities are naturally a mode of being—a fundamental mode—in that they are the focal centers of perspectives, experiencing subjects. In this sense, they are the "fundamental realities" of Whitehead's system because they comprise the essential elements of experient perspectives: they are the only prehensive entities. Here the primacy of the theory of experience is very strong. Kant's emphasis on subjectivity as the constitutive basis for experience is also very strong. Yet Whitehead also holds that actual entities are prehended by other actual entities: indeed, this mode of prehension—causal objectification—is essential to the continuity and solidarity of the succession of events. The past is prehended *as a past*; past occasions are prehended with their feelings and prehensions. The principle of perspective is very strong here. To be is to be in perspective: experiencing subjects and what they experience. Past occasions are real only to the extent that they are relevant to future occasions. There is a double but complementary mode of being involved in the concept of perspective: the focal center of a perspective and a prehensive datum of a perspective. Actual entities have a double mode of being: prehending and being prehended. This is precisely what Whitehead means by calling actual entities *subject-superjects*. The question is not how a dead or perished occasion can preside over its own future: it is simply not so dead as all that. More accurately, that is not what death means in a perspectival theory: sudden, total irrelevance.[17] The occasion exists for the future (according to the principle of relativity) *because* it constitutes future perspectives. The question is whether this double relation inherent in perspective is to be reserved for actual entities alone, or whether every mode of being should not be regarded perspectivally, as a focal center of relatedness and as a constituent of other perspectives.

In Whitehead's theory, only actual entities are perspectival centers:

all the other modes of being are prehended but do not prehend, are constituents of perspectives but not focal centers of perspectives: prehensions, nexūs, subjective forms, eternal objects, propositions, multiplicities, and contrasts. Whitehead's profound insight, that universals and particulars are not *kinds* of beings but distinct *functions* of eternal objects and actual entities, that actual entities function sometimes as actualities and other times as potentialities, that occasions are divisible in certain ways but indivisible in other ways—that is, that the traditional notions of universality and particularity, actuality and potentiality, divisibility and indivisibility, are functional, perspectival distinctions, from a point of view—is not carried over to his categories of existence. Actual entities and eternal objects are distinct *types* of beings, along with the other categories of existence. The most striking members of this group are nexūs and eternal objects. The former, comprising the ordinary objects of our everyday experience, require a principle defining them as a collective datum for some prehending occasion: the *principle of transmutation*. Yet where there is a nexus, it is not because its members are prehended together by another occasion, but because of the prehensions of the constituent members of the nexus. Here, then, a nexus is *both* a collective or aggregate datum by the principle of transmutation and *also* a collectivity in virtue of the feelings of the members of the nexus, a double relation closely analogous to the duality of center and multiplicity inherent in the concept of perspective.

> Just as, for some purposes, one atomic actuality can be treated as though it were many coordinate actualities, in the same way, for other purposes, a nexus of many actualities can be treated as though it were one actuality. This is what we habitually do in the case of the span of life of a molecule, or of a piece of rock, or of a human body. (PR 287)

An actual entity is a prehending focal center synthesizing its many constituent elements into one occasion; a nexus is a prehensive aggregate of constituent occasions comprising a collectivity. It is not obvious why one is a primary reality over the others, why the concept of perspective should be restricted to actual entities and not include nexūs.

Eternal objects are pure potentials available for prehension by occasions but not themselves prehensive.[18] Yet they can function as such potential forms of definiteness only to the extent that they are related to each other constitutively. As pure as they may appear to be from the standpoint of actual occasions, eternal objects thoroughly conform to the second element of the principle of perspective that no mode of being is unqualified, but is from a point of view—here qualified by other eternal objects. Whitehead resolves this qualification through the primordial nature of God: God defines the perspectival standpoint for eternal objects, constituting their mutual and systematic relevance so that they may function as potentials for actual occasions. The primordial nature of God, along with the ontological principle that defines the need for God relative to eternal objects, is a cosmological principle. The principle of perspective requires only the qualification of eternal objects by other modes of being—other eternal objects or actual occasions in particular. It entails, however, that insofar as eternal objects comprise constituent elements of perspectives, they are conditioned and qualified by their relations, that purity of potentiality is unintelligible. I will argue that a modified theory of the primordial nature of God in which eternal objects are qualified both by other eternal objects and by other occasions is more plausible than Whitehead's. A consequence of this view is that eternal objects comprise focal perspectival centers. The principle of perspective, that to be is to be in perspective, generalizes to the principle that to be is *both* to be constitutive of perspectives and to be a perspectival center. This view is not so very alien to Whitehead's, since he holds that eternal objects have both individual and relational essences. I will argue that only the extension of the principle of perspective to eternal objects as perspectival centers can make sense of this double essence. Whitehead comes very close to this view in some passages:

> An actual entity considered in reference to the publicity of things is a "superject"; namely, it arises from the publicity which it finds, and it adds itself to the publicity which it transmits. . . .
> An actual entity considered in reference to the privacy of things is a "subject"; namely, it is a moment of the genesis of self-enjoyment. . . .
> Eternal objects have the same dual reference. An eternal object considered in reference to the publicity of things is a "universal". . . .
> An eternal object considered in reference to the privacy of things is a "quality" or "characteristic"; namely, in its own nature, as exemplified in any actuality, it constitutes an element in the private definiteness of that actuality. It refers itself publicly; but it is enjoyed privately.
> The theory of prehensions is founded upon the doctrine that there are no concrete facts which are merely public, or merely private. (PR 289–90)

Of the remaining categories of existence, prehensions and subjective forms are essential components of perspectives where the paradigm of perspective is an experiencing subject: Kant's synthetic unity of apperception. An important issue for consideration is whether this notion of experience is essential to the concept of perspective, or whether in fact it is not the source of difficulties in Whitehead's theory. I will argue that these difficulties are mostly apparent, and that "experience" in Whitehead's theory is neither anthropomorphic nor idealistic. Yet a consequence of my argument is that the concept of perspective may be generalized far beyond the range of Whitehead's own generalizations to the point where the principle of experience is no longer plausible.

Contrasts and propositions are categories of existence that follow directly from the relational character of prehensive perspectives. The concept of perspective defines a synthetic unification of a multiplicity of elements or data. In this synthesis, there will be engendered novel conjunctions: propositions on the one hand, conjunctions of actuality and potentiality; contrasts on the other, conjunctions of modes of definiteness in terms of their conjoint similarities and differences. Both of these modes of being play important roles in higher experience, and are needed for an adequate theory of mind and knowledge. The question is whether they require so general a theory of experience as Whitehead develops. In both cases, from the standpoint of experience, neither seems to be able to function as a subject: both are only objects for a prehending subject. Each, however, has elements and comprises a synthetic conjunction of its elements. In the case of propositions in particular, as lures for feeling, they have a kind of existence even when not felt. This is a difficulty that leads in resolution to a wider notion of perspective than experience and prehension naturally give us.

Finally, the eighth category of existence, multiplicities, defines for us types of beings whose existence is deeply and without reservation dependent on perspectives but which are not constitutive of the focal center of a perspective. Multiplicities are "Pure Disjunctions of Diverse Entities." As such disjunctions, they cannot be perspectival centers. The question is whether they can be anything at all, whether they are truly a mode of being, in such disarray and heterogeneity. If they comprise a common if disjoint datum of a prehending subject, is that not a natural conjunction? The question is whether there are "mere" multiplicities that can comprise no togetherness beyond that of datum for some experience. This very question suggests the limitations of the experience model of perspective, as if any (combination of) objects might comprise a unifying ground for experience, whereas experience is a joint function of both natural orders and its own unifying properties. From this point of view, the concept of perspective with its associated principle is the more general basis upon which experience rests, and there "are" *no pure multiplicities*. "Purity" is incompatible with the principle of perspective. *A* multiplicity is qualified by some togetherness, defining singularity amidst disjunction. *Mere* disjunction as a mode of being is unintelligible. The concept of perspective here is generalized to include all modes of being as a conjunction of unitariness and multiplicity.

There remain for preliminary consideration the various categories and principles Whitehead defines as essential to his theory. I have mentioned several as expressions of the principle of perspective. Many more may be considered from the same point of view. Of the twenty-seven categories of explanation, some are principles of *process*, in particular, category (i) "that the actual world is a process, and that the process is the becoming of actual entities" (PR 22), and category (ix) "that *how* an actual entity *becomes* constitutes *what* that actual entity *is*; so that the two descriptions of an actual entity are not independent. Its 'being' is constituted by its 'becoming' " (PR 23). Yet the latter is not only a principle of process, but a principle of perspective: what the actual entity *is* is given by the perspective it imposes on what constitutes it.[19] In other words, the principle of process is a limited application of the principle of perspective: the being of an actual entity is a perspective defined by its becoming. Being is qualified by becoming. This understanding is supported by Whitehead's category of explanation (x): "that the first analysis of an actual entity, into its most concrete elements, discloses it to be a concrescence of prehensions, which have originated in its process of becoming" (PR 23). Prehensions are vectoral and perspectival. What is disclosed, upon analysis, to constitute concretely the becoming, therefore the being, of an actual entity are perspectival elements.

Category of explanation (ii) asserts that an "actual entity is the real concrescence of many potentials" (PR 22). This category is therefore a repetition of Creativity, and defines one of the conditions of perspectives: that many enter into and comprise a synthetic unity. Category of explanation (iii) is a principle of novelty, and asserts that "in the becoming of an actual entity, novel prehensions, nexūs, subjective forms, propositions, multiplicities, and contrasts, also become; but there are no novel eternal objects" (PR 22). Novelty of perspective is a central feature of Whitehead's metaphysics, and is, I will argue, essential to the concept of perspective. Perspectives introduce an infinite inexhaustibility into a determinate array of modes of being. In this sense, category (iii) serves to define the novelty and inexhaustibility of perspectives, but denies them to eternal objects. This limitation on perspective in Whitehead's theory with respect to eternal objects is one of the most striking features of his system, and is the source of major difficulties. I will argue that it rests at bottom on a mathematical intuition that is mistaken with respect to novelty and perspective, and that it conforms more than necessary to the cosmological principle.

I have mentioned category of explanation (iv), "the principle of relativity": that "it belongs to the nature of a 'being' that it is a potential for every 'becoming' " (PR 22). This is a fundamental principle of perspective: to be is to be in relation to other beings, a constituent of their perspectives. This principle is a full answer to the problem of the reality of the past in relation to the future: it is real, exists, as a potential element for that future, a constituent of future perspectives. The requirement that a being is potential for *every* becoming is a cosmological requirement not entailed by the principle of perspective, and expresses the tension between the two principles that is characteristic of Whitehead's thought. The same point is enforced by some versions of the ontological principle: "the principle that everything is positively somewhere in actuality, and in potency everywhere" (PR 40). The tension is relaxed somewhat in category of explanation (v): "that no two actual entities originate from an identical universe; though the difference between the two universes only consists in some actual entities, included in one and not in the other, and in the subordinate entities which each actual entity introduces into the world. . . . The nexus of actual entities in the universe correlate to a concrescence is termed 'the actual world' correlate to that concrescence" (PR 22–23). This actual world is, by selection and exclusion, precisely that perspective each occasion defines relative to its past, and it is clearly limited relative to the entities included. The past is *potentially* relevant to all becoming but *actually* included only in some further concrescences. There are two different perspectives involved here, that of an occasion upon the complete past and the full primordial nature of God, and that of the occasion after selection and exclusion, inclusive of only some of these potentials as constituent elements. This contrast between potential and actual (constitutive) relevance is a repetition of the tension between cosmological and perspectival principles. Yet it is essential to emphasize that even the former mode of relevance—which Whitehead calls the "initial data" (PR 221)—is perspectival, for it is from a point of view defined by the occasion's location in the extensive continuum and is a function of its particular subjective aim. All of these matters will require extended discussion.

Category of explanation (vi) repeats the contrast between potential and actual relevance and looks forward to the second categoreal obligation: "that each entity in the universe of a given concrescence *can*, so far as its own nature is concerned, be implicated in that concrescence in one or other of many modes; but *in fact* it is implicated only in *one* mode" (PR 23). The process of concrescence brings an indeterminateness of relevance to determination. "This indetermination, rendered determinate in the real concrescence, is the meaning of 'potentiality' " (PR 23). As so conditioned, potentiality is perspectival, a function of the aim and location of the concrescent occasion. Concrescence here is not the imposition of a perspective upon its own perspectival elements, but the transformation of one perspective definitive of potentiality into another. Whether this transformation is properly to be regarded as one from indeterminateness to determinateness is a fundamental question that must be considered in detail. It is worth noting that the perishing of an occasion (wholly determinate in Whitehead's view relative to its past) makes it indeterminate relative to its future.[20] Properly speaking, determinateness is perspectival, from a point of view, qualified, and the determinateness of an actual entity is only conditional and from a particular point of view. In other respects and from other points of view, it is indeterminate in many ways. Every feeling, insofar as it may be felt by a future occasion, is indeterminate as to how it will be so felt.[21]

Category of explanation (vii) defines an eternal object as "a pure potential," but a potential relative to the becoming of an actual entity, part of and constitutive of its perspective, "the particular mode in which the potentiality of an eternal object is realized in a particular actual entity, contributing to the definiteness of that actual entity" (PR 23). This category clearly conforms to the principle of perspective. Category of explanation (viii) also follows the principle of perspective, this time from the point of view of actual entities. In fact, it defines two general points of view relative to each actual entity: "(a) one which is analytical of its potentiality for 'objectification' in the becoming of other actual entities, and (b) another which is analytical of the process which constitutes its own becoming (PR 23). These two points of view express the two dimensions of perspective: being in perspective and being the center of a perspective: from a datum or object to a perspectival center or subject. Category of explanation (xiii) continues the emphasis on subjective form and experience. Category of explanation (ix) reasserts the principle of perspective in relation to becoming: "*How* an actual entity *becomes* constitutes *what* that actual entity *is*" (PR 23). The emphasis on process, I will argue, is cosmological, defining a particular type of perspective as fundamental. But the principle generalizes to the principle of perspective: whatever comprises a perspective constitutes what that perspective is. A perspective is comprised of its elements from its point of view, and nothing more. Such an interpretation makes process perspectival, from the point of view of succession and becoming. What I am arguing is that Whitehead's theory is thoroughly a perspectival theory conjoined with a cosmological perspective in which becoming is made primary. Whitehead's profound insight that being is not primary over becoming, that process has an ontological primacy also, must be supplemented by a general principle of perspective in which being is perspectival, becoming is perspectival, but neither process nor endurance has greater primacy. Both are perspectival modes of being, different from but related to each other.

Category of explanation (x) introduces prehension as the fundamental element of occasions: "The first analysis of an actual entity, into its most concrete elements, discloses it to be a concrescence of prehensions, which have originated in its process of becoming. All further analysis is an analysis of prehensions" (PR 23). I have indicated that prehensions are thoroughly perspectival and constitute occasions as perspectives. Category of explanation (xi) defines the factors of prehension disclosed by analysis: "(a) the 'subject' which is prehending, namely, the actual entity in which that prehension is a concrete element; (b) the 'datum' which is prehended; (c) the 'subjective form' which is *how* that subject prehends that datum" (PR 23). Factors (a) and (b) comprise the vectoral character of perspectives, the ordering of constituents into a perspective. Factor (c) expresses the trivalent nature of experience, and such experience is the foundation of Whitehead's theory of perspective. We have, here, two distinct principles: of perspective and of experience. Actual entities are drops of experience and are comprised of subjective forms as well as objective data. I will argue that the principle of experience leads to unresolvable difficulties and that it is unnecessary in Whitehead's theory, that its central and most important function is to provide a foundation for the principle of perspective and inexhaustibility. Subjective forms (private matters of fact) and self-causation (categories of explanation [xxi], [xxii], and [xxiii]) are required for the uniqueness of actual entities, their self-significance, their transcendent creativity. This self-significance functions on the one hand cosmologically, to define a ground for the ontological principle, and is the foundation as well of the principle of experience (if not its direct expression). Self-causation is required in *Process and Reality* to establish the uniqueness of each occasion's perspective in the context of a cosmological principle in which contemporary occasions share a common world. I will argue that a stronger principle of limitation and exclusion on individual perspectives makes self-causation unnecessary, and provides individuality and uniqueness without the difficulties of arbitrary self-determination.

Category of explanation (xii) defines "two species of prehensions: (a) 'positive prehensions' which are termed 'feelings,' and (b) 'negative prehensions' which are said to 'eliminate from feeling' " (PR 23). This is a direct expression of the selectivity and limitation required by perspectives. Category of explanation (xxiv) defines the constituents of actual entities to include other actual entities and eternal objects—thus, perspectives constituted at least by such actual entities and eternal objects. Categories (xxv) and (xxvi) define an actual entity to be a full and complete determination relative to all its constituents: "This final phase is termed the 'satisfaction.' It is fully determinate (a) as to its genesis, (b) as to its objective character for the transcendent creativity, and (c) as to its prehension—positive or negative—of every item in its universe" (PR 26). "Each element in the genetic process of an actual entity has one self-consistent function, however complex, in the final satisfaction" (PR 26). Category of explanation (xxvii) defines this satisfaction to be an outcome of a process of becoming, culminating in the determinate satisfaction.

> In a process of concrescence, there is a succession of phases in which new prehensions arise by integration of prehensions in antecedent phases. In these integrations "feelings" contribute their "subjective forms" and their "data" to the formation of novel integral prehensions; but "negative prehensions" contribute only their "subjective forms." The process continues till all prehensions are components in the one determinate integral satisfaction. (PR 26)

This notion of phases in an actual entity is a difficult one, and has led to many criticisms. Actual entities are both divisible and indivisible. "Each actual entity is analysable in an indefinite number of ways" (PR 19). It is to be noted that perspectives are both multiple and unified: that is their nature. The difficulties here, I will argue, lie not with the principle of perspective and divisibility, but with the cosmological emphasis on the uniqueness of occasions relative to time and succession and with a nonperspectival—I call it "mechanical"—principle of analysis. The complete determinateness of the satisfaction of an occasion is also a difficulty, and betrays a cosmological neglect of qualification.

Category of explanation (xiv) defines a nexus as "a set of actual entities in the unity of the relatedness constituted by their prehensions of each other, or—what is the same thing conversely expressed—constituted by their objectifications in each other" (PR 24). There is a mixture here of the principle of perspective and the cosmological principle to the extent that a nexus is effectively a perspective (without a single subject) constituted by actual entities in prehensive relation, but is, by the ontological principle, relegated to derivative status in terms of the individual perspectives of actual entities. With categoreal obligation (vi)—the category of transmutation—nexūs (and societies) are made objects for prehension, thereby real as elements of perspectives, but they are not themselves perspectives though they possess all the requisite properties except that of subjective experience. Nexūs are constituted by prehensions and are prehended, but they do not themselves prehend (though their members do). Even a multiplicity is unified in relation to a particular condition: "Its unity is constituted by the fact that all its constituent entities severally satisfy at least one condition which no other entity satisfies" (PR 24). In this sense, there is a unitary condition defined among the members of the multiplicity in relation to a common eternal object. This too is a perspective, if not an experiential, prehensive, or subjective one, to the extent that both unitariness and relatedness are jointly constitutive. The principle of experience here serves to enforce the ontological principle and has cosmological implications.

The categoreal obligations have a similar relationship to the principle of perspective. Obligations (i)–(iii) define the constituents of an actual entity as compatible in every incomplete phase and as unitarily functional in the final phase or satisfaction. In other words, an actual entity is made up of precisely those elements or prehensions that make it up, without indeterminateness, though there is indeterminateness relative to incomplete phases. This elemental function of constituents in an occasion is essential to the concept of perspective. The interplay of determinateness and indeterminateness, which Whitehead defines as essential to concrescence, is equally fundamental to perspective, since the point of view of a perspective in relation to its elements always suggests other points of view, both with respect to these elements and with respect to the future of the occasion. The duality of indeterminateness and determinateness conforms to the principle of perspective, as does the principle of objectification. The total determinateness of an actual entity in its final satisfaction is a consequence of the cosmological principle and introduces difficulties that should be alleviated.

Categoreal obligations (iv) (conceptual valuation), (vii) (subjective harmony), (viii) (subjective intensity), and (ix) (freedom and determination) are grounded in the principle of experience, and manifest the features of experience that Whitehead takes to be essential to the uniqueness of individual perspectives and their subjective aims. Here the category of freedom and determination is essential. I will argue that, to establish uniqueness and novelty, the principle of perspective does not require a foundation in self-causation and freedom, and therefore neither does it require such a foundation in experience and subjectivity. What is needed is a strong principle of limitation upon perspectives—a principle that is incompatible with the cosmological principle and the total perspective upon the world provided by God.

I have schematically discussed most of Whitehead's fundamental principles in relation to the principle of perspective. My contention is that his theory is dominated by three major principles: perspective, experience, and cosmology. I have noted a fourth—the mechanical principle of analysis—but it plays a subordinate role in Whitehead's metaphysical theory, though it often leads to unnecessary confusion. The principle of experience, I have suggested, and will show in further argument, plays the double role of establishing a basis for the principle of perspective and for expressing the cosmological principle. In this sense, Whitehead's is a metaphysics of experience and suffers the liabilities—while enjoying the positive features—of such a metaphysics. I will examine Whitehead's theory of experience in great detail and will defend it against charges of idealism and anthropomorphism. Yet I will also argue that the positive features of the principle are embedded in the principle of perspective. I will therefore discuss in considerable detail the major features of Whitehead's theory in relationship to the principle of perspective, with close attention to the conflict that is generated by the limitation imposed upon it by the principle of experience and the cosmological principle.

The principle of perspective, I am suggesting, has two elements: (1) being is from a point of view; (2) being is always qualified. These conditions make being inexhaustible and complete determinateness unintelligible. Another way of putting this is that being in any sense—as subject or as constituent—is always qualified by status and function: what a being is is a function of the status of that being relative to other beings. The ontological principle in Whitehead's theory defines this status to be legitimate only in relation to actual entities, and a variety of difficulties follow from this restriction, which is essentially cosmological. The view that status is always prehensive and percipient, a function of experience, is a version of the principle of experience, and generates additional difficulties. These principles support each other in remarkable ways in Whitehead's theory, and make it a sublime achievement, but they also generate difficulties that appear to be unresolvable.

Since I will be continually raising difficulties in Whitehead's theory that are a consequence of the tension among the three principles I consider central to it, it may be thought natural to interpret my position as generally critical of his achievement. This would be a serious error. To the contrary, I am concerned with identifying those elements in his theory that are to be taken as enduring and permanent contributions to metaphysical thought beyond the confines of his own system. I will, therefore, in the concluding chapter, evaluate the criticisms I have raised as to their importance for Whitehead's system to determine those that are essentially minor and can be resolved within his theory with modest changes, and those that call for more substantial modifications. I will also examine the consequences of raising the principle of perspective to prominence in his theory, resolving its tension with the cosmological principle and the principle of experience largely in its favor. I will sketch two versions of such perspectivity, one in terms of the structure of Whitehead's own system, keeping the extensive continuum and the primordial and consequent natures of God, the second developing the far more radical implications of dismissing both the principle of experience and the cosmological principle in terms of wholesale and pervasive perspectivity. I think contemporary Whiteheadians and process philosophers and theologians are required to hold the former version, on the basis of Whitehead's principles and their own allegiance to cosmological principles; the latter is my own preferred version, developed in detail elsewhere and very different from Whitehead's view in structure, but immeasurably indebted to him.[22]

Notes to Chapter 1

1. Alfred North Whitehead. *Modes of Thought* (New York: Capricorn, 1958) (hereafter cited as MT).

2. Gregory Vlastos (1963) has criticized Whitehead for a doctrine of internal relations without dialectical resolution. I suggest that the principle of perspective offers a resolution of the problem of internal relations without dialectic, and does so without a total commitment to the absolute primacy of historical process. What the principle of perspective asserts is that to be is to be a perspective in the double and irreducible sense that it is constituted by its relations yet transcends them inexhaustibly. To be is always to be in constitutive relation to something else—to many other perspectives—which it transcends inexhaustibly in virtue of its inexhaustibly manifold perspectival locations and identities.

3. According to Ewing Shahan:

The word "perspective" is sometimes used in *Process and Reality* in connection with the experience of an actual entity, but this word is not to be taken in a spatio-temporal sense. It does not refer to a spatio-temporal perspective upon the world, and it does not mean that experience occurs under the limitation of such a perspective. The word "perspective" is rather a process-analysis concept, related to the broad view of experience. It is to be understood in terms of subjective aim. (1950, p. 58)

Shahan goes too far in emphasizing experience and process, for "perspective" has a complex meaning for Whitehead, including extensiveness.

4. *"How* one actuality can be 'present in' another actuality, is answered by Whitehead in terms of a general metaphysical theory of the nature of actuality as 'experiencing activity' " (Leclere 1958, p. 136).

5. A very strong principle of perspective is inherent in emphasizing creativity relative to the role an occasion plays in defining its past actual world. "An actual entity, by synthesizing a contrast of entities, produces (i.e., creates) that contrast of entities as a novel entity distinct from any of the entities in its actual world prior to its process of concrescence" (Lango 1972, pp. 50–51).

6. "The unification thus realized through the prehensive activity is the actual entity or actual occasion, a concrete, fully determinate, spatio-temporal perspective." (Kraus 1979, p. 20)

7. "The chief meaning intended by calling every actual entity a pulse of *experience* is that the entity is conceived as having an immediate existence in and for itself" (Lowe 1966, pp. 38–39). "Existence-for-itself" is perspectival; the experiential elements come in only where subjectivist interpretations of the *immediacy* of this existence are emphasized. Thus: "there is no feeler over and above the togetherness which is the feeling. . . . the togetherness of the feelings is after all only a certain kind of novel togetherness of the actual entities forming the universe at a given point" (Pols 1967, pp. 30, 31).

8. In *Appearance and Reality*, Bradley writes:

Every quality in relation has, in consequence, a diversity within its own nature, and this diversity cannot immediately be asserted of the quality. Hence the quality must exchange its unity for an internal relation. But thus set free, the diverse aspects, because each something in relation, must each be something also beyond. This diversity is fatal to the internal unity of each; . . . (1946, pp. 26–27)

9. "A prehension is not so much a relation as a relating, or transition, which carries the object into the make-up of the subject" (Lowe 1966, pp. 39–40). The unity of the subject allows Whitehead to criticize Bradley as follows:

Bradley's discussions of relations are confused by his failure to distinguish between relations and contrasts. A relation is a genus of contrasts. He is then distressed—or would have been distressed if he had not been consoled by the notion of "mereness" as in "mere appearance"—to find that a relation will not do the work of a contrast. It fails to contrast. (PR 229)

10. Wolf Mays comes close to the position I am advocating. Whitehead, in *Science and the Modern World*, "made it abundantly clear that a 'prehension' has a complex character, that he thought of it as a process of integration (or unification) of the diverse aspects of other events into some particular pattern grasped into the unity of a perspective standpoint here and now" (Mays 1959,

p. 132). However, Mays's overly logical reading of Whitehead leads him to a gravely diminished theory of perspective and relation.

> He is, however, saying little more than that an event is, after the fashion of a field of force, made up of (i) a focal centre, which is a combination of the aspects of other events (i.e. the event as in its own prehension), and (ii) its field of influence, the modifications it sets up throughout nature (i.e. the event as in the prehension of other events). (Pp. 132–33)

In particular, Mays overlooks the central feature of qualification and limitation in perspective, leading him to a concept of point of view without acknowledgment of the limitations of every point of view.

> Instead of having a perspective space (or system of points of view), we have an interrelated structure of events (or manifold of prehensions). Each event or spatiotemporal point of view can be thought of as mirroring the universe, since it stands in perspective relationship to every other event. (P. 133)

11. Perspectival limitations on the principle of relativity are recognized by John Lango: he reformulates the principle as "it belongs to the nature of *every* 'being' that it is a potential for *some* 'becoming.' This is the category of universal relativity" (1972, p. 23). Yet his reservations are only with respect to the future, and he takes virtually a cosmological, totalistic position. "Each entity in the universe is related to, but distinct from, every other entity." "Actual entities are the foci of universal relatedness" (P. 18). "Each entity in the actual world of an actual entity not only has the *potentiality* for being prehended but *is* prehended by that actual entity. . . . whether prehended positively or negatively, the entity is always relevant to that actual entity" (P. 23).

12. The ontological principle limits the principle of perspective, thereby, I will argue, diminishing its force and engendering a number of unresolvable difficulties in Whitehead's theory. The emphasis on actuality in the ontological principle is cosmological, and may be given an absolute, unconditioned, and therefore nonperspectival interpretation. "The doctrine that all actualities alike are in the grip of creativity suggests a general principle which Whitehead thinks every metaphysical scheme, so far as it is coherent, must follow. The principle is that there is ultimately but one kind of actuality" (Lowe 1966, pp. 36–37.)

13. Even so, many commentators have no difficulty in conceiving God as infinite and perfect, effectively absolute and unconditioned. "For Whitehead, God is the perfect 'actual entity' " (Pittenger 1969, p. 34).

14. See Leclerc, *Whitehead's Metaphysics*:

> The nature of an actual entity too, like that of an eternal object, has a two-fold aspect, also brought out respectively by the two words making up the term. . . . The former word stresses its "activity," and thus its "subjective immediacy," while the latter stresses its "potentiality" as involved in its role as "objectified." (1958, pp. 110–11)

This twofold aspect, if we emphasize the interpenetration and inseparability of the factors, is perspectival: activity and objectification always involve a point of view.

15. The principle of perspective as defined here is entirely free from the criticisms Hartshorne offers of "objective relativism" (see preface):

> The table which to me appears as red really does so appear to me; and this fact is as much a truth about the table as it is a truth about me. When things are in certain relations, they really are in these relations. Is this doctrine, which is called Objective Relativism, an adequate solution of the bifurcation question? Perhaps it is such a solution upon one condition, that objective relativism be combined with panpsychism. For suppose this condition not to be granted. Then whatever things do not happen to be present to sentient organisms, to be felt, will be without actual secondary qualities; and thus nature will consist after all of two parts, in but one of which qualities occur. (Hartshorne 1972, p. 23)

Objective relativism is far closer to the principle of experience than the principle of perspective, and lends itself to Hartshorne's view that panpsychism is necessary. I suggest an "objective perspectivism" rather than objective relativism. Uniqueness is essential to being and is inherent in perspectivity. Secondary qualities may be unique, relative to some perspectives and not to others, but when they are relevant they pertain to whatever they qualify, percipient organisms and perceived objects alike.

16. I am referring particularly to the difficulties thought to exist for the reality of past occasions and for unfelt propositions (see discussions, pp. 32–33).

17. See further discussion, pp. 32–33, 53–55.

18. The *purity* of eternal objects is a weakening of perspective, founded on the ontological principle. "The ideal is nothing more than a *possibility* (good *or* bad) *for* the actual" (Lowe 1966, p. 43). Yet the limitation of perspective here is only relative to actual entities, for eternal objects are perspectival relative to each other to the extent that they are intrinsically related and mutually constitutive. However, the perspectivity of eternal objects must be defined apart from prehension, which is a severe weakening of the principle of experience.

19. For a direct expression of the perspectivity inherent in Whitehead's notions of process and creativity, see Donald Sherburne's *A Whiteheadian Aesthetic*: "Whitehead's treatment of the Category of the Ultimate implies *one* process with two distinguishable species. . . . Ontologically speaking, transition and growth are faces of the same coin. . . . microscopic and macroscopic process are equally fundamental as features of that which is really real, since at bottom they are inseparable, though distinguishable" (1961, pp. 22, 23).

20. Very few commentators have recognized this important truth, though some have spoken of the "externality" of the relation of an actual occasion to future occasions. One writer who has recognized it is John Lango: "Whitehead states that an actual entity has a kind of completeness that a prehension lacks. . . . But a kind of incompleteness infests an actual entity as well; an actual entity refers beyond itself (through its 'superjective' nature) to those actual entities in the future which prehend it" (1972, p. 14).

21. This indeterminateness I consider essential to perspectivity. To be perspectival is to be conditioned, thereby relative and limited. However, I reject the view that limitation is equivalent with *finitude*. God and the extensive continuum are infinite but conditioned, as are all other infinites including the real number system—infinite in some respects, limited in others. When Lango claims that "only eternal objects (and God) are eternal; all other entities are created. Only God is infinite; all other entities are finite" (1972, p. 16), actual entities must be understood to be finite *in some respects*—in this case, relative to time. I suspect that Whitehead's confusion on this point is a consequence of his cosmological emphasis on the infinitude and perfection of God. Otherwise his position is clear.

All forms of realization express some aspect of finitude. Such a form expresses its nature as being *this*, and not *that*. In other words, it expresses exclusion; and exclusion means finitude. (MT 107)

22. See my *Transition to an Ordinal Metaphysics* (1980) and *Philosophical Mysteries* (1981).

CHAPTER TWO
CAUSATION

Actual entities are the center of Whitehead's theory and the locus of his theory of perspective. Conformal with the principle of experience, the "internal" becoming of actual entities is perspectival, from the standpoint of a subject. Relative to other actual entities, however, in particular those of the past, actual entities are as thoroughly perspectival, based on the vectoral nature of prehension. The prehension by an actual entity of the past is a causal relation: the past occasion is constitutive of a future occasion; conversely, the subsequent occasion is a perspective on the past. Such causal prehension is selective and restrictive, conferring status upon the past occasion relative to the subsequent occasion.

The prominence of causal relations in Whitehead's theory of actual occasions is testimony both to the role of the principle of perspective in his theory and to its fundamental limitations. I am referring to the essentially cosmological implications of the principle that the most fundamental and concrete elements of the world are causally located, that actuality involves a temporal location, at least to the extent that successiveness and inheritance are thereby made fundamental notions. The cosmos here is a world of succession. Closely related to the prominence of causation in Whitehead's theory is the restriction of perspectival centers to actual entities, though all his categories share the multifariousness that demands perspectivity for full expression. The principle of process is relevant here, and it is thoroughly cosmological, imposing a principle of primacy upon actuality and the world: "*how* an actual entity *becomes* constitutes *what* that actual entity *is*" (PR 23); "the actual world is a process, and . . . the process is the becoming of actual entities" (PR 22). In a fully perspectival theory, there can be no unqualified primacy to process nor to substance, for each of them is relative and conditioned.

Whitehead's causal theory is a perspectival theory. This alone should indicate how radically he requires us to rethink our traditional views of causation. Those commentators who find in his theory of causal prehension an inadequate answer to Hume largely fail to understand his answer—and more important, his recasting of Hume's questions.[1] There is no answer to Hume's questions concerning necessary causal connection and the validity of induction if we grant Hume's premises that only deductive validity and necessity are legitimate and that the present separates the past from the future. Whitehead offers a metaphysical explanation of what it means for there to be a genuine connection among past, present, and future. Such an explanation establishes causality, natural uniformity, and even a natural basis for our knowledge of such uniformity. Yet there can be no *proof* of natural order that does not presuppose order, as there can be no proof of a metaphysical theory without rational presuppositions. Perspectivity demands that we ascertain and acknowledge conditions, not that we seek a mode of proof that is absolute, devoid of conditions. Hume's criticisms of causality and induction are effectively unconditioned and nonperspectival (though, as Whitehead points out, conditions return in Hume's theory of habit and memory). Whitehead's response to Hume is thoroughly perspectival, accepting the importance and relevance of conditions in all judgment, the perspectivity of all being. Nevertheless, though the principle of perspective is essential to Whitehead's entire theory of causation, it is often weakened by positions drawn from the principle of experience and the cosmological principle. These issues must be considered in detail.

Causal Relations

The issue of causation is largely one of the togetherness of actual occasions, a relation through succession. The principle of perspective entails that all being is qualified and relational. The becoming of actual occasions is therefore conditioned not only by the past but also by the primordial nature of God. That latter relation is "conceptual"; the former is "physical," and is the foundation of causality. In addition, however, each actual entity is self-causative, transcending causation in its own becoming. There is a doubly double mode of relational conditions for the becoming of occasions: physical and conceptual prehension, causal prehension, and self-causation. The unification of these different moments into a single act of becoming is perspectival, resolved by Whitehead through the principle of experience in terms of the prehending occasion's subjective aim. Causal prehension is from the point of view of the prehending subject; the prehending subject's becoming is constituted—at least in part—by its causal relations.

The primacy of causal inheritance in becoming is manifested in the notion of *data* for the initial phase of every actual occasion. Category of explanation (xi) asserts "that every prehension consists of three factors: (a) the 'subject' which is prehending, namely, the actual entity in which that prehension is a concrete element; (b) the 'datum' which is prehended; (c) the 'subjective form' which is *how* that subject prehends that datum" (PR 23). I have noted that conditions (a) and (b) are perspectival conditions imposing a qualified status upon prehended data—in this case, the objectified occasions of the past. Condition (c) is derived from the principle of experience and suggests that perspectives require privacy for legitimacy. I will argue, in discussing self-causation, that uniqueness is essential to the concept of perspective, but that it does not require privacy or arbitrariness—both of which are finally unconditioned. In other words, the subjective form of prehension is a condition for prehension but violates the principle of perspective in being itself unconditioned (or based on conditions that are inexplicable in being private).

Another formulation of the factors of prehension is that "an actual entity has a threefold character: (i) it has the character 'given' for it by the past; (ii) it has the subjective character aimed at in its process of concrescence; (iii) it has the superjective character, which is the pragmatic value of its specific satisfaction qualifying the transcendent creativity" (PR 87). Here factors (i) and (ii) express the same directed status inherent in perspective and prehension, but (iii) adds another perspectival element: the status of an actual occasion for "transcendent creativity," or for the future. This version is entirely perspectival, containing only a rudimentary reference to subjective character in condition (ii), and is far closer to Whitehead's explicit requirements than the former.[2]

The data are the inherited characteristics of the settled world—that is, the immediate past directly, the remote past indirectly via diverse routes of inheritance (PR 120). This multiplicity of routes of inheritance of a remote past occasion through different mediating occasions is perspectival: the prehension of an occasion as mediated by different intermediaries synthesized into the final act of becoming. The prehensions of prehensions involved here are perspectives of perspectives. Causation from remote events is multiply perspectival. The status of a datum in an occasion is a function of its many different statuses for many different occasions. Objectification is here a very complex and perspectival notion, the functioning of an occasion for its future.[3]

Every actual occasion originates in a prehension of the past as datum, "objectified" for it. "The 'objectifications' of the actual entities in the actual world, relative to a definite actual entity, constitute the efficient causes out of which *that* actual entity arises" (PR 87). Objectification is the prehension of one entity by another through the mediation of eternal objects. This involves the participation of two entities: (1) an object with its ingressed eternal objects, and (2) a subject with its subjective aim. The relevance of the two conditions is an expression of the principle of perspective, since the object is always from the point of view of the prehending subject. The former component embodies Whitehead's modified version of the subjectivist principle—that it is *entities* which are prehended, not just their qualities. It is the basis of the principle that an occasion is a perspective upon its actual world, upon past occasions, not just a conceptual perspective upon eternal objects, a synthesis of forms of definiteness. Whitehead's theory of causation depends on the rejection of being as qualified solely by predicates, and includes other occasions as relevant constituents of the perspectives defined by concrescences. His doctrine of internal relations (constitutive of their terms) is a perspectival theory; and it is the perspectivity which obviates any suggestion of a regress.

The second component is an expression of the principle of experience and Whitehead's conviction that perspectivity depends on experience for its intelligibility. He formulates his position in terms of a complete rejection of the "sensationalist principle": "that the primary activity in the act of experience is the bare subjective entertainment of the datum, devoid of any subjective form of reception. This is the doctrine of *mere* sensation" (PR 157). The entertainment of the datum has a subjective character which makes it possible for Whitehead to say that each actual entity presides over its own becoming. *Mere* sensation is unqualified sensation. Whitehead's conviction that sensation cannot be bare entertainment of a datum is another expression of the principle of perspective—conferring status through subjective feeling upon the sensation—in relation to the principle of experience.

The subjectivist principle is what concerns us here: "that the datum in the act of experience can be adequately analyzed purely in terms of universals " (PR 157). In Whitehead's view, if causal relatedness could be fully analyzed in terms of universals, it would fall apart into discontinuity. The subjectivist principle consistently applied entails solipsism. Again, what is rejected is an unqualified, nonperspectival theory of relation in which universals and their exemplifications confer no status upon each other and have no status conferred by their relations to subjects. If prehension were reducible to the apprehension of universals, then relatedness among entities would be spurious, and all relations would be only with universals. Status relative to the past would be unintelligible; moreover, status relative to universals would be equally problematic since they are presumably unaffected by their exemplifications. The great tradition of regarding universals as self-sufficient and unaffected by events is thoroughly antiperspectival. Whitehead's theory is directed against the limitations of this view, though his rejection is incomplete in important ways relative to eternal objects.

> In contrast to Hume, the philosophy of organism keeps "this stone as grey" in the datum for the experience in question. It is, in fact, the "objective datum" of a certain physical feeling, belonging to a derivative type in a late phase of a concrescence. But this doctrine fully accepts Descartes' discovery that subjective experiencing is the primary metaphysical situation which is presented to metaphysics for analysis. This doctrine is the "reformed subjectivist principle," mentioned earlier in this chapter. Accordingly, the notion "this stone as grey" is a derivative abstraction, necessary indeed as an element in the description of the fundamental experiential feeling, but delusive as a metaphysical starting-point. This derivative abstraction is called an "objectification." (PR 160)

The basic elements are the following: (1) A generalized sense of experience such that the relation of past to present is via experience, prehension, or feeling, and which accommodates the objective content of a past actual entity as datum. This is the contribution of the principle of experience. (2) The principle that the datum may be analyzed in terms of the eternal objects which mediate in its prehension, but that such analysis neglects the prehensive character of actual entities. Actual entities originate in a datum phase which is the prehension of the past as possessing a particular character—but it is not this character alone which is prehended. (3) Nevertheless, there is an abstraction in which the objective content of a causal prehension is singled out. This is the partial truth of the subjectivist principle. Far more important, (4) there is a derivative abstraction already inherent in the notion of a past entity qualified by a universal—as in "the stone as grey." This is an abstraction from two prehensions: of the stone and of the form of greyness by the entities that constitute the stone. In this view of prehension, a perspective upon past occasions is the primary datum from which an abstraction is made to the relevant determinate content. In other words, causal prehension is understood as a double perspective: upon past events and upon relevant eternal objects.

Sense-data are eternal objects playing a complex relational rôle; they connect the actual entities of the past with the actual entities of the contemporary world, and thereby effect objectifications of the contemporary things and of the past things. For instance, we see the contemporary chair, but we see it *with* our eyes; and we touch the contemporary chair, but we touch it *with* our hands. Thus colours objectify the chair in one way, and objectify the eyes in another way, as elements in the experience of the subject. (PR 62)

Whitehead's ontological principle asserts that actual entities are ontologically primary: "the only reasons." In terms of the present discussion, this is equivalent to the claim that all explanation must ultimately reflect a subjective character—a prehension or feeling. This is again the principle of experience. What is lost in the perishing of an actuality is its own immediacy of feeling. What takes its place is the subjectivity of subsequent actualities. The past is always prehended (objectified) from some other subjective standpoint. But we neglect the subjectivity of the past in our subjective apprehension of it. This is objectification.

Actual entities become and they perish. It has frequently been thought problematical that Whitehead should maintain the reality of a perished entity.[4] If agency and actuality are primary, what is an actual entity that lacks actuality? The criticism, it seems to me, is based on a misunderstanding, overlooking the principle of perspective. Whitehead repudiates reality *simpliciter*. Being is perspectival, that is, significant. And there are two forms of significance: for oneself and for another. An actual entity is significant for itself when a subject; it is significant for future occasions as an object.[5] This is fully expressed by the principle of relativity. Past occasions *are*, though perished, because they are potentials for future events. Whitehead does not deny the reality or being of the past, but he does deny its being *simpliciter*. The past exists *for* the future (excluding God).[6] The general formula for existence here is 'X is *for* Y,'' where Y is an actual entity functioning as a subject prehending X;[7] X participates in Y through being prehended. The special case where X is both subject and object is the case of self-significance and the foundation of what is primary in Whitehead's system.[8] That an actual entity functions as a superject "presiding over its own becoming" establishes that it provides its own transition from self-significance to significance as an object for subsequent prehensive occasions. Overemphasis on subjectivity in Whitehead's theory neglects the perspectivity of experience: that both an object and a point of view are required. In this sense, the principle of perspective entirely resolves the question of the status of the past.[9]

The notion of "objectification" provides the basis of causal order in nature. "The primary stage in the concrescence of an actual entity is the way in which the antecedent universe enters into the constitution of the entity in question, so as to constitute the basis of its nascent individuality" (PR 152). "Every actual entity springs from *that* universe which there *is for it*. Causation is nothing else than one outcome of the principle that every actual entity has to house *its* actual world" (PR 80). These references to the past world may be perspectival or cosmological: causation requires only the emergence of subsequent occasions out of conditions determined by past occasions. This conditionedness is perspectival. It is cosmological where the past world is total and unconditioned by the present.[10] The origination of an entity in the context of the past circumscribes the range of possibilities available for that entity. "No actual entity can arise beyond what the actual world as a datum from its standpoint—*its* actual world—allows it to be (PR 83). This formulation is entirely perspectival.

We are led to the issues of novelty and freedom, for causation and freedom are reciprocal and complementary concepts. This complementarity, which Whitehead recognizes dimly and incompletely, is a fundamental feature of perspectivity. Causation and freedom are conditions for each other. The factors that establish causal inheritance define the possibilities of novel becoming. The past is given for becoming. "The character of an actual entity is finally governed by its datum; whatever be the freedom of feeling arising in the concrescence, there can be no transgression of the limitations of capacity inherent in the datum" (PR 110). If that given qualifies further becoming, we must explain how its limitations afford a prospect of novelty. If the past does not qualify later becoming, then causal inheritance is merely nominal. But the notion of causal inheritance must not be understood to preclude novelty and freedom—and, in Whitehead's theory, it cannot do so. The past circumscribes the possibilities available, but each actual entity makes its own decision as to what it will become. This is what Whitehead means by saying that each actual entity is *causa sui*. This self-causation, founded on the principle of experience, defines a very strong principle of perspective relative to causal determination. Each actual entity, in determining its subjective aim, defines its own actual world in terms of its past, making a transition from the " 'initial data' which are to be felt" to "the 'objective datum' which is felt" (PR 221).

I am concerned here with Whitehead's perspectival recognition that causation and freedom are complementary notions, and that we cannot understand one without the other. His position is a direct consequence of the principle of perspective in relation to the past: the conditions of determinateness are perspectivally or vectorally related to origination and freedom, for the individual perspectival center is a joint outcome of both the past conditions and its self-identity. Causal relations to the past are established on the basis of a perspectival center of experience *constituted* by those relations, yet one which cannot be altogether, without qualification, so constituted, thereby opening the possibility of freedom and self-determination. The double character of perspectival relations establishes causation and freedom together as complementary and reciprocal notions.

Whitehead's theory of causation is an example of both his debt and his reply to Bradley. Bradley's critique of relations is founded on the principle that terms and relations must constitute each other, but cannot do so. In Whitehead's theory, each actuality arises in the prehension of past actualities; nevertheless, each actual entity is also *causa sui*. This self-causation, embodied in its subjective aim, establishes an identity for an entity irreducible to its multiplicity of elements. Self-causation is the foundation of the perspectival focus that is the basis of the concept of prehension, a vectoral constitutive relation that is Whitehead's reply to Bradley (who never imagined such a mode of relation, for he had no conception of a metaphysical perspectivism). Self-causation, here, is the basis of the principle of perspective, and is grounded in the principle of experience. The limitations as well as the strengths of Whitehead's theory of causation, freedom, and self-identity depend on this notion. My detailed discussion of the weaknesses of Whitehead's theory of causation is therefore to be found in chapter 3.

Providing a metaphysical basis for a general principle of causation does not of itself make intelligible the lawful character of events. Both the determinateness of causal connections and the possibilities necessary to freedom must be considered. Whitehead accommodates in his analysis both a causal inheritance that can promote uniformity in nature and a subjective perspectivity that can promote novelty. Uniformity and variance are also complementary notions that depend on established conditions for their particular prominence. What is involved are the conditions in events that accommodate successful scientific inquiry.

The Uniformity of Nature

The question of the uniformity of nature is a complex one with many facets. In modest form, as Hume conceives it, it is a question of the grounds for inferences to the future from experienced instances. Yet it may be generalized to address, on the one hand, the basis of natural law and, on the other, the question of continuity through time. Both of these uniformities appear cosmological, a condition imposed absolutely on the universe without natural conditions or qualifications.[11] Yet the perspectivity of actual occasions is inherent in natural uniformity as well as in causal prehension and succession. The causal relations of occasions do not of themselves establish natural uniformity, since each actual entity is self-determinative in part, a seat of novel creativity. The striking feature of Whitehead's theory, however, rooted in the principle of perspective, is that the apparent disruption of causal connection produced by self-determination is the ultimate basis of both causation and natural uniformity. The fundamental point again is the complementary relationship of freedom and causation, expressed in the perspectival nature of prehension in which an occasion is simultaneously a self-determining focus of a prehensive perspective and constituted by its prehensions of objectified occasions of the past.

In the small, causation is founded on objectified prehension. A multiplicity of past occasions is prehended as data for the becoming of a future occasion. This is nothing less than the movement of creativity from past to future. In the large, however, natural uniformity depends on a community of occasions. Either such togetherness is imposed from without upon natural events or it must be a function of prehension, imbued thereby with prehensive perspectivity. Hume's solution to the problem of this togetherness is based on the notion of *repetition*, a solution that Whitehead criticizes in a number of ways.

One criticism is that Hume dismisses the possibility of any impression of connection, yet requires that notion in his conception of repetition. "Hume seems to have overlooked the difficulty that 'repetition' stands with regard to 'impressions' in exactly the same position as does 'cause and effect.' Hume has confused a 'repetition of impressions' with an 'impression of repetitions of impressions' " (PR 134). As Kant argues, no solution to an epistemological problem is possible without a ground in connection and relation. On the one hand, Hume repudiates any ground of togetherness in experience. On the other, his solution rests upon the continuity through time embodied in the notions of habit and repetition. "Hume's philosophy is pervaded by the notion of 'repetition,' and that memory is a particular example of this character of experience, that in some sense there is entwined in its fundamental nature the fact that it is repeating something. Tear 'repetition' out of 'experience,' and there is nothing left" (PR 136). Either there is no connection among elements of experience, in which case we have an extreme solipsism and nothing can be explained, even experience, or some principle of connection must be found—which Hume defines as custom, habit, or repetition.

Repetition has another feature besides connectedness: that of similarity. Not only do later events arise out of earlier ones, but they preserve important traits of that past. Not only is the past a factor in later becoming, in constituting its source, but the past provides characteristics that subsequent events perpetuate. In Whitehead's view, actual entities inherit from the past; but they are also free and can supplement their inheritance through conceptual reversion. Causal prehension alone cannot establish sustained uniformity. It is societies which provide enduring uniformity in nature.

The important thing, Whitehead tells us, is that a society is self-sustaining. "It is its own reason" (PR 89). This identity, which a society both possesses and imposes, is perspectival in nature, in a variety of ways.

> The members of the society are alike because, by reason of their common character, they impose on other members of the society the conditions which lead to that likeness.
>
> This likeness consists in the fact that (i) a certain element of "form" is a contributory component to the individual satisfaction of each member of the society; and that (ii) the contribution by the element to the objectification of any one member of the society for prehension by other members promotes its analogous reproduction in the satisfactions of those other members. Thus a set of entities is a society (i) in virtue of a "defining characteristic" shared by its members, and (ii) in virtue of the presence of the defining characteristic being due to the environment provided by the society itself. (PR 89)

The defining characteristic shared by members of a society, a common element shared through time and space, is what we call the uniformity of nature. There is no reason to emphasize time here at the expense of space. Uniformity requires common features pervasive throughout regions extended in both space and time.

A society is not simply a set of entities with a common form, but is "self-sustaining" and "its own reason." It can be so self-determining only through the environment it engenders for its members. "A society is, for each of its members, an environment with some element of order in it, persisting by reason of the genetic relations between its own members. Such an element of order is the order prevalent in the society" (PR 90). A society creates an environment that is favorable for its own existence—which means its reproduction in subsequent members; and when that environment ceases to be favorable, the society passes away. This imposition of social environment is doubly perspectival: it is a sustained and ordered multiplicity prehended by member occasions (and other occasions as well, through the principle of transmutation), in this sense *in perspective*; but it is also an environment *imposed* on its members, actively sustaining a coherent character. A society here has both individual character and multiplicity, closely interrelated by ordered relations. Like an actual occasion, a society is constituted by its members, yet imposes itself upon them through the environment it provides for them.

The concept of an "environment" is an important one, particularly in relation to the principle of perspective. It is worth noting the system of environments within which any local environment possesses its character. "Every society requires a social background, of which it is itself a part. In reference to any given society the world of actual entities is to be conceived as forming a background in layers of social order, the defining characteristics becoming wider and more general as we widen the background" (PR 90). Not only, then, do actual entities define a perspective upon the entire actual world, but they define multiple and overlapping perspectives in which particular characters are possessed by multiple inclusion.

> The character of an organism depends on that of its environment. But the character of an environment is the sum of the characters of the various societies of actual entities which jointly constitute that environment; although it is pure assumption that every environment is completely overrun by societies of entities. Spread through the environment there may be many entities which cannot be assigned to any society of entities. The societies in an environment will constitute its orderly element, and the non-social actual entities will constitute its element of chaos. There is no reason, so far as our knowledge is concerned, to conceive the actual world as purely orderly, or as purely chaotic. (PR 110)

Each actual entity is the focal center of many perspectives of varying degrees of inclusiveness. This is a fundamental element of the principle of perspective, to be conjoined with the two elements discussed in the first chapter: point of view and qualification. The three conditions together define the multiple locatedness definitive of the inexhaustibility of perspectives. Whitehead thinks of social location as providing order and stability; he does not see that multiple social locatedness is the source of inexhaustibility and indeterminateness as well.

Actual entities are focal centers of inclusive and overlapping perspectives, but so are nexūs and societies. Indeed, the location of a society within many environments is essential to social character. A corollary of such multiple location, however, is that a society can only in part define its own environment, for that environment has a role in a wider context of conditions favorable or unfavorable to it. This indeterminateness of determination, produced by the multiple location of actual entities in diverse environments and perspectives, is a property of societies and occasions alike, and is a central characteristic of their perspectivity. Societies as well as occasions play this double (or multiple) role of being constituted by their environments and constituting their environments—*many* environments—so that the relations in which they participate are always multiply qualified and referent to the characters of the individuals involved.

The universe comprises the widest environment in Whitehead's theory and engenders the conditions that smaller societies adopt. This condition, of a widest perspective, is cosmological, and it is in continual tension with the multifarious modes of determination produced by overlapping perspectives. Nevertheless, even in Whitehead's cosmological terms, there are tenuous and indeterminate relations among environments or perspectives at different levels of inclusiveness. We cannot infer from the societies which we encounter that the universe conforms to our local conditions—only that such conditions must be encouraged by the complex relations smaller environments bear to larger ones. Thus, Whitehead distinguishes between the metaphysical characteristics of entities and the traits that are implicated in natural laws.

> The metaphysical characteristics of an actual entity—in the proper general sense of "metaphysics"—should be those which apply to all actual entities. It may be doubted whether such metaphysical concepts have ever been formulated in their strict purity—even taking into account the most general principles of logic and of mathematics. We have to confine ourselves to societies sufficiently wide, and yet such that their defining characteristics cannot safely be ascribed to all actual entities which have been or may be. (PR 90)

Natural laws represent the dominant characteristics of social order at any time. Yet even this general social order may be transitory. "A system of 'laws' determining reproduction in some portion of the universe gradually rises into dominance; it has its stage of endurance, and passes out of existence with the decay of the society from which it emanates. The arbitrary, as it were 'given,' elements in the laws of nature warn us that we are in a special cosmic epoch" (PR 91). Within a cosmic epoch, some laws of nature are dominant, representing the prevalence of wide and enduring societies. Yet it is an error to suppose either that our cosmic epoch will endure forever, or that it may change abruptly.

This complex and multiple social character in Whitehead's theory, which enables us to entertain the possibility that no known or even formulatable natural laws will prevail over all cosmic epochs and throughout the extended universe, is a direct consequence of the principle of perspective and a continual difficulty for the cosmological principle. The multiply perspectival and social character of each occasion, located as it is in an indefinite number of social environments, works against any all-inclusive social environment or pervasive character. Indeed, the universe need be no society—thereby, no (single) environment—with a dominant character, but a multiplicity of nexūs or perspectives with inclusive and overlapping relations. Every perspective here would be limited and restrictive—part of the very notion of qualification. The concept of a society extends the notion of perspective in Whitehead's theory beyond that of actual entities, yet also calls into question the cosmological assumption that the universe has a comprehensive identity. The perspectivity of societies is a central issue for Whitehead's cosmology. Social orders extend the perspectivity of being throughout the natural world.

Natural Teleology

The double movement in perspectivity of multiplicity and identity is paralleled by the double movement of determinateness and indeterminateness. I have noted the perspectival complementarity in Whitehead's theory of causation and self-causation. It is closely paralleled by the double (or multiple) role of environments of differing inclusiveness as determining conditions of social order but also as indeterminants, opening social order to modification and variation. The capacity of social environments, diversely inclusive perspectives, to serve simultaneously as determining conditions of order and as loosening conditions of variation is a central feature of their perspectivity. Generalizing, we may conclude that perspective in Whitehead's theory is so thoroughgoing and pervasive that necessity is always coupled with, complementary with, indeterminateness and variation. This perspectival complementarity is repeated at every phase and level of Whitehead's theory, a reflection of the multiplicity of determination inherent in the second element of perspective identified above.

I have discussed the grounding of natural uniformity on social order—thereby both a function of established conditions and variant with changing conditions. What is needed in addition is an explanation of the trend toward uniformity, toward social order. Societies are the basis of cosmic order; what is the basis of societies? The question is a cosmological one and is given a cosmological answer conjoined with strong perspectival elements. On the one hand, while the natural laws of our epoch may be contingent, and other epochs pervaded by different societies, social order as such does not appear to be entirely accidental. Yet in Whitehead's view, "there may evidently be a state in which there are no prevalent societies securing any congruent unity of effect. This is a state of chaotic disorder; it is disorder approaching an absolute sense of that term"(PR 92). Chaos is not unthinkable—to the contrary, it is often proposed as the initial or final stages of our universe. It is then essential to explain how order could come to pass from such chaos. Social order here is simultaneously determined by fundamental conditions, yet loosened by those same conditions. The reciprocity and complementarity of perspective is again essential. Order and disorder are complementary and inseparable notions.

As have so many philosophers before him, and for similar cosmological reasons, Whitehead takes God to be the ultimate ground of order. Such ultimate grounds of order seem to contradict the possibility of disorder and to weaken the complementarity of perspective. "The immanence of God gives reason for the belief that pure chaos is intrinsically impossible" (PR 111). Whitehead holds this principle to be an ultimate conception of religious thought, though too often in the fallacious form that the universe strives for a particular, ultimate order. He goes on to say that "the immensity of the world negatives the belief that any state of order can be so established that beyond it there can be no progress. This belief in a final order, popular in religious and philosophic thought, seems to be due to the prevalent fallacy that all types of seriality necessarily involve terminal instances" (PR 111). Even here, then, the ultimate grounds of order must leave room for variation. This intimate relationship of determinateness and indeterminateness is perspectival, even in its cosmological form. Nevertheless, the central question from the standpoint of perspectivity is whether a cosmic form of order can be sustained. I will argue that even God's primordial nature must be conditioned by the events to which it applies, and that there can be no ultimate, cosmic order beyond established social communities. This conclusion is required by the principle of perspective, and is not altogether incompatible with the bulk of Whitehead's theory.

Like other actual entities, God "transcends the rest of actuality," and is "transcended by the creativity which it qualifies" (PR 88). Since he is transcended by actuality, God's aim cannot be a determinate end toward which the universe evolves. Nevertheless, he is ultimate in some sense, and "is considered as the outcome of creativity, as the foundation of order, and as the goad towards novelty. 'Order' and 'novelty' are but the instruments of his subjective aim which is the intensification of 'formal immediacy' " (PR 88).[12] God is the ground of novelty in being the source of all possibility. He is the ground of order in establishing the relevance of these possibilities to every becoming. God is the supreme and ultimate perspective upon the entire universe, all its conditions and its becomings. The strength of Whitehead's theory—but also one of its most prominent limitations—is the perspectivity of God, who is simultaneously a condition for all becoming and conditioned by that becoming. The same complementarity of dependence and independence, determinateness and indeterminateness, inherent in all perspectives is central to the nature of God.

What requires discussion here is the notion of the "intensity" at which God aims. "The primordial appetitions which jointly constitute God's purpose are seeking intensity, and not preservation" (PR 105). Intensity is grounded in the principle of experience by the category of subjective intensity. Yet it does not depend on that principle alone, since it is inherent in the play of multiplicity and identity that is entailed by the principle of perspective. Contrasts are defined as *patterned entities* or *modes of synthesis of entities in one prehension* (category of existence [viii]) (PR 22). The principle of experience is implicated in the latter description but unnecessary to the former. Perspectivity entails a unity in multiplicity that leads directly to contrasts.

The clearest description Whitehead offers of intensity is

the reward of narrowness. The domination of the environment by a few social groups is the factor producing both the vagueness of discrimination between actual entities and the intensification of relevance of common characteristics. These are the two requisites for narrowness. The lower organisms have low-grade types of narrowness; the higher organisms have intensified contrasts in the higher categories. (PR 112)

It is "common characteristics," dominant elements of form, that are intensified. Low-grade types of narrowness couple vagueness with intensity: differences among members of a society are neglected, intensifying the dominant characteristic. Intensity, here, is a property of social order, a function equally of the individual members of a society and of the common and enduring nature of a society. Whitehead locates the intensity in the satisfaction of the component actual entities by the principle of experience. Alternatively, we may regard intensity as an outcome of the multiple nature of any mode of existence with its intrinsic identity and its multiple relatedness. Intensity is a potential for every being, including eternal objects in their multiple gradations of relevance and ingressions. But this view would require a more thoroughgoing perspectivism than Whitehead defines through prehension.

The second type of intensity, "contrasts in the higher categories," is typical of those forms of experience with which we are most thoroughly acquainted. "The problem for Nature is the production of societies which are 'structured' with a high 'complexity,' and which are at the same time 'unspecialized.' In this way, intensity is mated with survival" (PR 101). "There are two ways in which structured societies have solved this problem. Both ways depend on that enhancement of the mental pole, which is a factor in intensity of experience" (PR 101). The first way "is by eliciting a massive average objectification of a nexus, while eliminating the detailed diversities of the various members of the nexus in question" (PR 101). "There is some initiative of conceptual integration, but no originality in conceptual prehension" (PR 101). This is the first type of intensification mentioned: narrowness by exclusion. "These material bodies belong to the lowest grade of structured societies which are obvious to our gross apprehensions. They comprise societies of various types of complexity—crystals, rocks, planets, and suns. Such bodies are easily the most long-lived of the structured societies known to us, capable of being traced through their individual life-histories" (PR 102). Intensity here is endurance of character by minimization of responsiveness, idiosyncrasy, and contrast. A society that so massively endures "employs the device of blocking out unwelcome detail" (PR 101). We have perspectives in which stability of social form is the predominant element.

The contrasts that arise in higher mental operations require originality.

> The second way of solving the problem is by an initiative in conceptual prehensions, i.e., in appetition. The purpose of this initiative is to receive the novel elements of the environment into explicit feelings with such subjective forms as conciliate them with the complex experiences proper to members of the structured society. Thus in each concrescent occasion its subjective aim originates to match the novelty of the environment.
> In the case of higher organisms, this conceptual initiative amounts to

thinking about the diverse experiences; in the case of lower organisms, this conceptual initiative merely amounts to thoughtless adjustment of aesthetic emphasis in obedience to an ideal of harmony. In either case the creative determination which transcends the occasion in question has been deflected by an impulse original to that occasion. (PR 102)

Intensity here is not emphasis on a particular form, but a tension among elements of a contrast requiring original conceptual integration. The narrowness of intensity is realized either in a sharp contrast between the individual members of a society and its dominant form or by a complex contrast in which the fusion of elements held in integration by mental activity is intensified. In both cases, the contrast between the individuality of the perspective and its plural conditions is the basis of intensity, in one case by stability, in the other by variation and adaptation. In both cases, as a consequence of the principle of experience, intensity is a function of subjectivity. Only the second, however, is typical in human and animal experience.

We may now return to the claim that the subjective aim of God is toward intensity, not preservation. "God's purpose in the creative advance is the evocation of intensities" (PR 105). This conclusion follows from the conception of God as an experiencing subject. It is based on the application of the category of subjective intensity to the actual entity which is God. "The subjective aim, whereby there is origination of conceptual feeling, is at intensity of feeling (α) in the immediate subject, and (β) in the *relevant* future" (PR 27). This category defines the completion of an actual entity as a satisfaction—the integration of the complex elements of concrescence into a unified whole with intensive qualities. As experiencer, God aims at the fulfillment of his consequent nature, which is the conscious contrast of what is and has been against what might be as determined by his primordial nature, a satisfaction enhanced by all other contrasts.

God's primordial nature is a system of relations among eternal objects partially ordered in complex hierarchies. This system contains not only relatively simple forms, but complex patterns of indefinite complexity. A world without societies could realize only the lower orders of eternal objects and relations among them. A chaotic universe would be one of constantly shifting characteristics, lacking the complex forms endurance can bring to pass. God's primordial nature therefore imposes an urge upon the world toward intensity. The principle of experience, in application to God, provides a foundation for the macrocosmic order of the universe. The complex hierarchical system of eternal objects calls for maximal realization in the world. This is God's "yearning after concrete fact—no particular facts, but after *some* actuality" (PR 33). Higher and more complex grades of eternal objects can be realized only in the most intense modes of experience, and the instrument of such intensification is social order.

Intensity of experience is Whitehead's ultimate explanation of the social order that underlies natural law. Here the principle of experience appears essential, for atomism and causal prehension appear compatible with social chaos. Intensity preserves the two relevant poles of freedom and stability: social order is significant only in the context of the alternative of disorder; the determinateness of natural laws is coupled with the indeterminateness of instability. The teleology here is based on God and has a marked cosmological and theological character: the direction or purpose of the universe based on God's experience.

As an alternative, we may consider the possibilities of order inherent in the principle of perspective independent of the cosmological principle and the principle of experience. The relevant premise is the inexhaustible multiplicity of perspectives and environments for any individual perspective. Intensity is inherent in all perspectives due to the complementarity of unity with multiplicity, but is realized in its more complex forms only at higher levels of organization. Nevertheless, chaos is impossible and unintelligible from the standpoint of perspective—chaos as disorder, as nonperspective. Perspectivity is order—but order immersed in disorder and conversely. Order is inherent in perspectivity—but not necessarily the orders we find around us. I am suggesting that perspectivity of itself is a basis for macrocosmic order and intensity, but that there is no explanation beyond the perspectives that there are, the kinds of order that there are (or were) for further intensity and cosmic order. Some social environments tend toward greater intensity and structure, others toward greater intensity through origination and adaptation, some toward dissolution and decay: but there is no universal order, no universal, comprehensive experience, no universal trend toward particular forms of order. The possibility of social decay in the physical universe as we know it is no denial of either perspective or intensity, for the dissolution may be intense: but it is a disconfirmation of the order God's experience imposes on the world.

The fact that two major forms of intensity are possible creates an interesting and ironic situation. The intensities generated by massive endurance promote the greatest possible uniformities, providing both secure environments and stable objects for living organisms. But the intensity of experience generated in living and complex organisms who live in a stable and secure world, since it is an intensity based on contrasts in the mental pole, is dependent on the greatest originality possible. The two modes of experience aim at opposite goals—the one toward uniformity, the other toward novelty. Together, they promote an even greater intensification: social uniformity in tension with social adaptation and variation. This intensification is a predominant feature of reflective life, but it manifests a pervasive, even metaphysical feature of perspectivity: the tension of stability with origination in complex organisms and institutions, the perspectivity inherent in the most complex forms of organization.

Inductive Knowledge

I have discussed the metaphysical components of Whitehead's theory of causation and their relationship to the principles of experience, cosmology, and perspective. It would be appropriate to consider some aspects of Whitehead's theory of knowledge in this context; further discussion will be found in chapter 5. A natural consequence of the principle of perspective is that knowledge, causal and in general, is a perspectival outcome, heavily dependent on the standpoint of an agent or judge.

The foundation of Whitehead's explanation of inductive knowledge is that order prevails. Whatever may be our evidence for belief in particular principles of natural order, order in general is required by any theory of the universe. Whitehead criticizes Hume far more for his inadequate metaphysical principles than for his epistemological assumptions. The main purpose of cosmology, to Whitehead, is to restore to our sense of the world those principles that constitute it an intelligible order. This is part of what he means when he says:

> The philosophy of organism is the inversion of Kant's philosophy. *The Critique of Pure Reason* describes the process by which subjective data pass into the appearance of an objective world. The philosophy of organism seeks to describe how objective data pass into subjective satisfaction, and how order in the objective data provides intensity in the subjective satisfaction. For Kant, the world emerges from the subject; for the philosophy of organism, the subject emerges from the world. (PR 88)

This passage is a constellation of the three principles I have been emphasizing: the principle of experience in the passage of data into subjective satisfaction, the cosmological perspective upon the world, and the perspectivity inherent in the emergence of a unique individual.

I have discussed the social nature of the world and resulting natural uniformities. This social nature, including the social character of the knowing and judging subject, is what makes inductive inference possible.

> Every actual entity is in its nature essentially social; and this in two ways. First, the outlines of its own character are determined by the data which its environment provides for its process of feeling. Secondly, these data are not extrinsic to the entity; they constitute that display of the universe which is inherent in the entity. Thus the data upon which the subject passes judgment are themselves components conditioning the character of the judging subject. It follows that any general presupposition as to the character of the experiencing subject also implies a general presupposition as to the social environment providing the display for that subject. (PR 203)

This passage merits extended consideration.

An actual entity as judging subject originates within a world which provides data for its becoming. This world is its environment and is a determinative factor in the character of its experience. Nevertheless, an actual entity also determines its actual world by selection and exclusion. It follows that the character of an actual entity and its actual world are mutually implicated. In its own experience, a subject finds traits that reveal the world. Setting aside the experiential elements here, we have a clear expression of the principle of perspective with some of its most powerful implications. The perspectival standpoint of an experiencing subject is multiply conditioned by diversely overlapping environments, each of which is itself multiply perspectival. Inference is a function of perspectival standpoint, but it is a standpoint grounded in complex and perspectival patterns of natural order.

Minimally, inductive inference presupposes a persistence in the experiencing subject through time. But the persistence of the experiencing subject entails the persistence of an environment for that subject, therefore a continuity of inheritance.

> ... in every forecast there is a presupposition of a certain type of actual entities, and that the question then asked is, Under what circumstances will these entities find themselves? The reason that an answer can be given is that the presupposed type of entities requires a presupposed type of data for the primary phases of these actual entities; and that a presupposed type of data requires a presupposed type of social environment. But the laws of nature are the outcome of the social environment. Hence when we have

presupposed a type of actual occasions, we have already some information as to the laws of nature in operation throughout the environment. (PR 204)

Whitehead's argument is that to posit a question of inductive inference is to presuppose the endurance as well as the standpoint of the subject who poses the question. Induction presupposes a perspectival standpoint grounded in social order. There are no questions without such standpoints. The standpoint of the question, "Will the future be like the past? " entails a persistence into that future. More generally, inferences and questions are conditioned—as are all modes of perspectival being—and are both limited by and fulfilled by those conditions. The social order—the perspectival conditions—which permits us to ask questions also defines conditions for their solution. The very notion of inductive inference rests upon the precondition of sufficient order in the environment to make some such inferences legitimate.[13] The social order presupposed in offering an inductive inference rests on an environment with sufficient order to reproduce itself into the future. "The completely unknown environment never enters into an inductive judgment" (PR 205).[14]

In every inductive judgment, there is therefore contained a presupposition of the maintenance of the general order of the immediate environment, so far as concerns actual entities within the scope of the induction. The inductive judgment has regard to the statistical probabilities inherent in this given order. The anticipations are devoid of meaning apart from the definite cosmic order which they presuppose. (PR 204–205)

I suggest again that the conditions inherent in every perspectival determination in which questions of order arise provide a basis for intensity and social order that is sufficient to our purposes without God and his subjective experience. The question of the future is conditioned by the present, from its perspective. The question of why there is order is not unconditioned, but rests on the perspectival conditions from which it emerges. The general answer to the problem of induction is that no such problem can be formulated absolutely and nonperspectivally, while there is no problem of induction relative to any conditioned standpoint.

The category of transmutation provides Whitehead with a principle of transition from the multiplicity of actual entities that comprises a society to the entire society as felt through its dominant form. This principle converts the togetherness of members of a society in their prehensions to a togetherness from other perspectival standpoints. "Some category is required to provide a physical feeling of a nexus as one entity with its own categoreal type of existence" (PR 251). We project our expectations into the future on the basis of the experience of enduring objects, societies of entities experienced under the principle of transmutation. Such transmutation is perspectival and selective.

> Transmutation is the way in which the actual world is felt as a community, and is so felt in virtue of its prevalent order. For it arises by reason of the analogies between the various members of the prehended nexus, and eliminates their differences. Apart from transmutation our feeble intellectual operations would fail to penetrate into the dominant characteristics of things. We can only understand by discarding. (PR 251)

The category of transmutation also enters into that type of intensification which is massive endurance. A world that accommodates massive and frequent transmutation is one in which inductive knowledge has a basis in the facts of social order.

The social relations that establish order as the ground for inferences regarding the future are the basis of the vague immanence of contemporary entities in each other in virtue of common elements of the past.

> There is thus a certain indirect immanence of contemporary occasions in each other. For if A and B be contemporaries, and C be in the past of both of them, then A and B are each in a sense immanent in C, in the way in which the future can be immanent in its past. But C is objectively immortal in both A and B. Thus, in this indirect sense, A is immanent in B, and B is immanent in A. But the objective immortality of A does not operate in B, nor does that of B operate in A. As individual complete actualities, A is shrouded from B, and B is shrouded from A.[15]

Since contemporary occasions do not prehend each other, the relationship can be no stronger than that provided by common elements of social order.[16]

As is to be expected by the cosmological principle, God provides the ultimate ground for inductive inference and for all inferences involving novelty. God's primordial nature is the ultimate basis of the relevance of eternal objects to the data of the actual world. Each actual entity prehends "the graduated order of appetitions constituting the primordial nature of God" (PR 207). This prehension supports an intuition which permits inferences from the past to novelties of the future. "In this way, there can be an intuition of probability respecting the origination of some novelty" (PR 207). It is a fundamental question for later examination whether a cosmic perspective is required as a basis for natural laws and scientific knowledge. The alternative is that since perspectivity, including novelty, is pervasive throughout natural existence, we anticipate novel variations in the future through perspectival interaction, but fallibly and incompletely. No cosmic intuition is needed to explain a perspectival projection from complexly overlapping environments into a novel future, provided that such a projection is limited, relative, and fallible.

Causal Perception

Whitehead repudiates Hume's theory of impressions and his requirement of logical necessity in causal relations; but Whitehead does appear to accept the view that our belief in causal connection is rooted in perception. Although his entire theory is based upon causal connection, he seems unsatisfied with the theoretical principle that actual entities originate in an inheritance from the past. His perspectival ontology is closely associated with a perceptual epistemology in which the primary paradigm of perspective is given by conscious perception, and the question of *proof*, which is largely irrelevant to his metaphysical concerns, emerges into prominence. He claims, for example, that "elucidation of immediate experience is the sole justification for any thought" (PR 4), and seems to seek an ultimate epistemic ground of our belief in causal inheritance in conscious perception. Part of his conviction here is based on a concern for understanding perspectives through the paradigm of perception—a natural enough paradigm, though often a misleading one. Part of his conviction, however, is concerned with grounding metaphysical principles in immediate human experience. This latter part, essentially an epistemological concern, requires detailed examination, for I believe it badly distorts both the nature of metaphysical generalization and the principle of perspective.

Whitehead's account of perception is recurrently affected by this epistemological concern. On the one hand, perception is a highly derivative notion, applicable only to higher experience; on the other hand, it plays a central role in all actualities as the paradigm of prehension, thereby the foundation of perspectives. It is often difficult to tell whether presentational immediacy and causal efficacy are modes of *perception* or *prehension*, whether they are restricted to human experience or applicable to all actual entities. The principle of causal inheritance—that an entity originates in the prehension of the past world as datum—is true for all occasions. However, Whitehead also seems to say that we consciously perceive causal connections. It is difficult to see why he believes causal connection is to be grounded epistemologically in conscious experience. A possibility is that he follows the principle of experience ambiguously, sometimes recognizing that the principle of perspective embodies the major force of the paradigm of experience, sometimes looking to human experience as a full ground of the principle of perspective.[17]

All relations involving actual entities are prehensions in Whitehead's system, including the physical prehension of the past. The question is whether such prehension can be identified with human perception—with so complex, sophisticated, and cognitive a mode of experience. Whitehead's concern for feeling in experience may be divided in two: feeling as a constituent of experience and becoming, a category complex enough to serve for all relatedness, essentially a perspectival notion; and feeling as the specific ground of veridical judgment. The very notion of prehension as *feeling*—in conformity with the principle of experience—seems to force us to consider both of these, while the principle of perspective, expressed through prehension, seems to avoid the epistemological factor at this level of generality. It is not clear how causal efficacy as a perspectival element in becoming can serve as a ground of judgment. It is too inchoate, vague, and unreflective.[18] Even more difficult to understand is why Whitehead calls it a mode of "perception."

In his first formulation in *Process and Reality*, Whitehead defines causal efficacy as the sheer physical inheritance of the character of the past.

> The experience of the simplest grade of actual entity is to be conceived as the unoriginative response to the datum with its simple content of sensa.... There is thus a transmission of sensation emotion from A, B, and C to M.... Thus the (unconscious) direct perception of A, B, and C is merely the causal efficacy of A, B, and C as elements in the constitution of M. (PR 115–16)

Causal efficacy is unconscious and vague, relevant to the simplest grade of actual entity. Energy transmission is a form of perception in the mode of causal efficacy. Here "perception" is simply a nontechnical translation of "prehension," while "prehension" simply designates the constitution of emergent perspectives by past occasions.

> The perceptive mode of causal efficacy is to be traced to the constitution of the datum by reason of which there is a concrete percipient entity. Thus we

must assign the mode of causal efficacy to the fundamental constitution of an occasion so that in germ this mode belongs even to organisms of the lowest grade; while the mode of presentational immediacy requires the more sophistical activity of the later stages of process, so as to belong only to organisms of a relatively high grade. (PR 172)[19]

All actual entities inherit perspectively from the past; but only in higher organisms can we find "the enhancement of the importance of relationships which were already in the datum, vaguely and with slight relevance" (PR 173). Since this "enhancement" depends on higher mental operations, we may wonder whether causal efficacy is to be thought of merely as causal inheritance, perspectival constitution, and not a form of perception at all—lacking complex mental operations—or as such a form, in which case it does not seem fundamental in any respect. It is not causal *perception* that is fundamental, but causal *inheritance* or physical *prehension*. In the latter sense, it is the constitution of occasions by past occasions, a consequence of the principle of perspective uncorrupted by the principle of experience. Here our vague sense of causal perception offers no secure evidence of causal connection but is rather an exemplification of a general metaphysical principle, thereby receiving grounding and interpretation.

The difficulty takes its most critical form in some of Whitehead's examples. He considers the turning on of an electric light and the blinking of an eye. "According to the philosophy of organism, the man also experiences another percept in the mode of causal efficacy. He feels that the experiences of the *eye* in the matter of the flash are causal of the blink" (PR 175). "The man will explain his experience by saying, 'The flash made me blink'; and if his statement be doubted, he will reply, 'I know it, because I felt it' " (PR 175). Here we find the double sense of causal efficacy and a strong emphasis upon its epistemic role. Yet Whitehead, only three pages later, refers to perception in the mode of causal efficacy as vague, unclear, unformed. It

produces percepts which are vague, not to be controlled, heavy with emotion: it produces the sense of derivation from an immediate past, and of passage to an immediate future; a sense of emotional feeling, belonging to oneself in the past, passing into oneself in the present, and passing from oneself in the present towards oneself in the future; a sense of influx of influence from other vaguer presences in the past, localized and yet evading local definition, such influence modifying, enhancing, inhibiting, diverting, the stream of feeling which we are receiving, unifying, enjoying, and transmitting. This is our general sense of existence, as one item among others, in an efficacious actual world. (PR 178)

It is incredible that Whitehead should suppose that such causal perception could provide a ground for cognitive claims, even as testimony of itself. Presentational immediacy is rather the source of testimony. It is essential to knowledge because of its clarity and precision. But presentational immediacy cannot be separated from inheritance of the past. Conscious perceptions are always a mixture of modes. It is impossible to perceive an extensive region without temporal endurance or pure inheritance without extension. A perspectival ontology requires the constitution of present events by past occasions; an epistemology based on observation and perception requires that present perceptions be constituted by relations to the past, but not necessarily to display these constitutive relations in conscious awareness. This is precisely the difficulty of conscious perception: it is complicated by factors drawn from multiple perspectives and environments of human experience. In this respect, of course, it is simply perspectival, manifesting the complex and overlapping environments of all standpoints. Purity in the modes of perception is incompatible with the principle of perspective. Yet this purity is thought necessary by Whitehead to establish testimony as to the nature of things.

Whitehead calls the interplay between causal efficacy and presentational immediacy "symbolic reference." If the above argument is correct, all perception is symbolic reference. But that is not Whitehead's position. He frequently speaks of "pure" causal perception. Yet the only reason I can see for postulating the existence of a pure mode of causal efficacy in human perception is to ground causal claims; and it is unnecessary. The important mode of conscious perception is symbolic reference, and all human perception is in this mode. The significant reply to Hume's theory of perception is that no pure mode of presentational immediacy exists. Nor is it necessary to presuppose a pure mode of causal efficacy.[20] As a consequence, the grounds for belief in causal relations are systematic, based on the incoherence of disconnection between past events and the future, not based on the testimony of everyday experience. As a further consequence, all claims about the past are interpretive, complex judgments, not based on the simple reproduction of characteristics from that past. I will resume this discussion in chapter 4.

Notes to Chapter 2

1. A typical example is Gary Gutting, in his article "Metaphysics and Induction". "The doctrine of internal relations is not a sufficient condition for

solving the problem of induction because, like the doctrine of causal production, it gives no information on the crucial question of the essential similarity of the past and the present cause" (1971, p. 178). See Ann Plamondon's reply, that Whitehead is concerned less with validation of induction and more with "explanation of the concept of 'valid induction.' " Her conclusion is that "it seems that any explication of 'valid inductive inference' requires as a necessary condition the metaphysical doctrine of internal relations. This doctrine is a necessary condition for the limitation of independent variety, which is, in turn, a necessary condition for 'valid inductive inference' to predictions and to theories" (1973, p. 99).

I am arguing that what is necessary is a principle of perspective that entails constitutive relations from a point of view. This is not the traditional understanding of internal relations.

2. Many commentators have been led astray by the tension between the principles of perspective and experience and fail to understand the force of condition (iii) in the second formulation. The status of an occasion for the future then becomes a problem. See William Christian (1959), discussed below.

3. There is some question as to whether occasions of the remote past are prehended directly or only by transmutation and mediation. The principle of relativity, taken in a strong sense, would appear to demand direct objectification as well as indirect transmission. Otherwise there could be total and irremediable loss in the transition. Whitehead seems to acknowledge this:

> In the transmission of inheritance from A to B, to C, to D, A is objectified by the eternal object S as a datum for B; where S is a sensum or a complex pattern of sensa. Then B is objectified for C. But the datum for B is thereby capable of some relevance for C, namely, A as objectified for B becomes reobjectified for C; and so on to D, and throughout the line of objectifications. Then for the ultimate subject M the datum includes A as thus transmitted, B as thus transmitted, and so on. . . . Some of the line, A and C for instance, may stand out with distinctness by reason of some peculiar feat of original supplementation which retains its undimmed importance in subsequent transmission. Other members of the chain may sink into oblivion. (PR 120)

The absolute and total relevance of the past to the future, as expressed in the principle of relativity, is unconditioned and absolute, nonperspectival. Perspectivity is selective, and a consequence is that some occasions of the remote past may have faded into irrelevance for some subsequent future. The totality and unity of the universe through time is at stake, a cosmological concern.

4. The most well-known discussion of this issue is Christian's *An Interpretation of Whitehead's Metaphysics* (1959). Christian defines the problem in such a way as virtually to prohibit solution, since he quite misses the force of the principle of perspective. He emphasizes the principle of experience instead.

> No two actual occasions have any immediacy of feeling in common. Among actual occasions there is no sharing of immediacy. No two actual occasions mutually enjoy any feeling. . . . the experience of a subject as felt from within is private to that subject and is not, as immediate feeling, shared in by any other subject. (P. 52)

Thus:

> How is it that what was decided in the past is given *now* for the present experience? This would apply the ontological principle not only to the character given for A but also to the fact that this datum is now given for A. (P. 321)

Oddly, Christian misses the force of the principle of relativity in relation to being: he claims that the principle of relativity only "means that no actual entity is beyond logic, beyond the world, or beyond experience. . . . it brings all entities into connection with experience" (P. 365). He does not recognize that relativity as perspectivity entirely solves the problem of the past (which arises due to an overemphasis on God and experience).

Whitehead's own words to Dorothy Emmet, quoted in her *Whitehead's Philosophy of Organism* (1966), should be noted here:

> You seem to me at various points to forget my doctrine of "immanence" which governs the whole treatment of objectification. Thus at times you write as tho' the connection between past and present is merely that of a transfer of *character*. . . . The doctrine of *immanence* is fundamental. (Pp. xxii–xxiii)

This immanence is an expression of the principle of relativity. How perspectives constitute other perspectives is essential. "All origination is private. But what has been thus originated, publicly pervades the world" (PR 310).

See also Leclerc, in *Whitehead's Metaphysics*:

> How, indeed, can there be an "individual" if there be only a continuous "becoming"; for does not the notion of "individuality" imply a "completed unity"? But how can there be a completed unity when an actuality exists only "in the process," and when, at the termination of that process, there just *is* no existent at all? (1958, p. 71)

Leclerc (1958, p. 109) notes Whitehead's answer:

> When they perish, occasions pass from the immediacy of being into the non-being of immediacy. But that does not mean that they are nothing. They remain "stubborn fact."
> *Pereunt et imputantur.* (AI 238)

Similar confusions, based on neglect of the principles of perspective and relativity, have been recurrent; for example: "When an occasion 'loses its subjectivity' it has lost *everything*." Therefore, "if an occasion cannot be prehended *before* it completes itself (since it is not yet a determinate prehendable reality) nor the instant *after* (since it then has perished and disappeared), it must be prehended *at the same instant* it attains satisfaction" (Johnson 1976, pp. 257, 262). Such a view imports a temporal metric where such a measure is quite inappropriate.

In his later writing, Christian seems to hold less strong objections to the relevance of the past in Whitehead's theory (1963, pp. 93–101). Nevertheless, he maintains the problematical nature of the past. "There are reasons for saying that the categoreal scheme does not introduce the concept of pastness either explicitly, by using and explaining it, or implicitly, by requiring it" (P. 96). Christian still seems to miss the force of the principle of relativity. Nevertheless, if his later reservations manifest an awareness that perspectivity is separable from temporality (and spatiality as well), that is an important insight. Succession seems to me to be an essential part of Whitehead's theory of occasions, weakening the generality of the principle of perspective in his theory.

5. Elizabeth Kraus adds to this duality of significance a cosmological element, transforming it into a triad. "The previous analysis of the concrete value achieved by an actual occasion revealed it to have an intrinsically trivalent character: being something in itself, for the others, and for the totality" (1979, p. 33).

6. This perspectivity provides a reply to those who suppose that there is a threat to being in every moment, the threat of dissolution. In Whitehead's theory, the principle of relativity makes dissolution unintelligible, since every actual entity needs future occasions to which it is relevant.

> There is no more reason to assume that becoming will cease than to think that being will suddenly lapse into non-being, *unless* one insists upon thinking in terms of a substance ontology. . . . Creativity functions to express why things *become* in the same manner in which prime matter functions as an explanation of why things *are*. There is a contingency about both ontological substances and processes. (Hall 1973, p. 27)

Perspectivity makes unqualified nonbeing unintelligible.

7. The meaning of significance (for oneself and for another) changed during Whitehead's career, and the notion of significance for oneself, which becomes central in *Process and Reality* and is the foundation of the principle of experience, is a relatively late entry.

> In the limited analysis of experience nothing is significant of itself. An entity is significant only in terms of its relations with other entities. This point of view is inverted in the process analysis and the broad view of experience. The later analysis begins with the postulation of entities which are significant in themselves, and then proceeds to the discussion of the relations between them.

> In the later works . . . this enlarged notion of experience becomes the basic principle of understanding and analysis of nature itself. Nature is now to be understood in terms of "life'—a "feeling" analysis has been adopted in place of the "extension" analysis of the early works. (Shahan 1950, pp. 31, 37–38)

Compare here Christian's claim that "an abstract entity is one which has no significance for itself" (1959, p. 20). Christian does not emphasize strongly enough the other pole of significance for another.

8. My position here is, I take it, similar to Hartshorne's when he says that "the pastness of an entity is the *same* as its being objectified by successors. It is not first past and then objectified; rather it first completes its process of becoming, and then it is objectified. There is nothing between" (1972, pp. 165–66).

9. This is grasped in part by Robison James and Jorge Luis Nobo:

Once actual occasions are firmly formed and finished, they are drawn instantly into a creative onflowing which is thereafter ceaselessly making something partly new of them. Actual occasions do impose their achieved character upon the creativity which rushes through them and drives beyond them; but they make their immortal mark in this fashion precisely in the act of exhausting their own creativity. And in this same act, which is their terminal act, they surrender their status as "final realities." They are thenceforth dependent for further existence upon the subsequent occasions which grasp them and are partly shaped by them. (James 1972, p. 112)

An occasion is a *becoming* when it is subject, and a *being* when it is a superject. In the former mode of existence, the occasion is a process of concrescence; in the latter mode, it is a concrete product; in both modes, it is *actual*. . . . The principle of process asserts that an occasion *qua* actual subject creates, or produces, that same occasion *qua* actual superject. (Nobo 1974, p. 275.)

I would not accept the latter's formulation of the *actuality* of the objectified occasion in terms of Whitehead's theory, though I think Nobo is correct from the standpoint of the principle of perspective.

10. See in this connection Hartshorne's interpretation:

Concerning the ancestors there need I think be no dispute: . . . Every actual entity prehends the entirety of its own actual universe and this actual universe consists of all entities in its causal past.

In spite of the difficulties, I venture to suggest, against Whitehead's own opinion, that the unqualified inclusiveness of prehension . . . is required by this system as a whole. For it is the only means which the system seems to provide by which the world can be constituted as such, as a real whole. (1972, pp. 30, 31)

The totality of relevance to the past, by the principle of relativity, is a cosmological totality, unnecessary for causation but essential to the unity of the world through time. Nevertheless, Hartshorne argues:

If there are determinate truths about the details of the past—and it is paradox to deny it—then the past is not simply dropped from the universe, in the passage to the present, but preserved.

The past is the realm of facts, and what has been will always have been. In other words, facts about the past are immortal. (1972, pp. 34, 51)

See here Whitehead's words:

In Descartes' phraseology, the satisfaction is the actual entity considered as analysable in respect to its existence "*objectivé*." It is the actual entity as a definite, determinate, settled fact, stubborn and with unavoidable consequences. (PR 219–20)

11. See in this connection Hartshorne's cosmological emphasis (1972, p. 133) quoted in note 4, p. xiii. God here provides the supreme basis for the order in the

universe. The most extreme ascription of a cosmological argument to Whitehead is found in Kenneth F. Thompson, Jr., *Whitehead's Philosophy of Religion*:

> The world requires God, then, because the intelligibility of its metaphysical character involves reference to antecedent limitations. The world is a process of concrete finite entities which are complex, interrelated, and unique. We must make reference to some antecedent ordering, however, to explain the actuality of this world among the possible alternatives which we can more or less vaguely imagine. This antecedent ordering can be described as a hierarchy of orders.... God is the ground of these limitations, and hence is the reason why the actual world has the metaphysical character it has. (1971, p. 42)

The cosmological argument is antiperspectival, since God is made the unconditioned ground of the universe, required absolutely.

12. God is ultimate *in some sense*, but not ultimate in *all* senses. When he is made so, perspectivity is entirely abandoned. (See Thompson [1971] for an extreme cosmological, thereby nonperspectival, reading of Whitehead.) Whitehead never abandons perspectivity, even in his most cosmological moments. Nevertheless, ultimacy of any sort is, as unconditioned, nonperspectival.

13. See Robert M. Palter:

> In order for a species to be viable, an appropriately sustaining environment (itself composed of various interdependent species of organisms) is required; the latter will be characterized by a locally dominant set of natural laws. Thus, an inductive judgment can derive at least a modicum of support from the set of natural laws presupposed in the very formulation of the judgment. (1964, p. 71)

14. This argument is not directed against Hume's demand for a noncircular ground for inductive inference. It is rather a metaphysical expression of Kant's reversal: if inductive inference could succeed, what would be its conditions? These lie not in a priori conditions of the understanding but in the real conditions of interrogative standpoints, a thoroughly perspectival answer. Certain criticisms of Whitehead's position are therefore quite misconceived; for example: "The doctrine of internal relations is not a sufficient condition for solving the problem of induction because, like the doctrine of causal production, it gives no information on the crucial question of the essential similarity of the past to the present cause" (Gutting 1971, p. 178). Gutting is correct that internal relations alone would provide no solution to causation and induction, but he fails to understand the relevance of social environments and the full application of the principle of perspective in Whitehead's account. Far more important, however, he makes the fundamental Humean error of treating inference absolutely and unconditionedly, as if epistemological questions could be given an unqualified answer. Once perspectival conditions are recognized, there can be no absolute justification of inductive inference, only justifications of particular inferences in particular circumstances; no absolute principles of natural uniformity, only those inferences that prevail under certain conditions; and no absolute barrier between past and future, only a separation relevant in certain

respects. There is no unqualified standpoint from which the problem of induction can be raised, although it is a problem only from such a standpoint.

15. Alfred North Whitehead, *Adventures of Ideas* (New York: Mentor, 1955), p. 198 (hereafter cited as AI).

16. But it is a *perspectival* order. Whitehead is limited by the principle of experience to the independence of contemporary entities.

An excellent example of what happens when Whitehead is read without understanding of the selectivity and limitations demanded by perspectivity can be found in William Alston's criticisms of internal relatedness and the immanence of the future in Whitehead's theory. Alston rejects the "abstractness of objectification" (perspectivity)—that "a given actual occasion, A, does not prehend the total nature of each of its objects, but only a part of each." To Alston, "any actual occasion, A, in prehending one component prehension, p, of another actual occasion, B, will thereby be prehending B in its full concreteness" (Alston 1952, pp. 555, 557). It follows that "reference to the future . . . can only consist of relations . . . to determinate future actual occasions" (p. 552). The conclusion is that there is a conflict between the principle of internal relations and Whitehead's pluralism.

> The former of these principles [internal relatedness] implies the negation of the latter [pluralism]. For, according to the latter, all of the relations in which any actual entity stands are internal to it, and this in turn implies that it contains within its experience all the other termini of these relations. In other words, the Principle of Internal Relatedness says that an actual entity contains all the entities to which it is related. (Alston 1952, p. 542)

Aside from the error involved in Alston's understanding of internal relations in Whitehead's theory, the absence of any sense of perspective is devastating. Whitehead's own words on this subject are telling:

> It is not wholly true that two contemporaries A and B enjoy a common past. In the first place, even if the occasions in the past of A be identical with the occasions in the past of B, yet A and B by reason of their difference in status, enjoy that past under a difference of perspective elimination. Thus the objective immortality of the past in A differs from the objective immortality of that same past in B. Thus two contemporary occasions, greatly remote from each other, are in effect derived from different pasts. (AI 198)

17. Many commentators emphasize the difference between perception and prehension, missing the epistemological flavor in Whitehead's writings. "When applied to actual entities, the term 'perception' must be understood as a metaphor" (Lango 1972, p. 54).

18. It is too inchoate and vague to constitute evidence of causal connections. If we demand evidence in conscious experience for causal relations, I am arguing, we will not be able to resolve the metaphysical issue of constitution in perspective. The epistemological issue of the grounds for our knowledge of causal relations is irrelevant to, and misleading concerning, the essentially

metaphysical issue of how events in process are intelligible—in Whitehead's view, by being constituted by their relation to past events.

19. Although the corrected edition of *Process and Reality* retains the word "sophistical," implying that higher-level stages of experience are *deceptive*, I have always supposed Whitehead to mean "sophisticated" in this passage.

20. "As adults it is doubtful whether our perceptions are entirely free of some sort of conceptual interpretation" (Mays 1977, p. 127).

CHAPTER THREE
FREEDOM

Self-causation is the ultimate basis of Whitehead's theory of perspective.[1] It follows from the importance of the principle of experience in establishing the foundation for perspectives in actual entities. The fact that Whitehead appears to need a basis for perspective in actuality, founded on an ultimate peculiar to actual entities, is an indication of the limitations of his theory of perspective. The concept of self-causation in Whitehead's theory is deeply problematical, and the most natural resolution of its difficulties is given by extending the principle of perspective and separating it from the principle of experience. One of the consequences of such extension is that actual entities are made both divisible and indivisible, from different points of view, that actual entities are analyzable into prehensive phases only perspectively.

One of the great values of the principle of perspective is that it defines the relationship between causation and freedom as complementary rather than in opposition. Neither can be understood without the other, for each expresses a side of the other required for intelligibility. This is a natural consequence of the principle of perspective, for every perspectival component is qualified by a relational point of view, a standpoint. Determinateness must qualify freedom if it is to be intelligible; conversely, possibilities and alternatives must qualify actuality if it is to have limits. Whitehead's theory of causal inheritance includes both the determinate contributions of past occasions as data and alternatives engendered by the diversity of future standpoints taken toward such data. Here, freedom as self-causation and novelty as creativity are closely related notions grounded in the principle of perspective. I will trace the conditions that establish novelty and creativity in Whitehead's system to their ultimate and arbitrary foundation in self-causation and indicate how a more thoroughgoing principle of perspective can eliminate the difficulties involved while preserving the effectiveness of Whitehead's creativity.

Novelty

It is one of Whitehead's finest achievements to establish principles of novelty in the very fabric of causal inheritance. Creativity, the "category of the ultimate," embodies both novelty and inheritance. It is the "ultimate principle by which the many, which are the universe disjunctively, become the one actual occasion, which is the universe conjunctively. It lies in the nature of things that the many enter into complex unity" (PR 21). The "many" are the entities of the past. The "unity" is the novel entity which becomes. Either the multiplicity persists, unqualified, or creation occurs, synthesizing this multiplicity into a novel entity. Thus, " 'Creativity' is the principle of *novelty*" (PR 21). It is the emergence of novel perspectives. "A set of all actual occasions is by the nature of things a standpoint for another concrescence which elicits a concrete unity from those many occasions. Thus we can never survey the actual world except from the standpoint of an immediate concrescence which is falsifying the presupposed completion" (PR 211).

Two categoreal obligations specifically express the place of freedom in becoming: *conceptual reversion* and *freedom and determination*. The latter is fundamental and relevant within every occasion, and it explicitly though incompletely asserts the complementarity of determination and freedom. "The concrescence of each individual actual entity is internally determined and is externally free" (PR 27). Whitehead explicates the category further by the words, "in each concrescence whatever is determinable is determined, but that there is always a remainder for the decision of the subject-superject of that concrescence" (PR 27–28). This is very important, for it expresses his conviction that freedom is not gained by introducing gaps into determinate relations. The word "whatever" is meant quite literally: *everything* determinable is determined; but there is nevertheless something more which involves a "decision." This completeness of determination conjoined complementarily with indeterminateness is a natural corollary of perspectivity. To be determined perspectivally is to contribute a point of view in which freedom as decision is inherent.

We may reformulate Whitehead's principle as follows: *In any becoming, everything that can be determined is determined; but there is also freedom.* The limitations of even this reformulation, from the point of view of perspectivity, are that freedom is conceived as an *addition* to determination rather than as included within it. Nevertheless, the reformulation does expand the generality of the principle of freedom, and does not refer specifically to determination by the past. Actual entities are determined by extensive relations, eternal objects, God, and prehensions of the past, as well as by every other relevant mode of existence. Indeed, by inverting the principle of relativity we have a principle of modes of determination: it belongs to the nature of a "becoming" that every being is a potential determinant for it. Each mode of determination is as complete and determinate as it can be, yet there is still something more: a "decision" by each actual entity to become what it will. This follows directly from the principle of perspective: every determination is from the actual entity's point of view. We may consider a simpler and more general formulation: in addition to all determinations of an entity by other beings, it must also determine itself. Its subjective aim is a factor in the determinateness of every one of its constituent elements. Here determination and self-determination express the two poles of prehension inherent in the principle of perspective. Nevertheless, it is important to decide whether self-causation is another mode of determination or a break with all such modes, a transcendence of their limitations. What is at stake is the full complementarity of determination and freedom, whether determinateness is intelligible without indeterminateness. The category of freedom and determination suggests that self-causation and external determination are separable factors, that becoming is attained in the supplementation of external determination by self-determination, by the addition of self-causation to external determination. This supplementarity, which is not equivalent with complementarity, indicates Whitehead's limited acceptance of the principle of perspective. An alternative is that freedom resides in the sheer multiplicity of possibilities of determination, in the sheer transformation of a multiplicity of perspectives into a novel, unitary perspective. That many perspectives become one requires a thoroughgoing perspectivity in which determinateness and indeterminateness are conceptually inseparable. A similar complementarity is expressed by the category of creativity in which many become one from a novel point of view. It is weakened, however, by the possibility in Whitehead's system that causal inheritance might be sheer reproduction, that something—self-determination or conceptual revision—must be *added* to causal inheritance to produce novelty.

"Each individual actual entity is internally determined and is externally free." In Whitehead's detailed discussion of this categoreal obligation, he states that "any flux must exhibit the character of internal determination. So much follows from the ontological principle" (PR 46). This is an explicit assertion that freedom is *self*-determination. The ontological principle asserts that all explanations lead ultimately to actual entities. Implicit is the conviction that there are always reasons: there is no arbitrary principle of rearrangement, no "swerve" of atoms in the void. Freedom is not *in*determination, but is the mode of determination in which an actual entity presides over its own becoming. A particular flux always has the particular character that it gives to itself. In this sense, every actual entity is internally determined—that is, self-caused. But every actual entity is also determined in its relationships to the past —though never completely. (By the principle of perspective, no mode of determination can be complete, nor can any modes taken together. All must be from a point of view that brings alternative possibilities into relevance.) Inheritance from the past always leaves room for further determination by the entity itself. Therefore, relative to the past, every concrescence is partly indeterminate and free. Both freedom and causal determination are essential to concrescence, for it must be both unique and qualified by its relations. This is a direct expression of its perspectivity.

The capacity of an actual entity to inherit from its past, yet to be capable of self-determination, is developed in complex and intricate detail in Whitehead's system. The principle of experience is a major factor here and the source of much of the complexity. It is a great temptation to construe causal determination so as to eliminate freedom—for example, by reference to God. Since God is the ultimate ground of intelligibility, it is tempting to make him responsible for all gaps in determination, and eliminate freedom. However, if my interpretation of creativity is correct, this would eliminate individual becoming as well, and is incompatible with Whitehead's position. I have noted that the principle of perspective entails a complementarity of determinateness and indeterminateness that makes unqualified determinateness unintelligible. The error of misconstruing the role of God to be that of completing determination is a consequence of a misapplication of the cosmological and ontological principles, and a limitation on the generality of the principle of perspective.

Contingency

Each concrescence is to be referred to a definite free initiation and a definite free conclusion. The initial fact is macrocosmic, in the sense of having equal relevance to all occasions; the final fact is microcosmic, in the sense of being peculiar to that occasion. Neither fact is capable of rationalization, in the sense of tracing the antecedents which determine it. The initial fact is the primordial appetition, and the final fact is the decision of emphasis, finally creative of the "satisfaction." (PR 47–48)

We have here a double freedom, of initiation and conclusion. The "free initiation" or "primordial appetition" is the ultimate arbitrariness of things. "No reason, internal to history, can be assigned why that flux of forms, rather than another flux, should have been illustrated" (PR 46). Whitehead also denies that this flux has any particular character of perfection. The Leibnizian theory of the best of all possible worlds, he calls "an audacious fudge" (PR 47). The references to "primordial appetition," the absence of reasons, the "unconditioned" nature of the primordial nature of God, are expressions of the cosmological principle. There is an "ultimate," "final" contingency rooted in the primordial appetition, on the one hand, and the "final reaction of the self-creative unity of the universe" (PR 47), on the other. Here freedom is made to depend on unconditioned factors, a cosmological indeterminateness. Yet Whitehead comes very close, in his understanding that freedom is doubly relevant to actual entities, to a full complementarity of determinateness and indeterminateness, once we can free his theory from the difficulties associated with the cosmological principle.

The notion of an "initiation" is somewhat misleading in suggesting a beginning to the universe. "The universe" with its "initiation" are cosmological notions, not so much in the question of time as in the absence of conditions for a *first* cause of *all* things. The universe is contingent in that, after all explanations have been given, *it* has not been explained, only determinations within it. The assumption that the universe is a legitimate object of thought, that it *could* have an explanation as a whole, is cosmological, and is incompatible with the principle of perspective and its requirement of qualification. Whether it includes God or not, the universe is ultimately unconditioned and unqualified. In the end, the universe is what it is. The cosmological principle is a filter through which many of Whitehead's conceptions of freedom and indeterminateness pass, and it is a major limitation of his conception of the principle of perspective. The cosmological principle addresses "the universe as a whole," demanding an ultimate ground of both determinateness and indeterminateness. Even here, in the primordial nature of God, determinateness and indeterminateness are complementary: the primordial nature is a ground for all determinations and for all creative departures. Nevertheless, it is itself unconditioned, reflecting Whitehead's incomplete acknowledgment of perspective.

In the microcosmic sense, each actual entity is ultimately *causa sui* and determines itself. However determinately causal inheritance rules over events, there is "the ultimate freedom of things, lying beyond all determinations" (PR 47).

> Every actual entity, including God, is something individual for its own sake; and thereby transcends the rest of actuality. And also it is to be noted that every actual entity, including God, is a creature transcended by the creativity which it qualifies. . . . It is finally responsible for the decision by which any lure for feeling is admitted to efficiency. The freedom inherent in the universe is constituted by this element of self-causation. (PR 88)

Every actual entity, including God, transcends the rest of actuality. This is a natural consequence of the principle of perspective if the transcendence means that each entity imposes its own point of view on its own constituents. It goes beyond the principle of perspective to the cosmological principle and principle of experience to the extent that this transcendence is supplemental, a going beyond, unconditioned and unintelligible, grounded in an unconditioned choice of subjective aim. One of the most important functions God fills in Whitehead's cosmology is to represent the ultimate limit to possibilities of rational understanding. "God is the ultimate limitation, and His existence is the ultimate irrationality."[2] That there is an *ultimate* irrationality is cosmological. The principle of perspective entails that irrationality is everywhere, permeating all modes of being, all modes of determinateness. But it is complementary with determinateness, and wherever there is irrationality, there is rationality as well.

Self-Causation

Freedom for actual entities is defined in terms of "self-causation" or "decision." This nontechnical term "decision" suggests a "selection" from possibilities and self-determination. Each actual entity is the result of its own decision, made in terms of the past, God, other actual entities, and the order of possibilities. These determine the entity as much as possible, but never completely. The notion of decision clearly stems from the principle of experience. Its major weakness is that it appears to identify a particular stage of concrescence in which freedom is to be located. Indeed, the principle of experience—especially when conjoined with a principle of analysis, entailing phases or stages of experience—suggests a *supplemental* view of self-causation, whereas perspectivity demands complementarity. The individuality of actual entities is a fundamental factor in Whitehead's theory of self-causation.

I have argued that Whitehead's sense of creativity does not include the possibility that an actual entity might be "completely" determined by the conjunction of causal inheritance and the primordial nature of God. To the extent that something is created, it is what it is. It is a unique perspective upon its determinants and conditions. Yet the concept of decision here suggests that we think of such creativity as grounded in a residuum of self-causation after all other determinations have been accommodated—*after* them rather than *through* them. If an actual entity were completely determined by the past plus the primordial nature of God, it would be nothing in itself, and nothing would have been created. It decides what it will be, above and beyond what is given to it, supplementing its conditions. There are two ways of conceiving this supplementation: as a further step of determination, performed by an occasion in concrescence, or as a condition permeating its concrescence and inseparable from any of its other conditions. The latter view is essential to the principle of perspective: the uniqueness and transcendence of an actual entity is inherent in its conditions. Here the very nature of an actual entity is implicated in its free decision: freedom is to be identified with the self-identity of the actual entity. In the former interpretation, the concept of self-determination is located in the principle of experience and the cosmological principle, as if the principle of perspective could not alone carry the meaning of creativity.

To enforce the sense that an actual entity is self-causative *beyond* or *subsequent to* all external determinations, Whitehead introduces a notion suggestive of the theory of relativity: the causal independence of entities in the contemporary world. "So far as physical relations are concerned, contemporary events happen in *causal* independence of each other" (PR 61). He notes that "this principle lies on the surface of the fundamental Einsteinian formula for the physical continuum" (PR 61n). Nevertheless, it is based, in Whitehead's view, entirely on metaphysical considerations. It is essential to his theory of self-determination. It is also at the heart of his complex and difficult theory of perception in the mode of presentational immediacy, in which "the contemporary world is consciously prehended as a continuum of extensive relations" (PR 61).

The reason for the causal independence of contemporary occasions is explained in the following passage:

> The process whereby an actual entity, starting from its objective content, attains its individual satisfaction . . . expresses how the datum, which involves the actual world, becomes a component in the one actual entity. There must therefore be no further reference to other actual entities; the elements available for the explanation are simply, the objective content, eternal objects, and the selective concrescence of feelings whereby an actual entity becomes itself. (PR 153)

Upon reception of its data, the actual entity must "become itself." A stage in becoming must be given over to the unification of the elements of the actual world into a complete entity. If entities were continuously in process of prehending each other, then the data would be constantly in flux, and no completion or decision, therefore no becoming, could take place. If the relevant data were constantly changing, impinging on each other, there could be no definite decision, for it is impossible for a decision to include itself as datum. "No actual entity can be conscious of its own satisfaction; for such knowledge would be a component in the process, and would thereby alter the satisfaction" (PR 85). Either no satisfaction can be reached, and nothing becomes, or the satisfaction must eventually "close up" the entity. (PR 84) A point is reached at which the "final 'satisfaction' of an actual entity is intolerant of any addition" (PR 45). Thus, there must be a stage of becoming that excludes any further additions from without, and allows the entity to complete itself.[3] To allow mutual interaction in the contemporary world would destroy the finality of satisfaction and the uniqueness of actual entities.[4] The satisfaction of one occasion cannot be datum for another, which is itself datum for the first, without instituting a vicious regress.[5]

An actual entity is self-caused in reaching its own satisfaction, in being its own unity amidst multiplicity. Whitehead conceives of the genetic analysis of becoming in terms of stages: "datum, process, satisfaction, decision" (PR 149–50). The datum is given by the past while the process, satisfaction, and decision are the internal stages in which the occasion completes itself and passes into later becoming. Causal inheritance resides in the prehension of the past and transmission to the future. Novelty and freedom are inherent in the stages of decision and satisfaction. Properly understood, novelty and freedom are inherent in the perspectivity of occasions, permeating concrescence. "Final causation expresses the internal process whereby the actual entity becomes itself" (PR 150). Final causation is a fundamental manifestation of Whitehead's perspectivity, except where it is undermined by considerations derived from the principle of experience.

Conceptual Reversion

As I have indicated, Whitehead's theory comes close to a perspectival, complementary relationship between novelty and determination in the notion of creativity, but it is weakened in many of its formulations to a supplementary relationship: freedom is *added to* determination by decision. Such addition is based on the category of conceptual reversion and grounded in the category of conceptual valuation: "From each physical feeling there is the derivation of a purely conceptual feeling whose datum is the eternal object determinant of the definiteness of the actual entity, or of the nexus, physically felt" (PR 26). To each actual entity an actual world of past entities is given with ingressed eternal objects. The entity can add other relevant eternal objects through conceptual reversion: "There is secondary origination of conceptual feelings with data which are partially identical with, and partially diverse from, the eternal objects forming the data in the first phase of the mental pole" (PR 26). There is an analogy here with imagination, which has the power to intuit new forms. To Whitehead, Hume's example of apprehending a missing color in a graduated color scheme is an instance of the power of conceptual imagination. "There is an origination of conceptual feeling, admitting or rejecting whatever is apt for feeling by reason of its germaneness to the basic data" (PR 87). Reversion here is clearly supplemental, particularly where we emphasize the successive stages within concrescence. There is incomplete acknowledgment in Whitehead's formulations that inheritance without origination would be unintelligible. There is selection and origination in the objective datum of a concrescence, but not in its initial datum. The analysis of an actual entity into stages tends to undercut the denial that no stage is intelligible apart from the concrescence as a whole. We need to remind ourselves continuously that actual entities are *indivisible drops* of becoming. From the latter point of view, reversion is less supplementation than it is an essential and determinative element of prehension.

The twin categories of conceptual valuation and conceptual reversion provide the means whereby novelty is introduced into the becoming of an occasion, and establish conditions for freedom. Freedom here is always conditioned. "There is no such fact as absolute freedom; every actual entity possesses only such freedom as is inherent in the primary phase 'given' by its standpoint of relativity to its actual universe. Freedom, givenness, potentiality, are notions which presuppose each other and limit each other" (PR 133). This is an overt expression of qualification and complementarity, and is a full manifestation of the principle of perspective. It is essential, however, that determination be understood to be qualified by freedom, not simply freedom by determinate conditions. Complementarity and supplementarity war for supremacy in Whitehead's theory of the relationship between determination and freedom.

The supplementarity theory requires a full range of subordinate notions if it is to be intelligible. Two questions must be answered if we grant the principle that supplementary stages of concrescence may include the addition of novel eternal objects relevant to the datum. The first asks for the ground of relevance. The answer is, the primordial nature of God. The second asks whether what is added is completely determined by God—in which case we eliminate self-causation—or whether it is effectively undetermined—in which case causal inheritance and freedom are sundered in the arbitrariness of imagination. Whitehead's answer to this question rests upon the nature of subjective aim. It is based on the principle of experience.

The ground of relevance for conceptual reversion is the primordial nature of God: "the unconditioned conceptual valuation of the entire multiplicity of eternal objects" which "in each derivate actual entity results in a graduation of the relevance of eternal objects to the con- crescent phases of that derivate occasion" (PR 31). In God, we find the entire multiplicity of eternal objects hierarchically if incompletely or- dered in a system of graduated relevance. "By reason of the actuality of this primordial valuation of pure potentials, each eternal object has a definite, effective relevance to each concrescent process. Apart from such orderings, there would be a complete disjunction of eternal objects un- realized in the temporal world. Novelty would be meaningless, and inconceivable" (PR 40).

I have noted that, if God provided a systematic and determinate order of relations among all possibilities, from which each actual entity derived its becoming, then freedom would be eliminated. The past con- joined with the system of eternal objects in the primordial nature of God would determine all forms of definiteness for a subsequent becoming. Yet there is Whitehead's continual reference to the fact that each actual entity "is finally responsible for the decision by which any lure for feeling is admitted to efficiency" (PR 88). Self-causation is the foundation of perspective for actual entities. It must clearly establish a correlative perspectivity for the primordial nature of God, an indeterminateness among the determinate relations of eternal objects to each other. It is possible to understand Whitehead's God, particularly his primordial nature, in terms akin to Spinoza's, as the principle of limitation that brings all determination into becoming from without. What is particularly misleading is Whitehead's assertion that "by the recognition of God's characterization of the creative act, a more complete rational explanation is attained. The Category of Reversion is then abolished; and Hume's principle of the derivation of conceptual experience from physical experience remains without any exception" (PR 250). If reversion is abolished, then with it seem to go all novelty and freedom. God becomes the basis of all determinateness.

Such an interpretation must be incorrect: we are told recurrently by Whitehead that actual entities are self-caused and free. " 'Decided' conditions are never such as to banish freedom. They only qualify it. There is always a contingency left open for immediate decision" (PR 284). Nevertheless, there is a central duality involving God which pervades Whitehead's cosmology. It supports the antitheses he describes in the final chapter of *Process and Reality*. Yet even this list fails to cover the relevant plurality, for it depends on a shift from God's primordial to his consequent nature. The duality I am concerned with involves the primordial nature alone. It is a duality deeply expressive of perspectivity.

The immanence of God in actual occasions is complex and perspectival, for he plays no unconditioned and unqualified role relative to occasions. God is immanent in all becoming in virtue of the relevance of possibilities he provides through his primordial nature and his "urge toward the future based upon an appetite in the present" (PR 32). But he is not immanent in the sense that he determines all becoming completely—that would eliminate freedom and would thoroughly undermine individual perspectives.[6] "God can be termed the creator of each temporal actual entity. But the phrase is apt to be misleading by its suggestion that the ultimate creativity of the universe is to be ascribed to God's volition" (PR 225). Likewise, God is the ground of novelty in making available possibilities not ingressed in past occasions. But he does not compel particular novelties to become as they do, either indirectly or directly: that too would eliminate freedom.

The *relevance* of an eternal object in its rôle of lure is a fact inherent in the data. In this sense the eternal object is a constituent of the 'objective lure.' But the admission into, or rejection from, reality of conceptual feeling is the originative decision of the actual occasion. In this sense an actual occasion is *causa sui.* (PR 86)

The past and God jointly constitute every determining condition other than the occasion itself. But there is always something more: "the final reaction of the self-creative unity of the universe" (PR 47).

We are therefore required to find an interpretation of God's primordial nature that allows it to function as a ground of novelty without eliminating self-causation. Can we understand a ground of relevance that does not impose completely determinate conditions on events? What is required is a system of relations that circumscribes without completely determining. It is clearly a perspectival system in which determinateness and indeterminateness are closely conjoined. The relations constitute an environment establishing the relevance of particular possibilities to any new becoming, but there is always room for the decision of the conditioned entity.

The past and the primordial nature of God together define a range of possibilities for every subsequent becoming. This principle—of the relevance of possibilities to every perspective—is fundamental to perspectivity and a manifestation of the indeterminateness in all determinations. All determinate conditions together, for any occasion, establish but a qualified range of relevant possibilities. In some societies, there is the greatest possible reproduction of the character of the past—as in lowest-grade physical societies. Reversion is limited to ineffective, subjective feelings. Nevertheless, even undifferentiated reproduction can accumulate to something new. "There is always change; for time is cumulative as well as reproductive, and the cumulation of the many is not their reproduction as many" (PR 238). A river washes away the base of a cliff year after year, until the cliff collapses. A new bank is formed. *Plus c'est la même chose; plus ça change.* Something always becomes, and in becoming there is novelty.

Causal inheritance is always mixed with origination, however minimal. Alternatives reside within any order of causation. These are conclusions required by the principle of perspective. Now the possibilities realized in reversion come from the primordial nature of God. If this comprises a complex system of relations admitting only one complex possibility from any actual standpoint, then freedom and novelty are abolished. Clearly Whitehead does not intend this. We must not, then, interpret God's primordial nature as a complete system of relations with a complete order, but rather as a system of relations with at most partial order.[7]

How then are we to understand Whitehead's claim that, through God, the category of conceptual reversion is abolished? Certainly not so that freedom is abolished with it. Freedom resides in self-determination, the decision by an actual entity to be itself, and there must be room for such a decision. Together, God and the past provide a multiplicity of possibilities, graded according to their relevance from the standpoint of a novel becoming. But only the decision of the occasion eliminates the indeterminateness that remains through all other modes of determination (though, by its becoming, it also introduces new indeterminatenesses for the future). There is no particular way in which the past must be viewed from a later perspective. Conceptual reversion is abolished only to the extent that the novel forms which arise in reversion can do so only through the primordial nature of God. God is the ground of origination but not of self-determination. If we include God, we may say that all conceptual experience is derivative from the experience of other entities, but no such experience can replace the self-determination inherent in concrescence. Whitehead's claim that conceptual reversion is abolished through God is cosmological, effectively bringing all determinations into a single order. Yet the principle of perspective is essential to the uniqueness of point of view of every actual entity, a point of view irreducible to any and all conditions outside itself.

Subjective Aim

Freedom for actual entities is self-causation, the "decision" an entity makes in its own becoming. This is to be understood in terms of the entity's subjective aim, a proper understanding of which brings us to Whitehead's unification of causal inheritance and freedom through the principle of experience. The subjective aim is the final cause within every becoming and, since an actual entity *is* its becoming, every stage must incorporate that aim within it. The subjective aim qualifies every prehension and unifies itself through those prehensions. This reciprocal qualification is an expression of the principle of perspective. Nevertheless, the importance of the subjective aim lies in the role of the ontological principle and the principle of experience in Whitehead's perspectivism.

Many feelings can belong to one subject only if the unity of the subject is an aim that characterizes every feeling. Thus, "the feelings are inseparable from the end at which they aim; and this end is the feeler. The feelings aim at the feeler, as their final cause. The feelings are what they are in order that their subject may be what it is" (PR 222). This unity of feeler and feeling is perspectival, but it is interpreted as a synthetic unity of prehension through the principle of experience. The subjective aim is doubly inseparable from the prehensions that constitute it. "This final cause is an inherent element in the feeling, constituting the unity of that feeling. An actual entity feels as it does feel in order to be the actual entity which it is. In this way an actual entity satisfies Spinoza's notion of substance: it is *causa sui*" (PR 222).

I have recurrently criticized the role of the principle of experience in Whitehead's theory, particularly for its diminution of the power of the principle of perspective. Yet Whitehead's theory of experience is a sublime achievement. It embodies a profound principle of unification, founded on subjectivity and closely related to the ontological principle. An actual occasion is a drop of experience, a single act. Its unitariness is a function of its aim. An occasion's subjective aim is implicated within every element contributing to it and is the final cause that unifies its diverse elements in one becoming. It is the qualification that establishes the perspectivity essential to prehensive unification. Every prehension is the reception of a datum by an actual entity so that its subjective aim may be realized.[8]

In ordinary experience, there are false starts, failed ends, and means gone astray. On Whitehead's view, such dissolutions are properties of enduring objects whose members cannot carry a project through in time because of inability or an inauspicious environment. A society contains a multiplicity that cannot be overcome; as a consequence, a society cannot be wholly self-caused. An actual entity is self-caused and free. It must, then, possess an aim that is effective and complete, implicit in every one of its prehensions.[9]

Thus, when Whitehead gives us his most detailed account of the stages of prehension, the "*subject* who feels" is mentioned first, since it is the factor that qualifies every feeling, physical or conceptual. From the standpoint of the subject, the occasion is indivisible. The entire past world constitutes "the 'initial data' which are to be felt" (PR 221). But the entity, based on its subjective aim, excludes some of these initial data as irrelevant to its standpoint, and selects from the rest the " 'objective datum' which is felt" (PR 221). The *entire* past, as such, is indeterminate relative to any particular prehensive standpoint. It is rendered determinate by selection and exclusion through the prehending occasion's subjective aim. The objective datum, which is the occasion's actual world, is a fusion of the initial datum and the aim of that occasion freely chosen. Only this objective datum is fully perspectival, based on the standpoint of the prehending occasion. The initial datum is only a potentiality for prehensive unification.[10]

We can now see how the datum operates in the determination of a novel occasion. The initial datum is a multiplicity of ingressions, from no standpoint, thus not perspectivally determinate. The objective datum is determinate because it includes the self-creative act of the prehending occasion. This self-creative act, based on the occasion's subjective aim, transforms a multiplicity of potential data into unified data from a particular perspectival standpoint. The objective datum determines the becoming if we include the primordial nature of God. But the new occasion has contributed to the objective datum. The initial datum of itself determines nothing, for it can only determine becoming relative to standpoints which prehend it, thus which transform it into an object for them. The standpoint or perspective *at* which becoming takes place is also the perspective *from* which an aim is provided and *toward* which all feeling flows. Perspectivity here is based on the principle of experience, and suffers to some extent from irrelevant anthropomorphic analogies.

There remains a final difficulty concerning subjective aim. Whitehead claims that "the initial stage of the aim is rooted in the nature of God" (PR 244). This difficulty is analogous to that discussed above involving conceptual reversion, and requires the same resolution. If we emphasize the word "initial," and realize that Whitehead does not intend that the aim be determined entirely by God—which would abolish freedom —then this is not an issue of freedom but of the immanence of God and ground for the future. It is a manifestation of the cosmological principle and a weakening of perspectivity, but it is not a violation of freedom. God provides the range of possibilities among which an entity determines its subjective aim. But these possibilities are, as a range of alternatives, not determining conditions of an occasion without its self-determining decision. I have rejected the view that God directly provides the movement from subjectivity to objectivity, from the present to the future. If all being is significance and perspective, then there is a double significance in every occasion: self-significance and significance for another. As superject, an occasion presides over its perishing and establishes its relevance for the future. This relevance defines the initial data for the future which become determinate conditions only through being prehended by occasions that define their own subjective aims. This double significance, with inseparable poles, is a manifestation of perspectivity that has misleading formulations through the language of experience.

The Ultimate Irrationality

In *Science and the Modern World*, Whitehead claims that God is the ultimate limiting principle, the ultimate irrationality. Throughout *Process and Reality*, he looks for ultimate reasons. And in many ways, his theory of freedom represents the crystallization of these final irrationalities. After he has defined causal inheritance, the origination of novelty in God, and even the origination of the subjective aim in God, there is still a further ground of freedom—the self-causation of each actual entity.

I have tried to show how carefully Whitehead works out the complementary interrelationship of determination and freedom, though his theory is weakened throughout by considerations based on the principles of experience and cosmology. I must at this point raise the question whether the notion of self-causation is not in the end arbitrary and unintelligible. Ultimately, an actual entity is what it is. Some aspect of its becoming lies wholly within itself and depends on nothing else. Is there not here a relic of the older theory that a substance is wholly in itself and conceived in itself, though Whitehead has thoroughly rejected that theory? The perspectival features of his theory of self-determination are incomplete. An actual entity is not literally "in itself"—for actual entities are prehensively related. But one phase or aspect of each entity seems to be entirely self-contained.[11]

To recapitulate, each actual entity originates in a prehension of data from the past and of all eternal objects graded in relevance within the primordial nature of God. Yet these two together do not determine the becoming of an occasion. It decides for itself. Since many such entities are inorganic, the "decision" here is not conscious. Is this not then merely a form of chance or spontaneity, wholly without foundation, an arbitrary basis for novelty or freedom? Although Whitehead is committed to the principle that freedom is not indeterminateness but self-determination, does not self-determination become arbitrary in the end? The choice or decision of an actual entity among a range of possibilities can have no further ground beyond these possibilities and must, then, be unintelligible and ungrounded. The error here lies in the supplemental mode of analysis, as if self-causation comes by way of addition to other determinants. The principle of experience suggests the separability of freedom from conditions, a notion that is unintelligible from the standpoint of the perspectivity of prehension. Only a full complementarity of determinateness and indeterminateness, embodied in a stronger principle of perspective, can make self-determination anything but arbitrary.[12]

A related issue is based on the arbitrariness of the primordial nature of God and the timelessness of eternal objects. It is expressed directly in Whitehead's principle that there are ultimately two modes of freedom, "a definite free initiation and a definite free conclusion" (PR 47). In one sense, both of these are forms of self-causation, God's and that of actual occasions. Yet God's decision is unconditioned, primordial, and everlasting. It is therefore nonperspectival and absolute. If self-causation is intelligible relative to an occasion's prehensions of the past, why not treat God's complete envisagement of eternal objects as a function of his consequent nature, his prehension of past actualities, changing with them? This would have two advantages: it would reduce two modes of freedom to one—the self-causation of actual entities relative to their inheritance from the past in terms of their subjective aim and satisfaction—and it would eliminate the independence of eternal objects and their relations from the development of the world. Even the primordial nature of God would here be conditioned and perspectival, and cosmological notions could be further eliminated. However, it is acceptable only if self-causation itself is intelligible. I am now questioning that intelligibility.

The central principle of Whitehead's theory of self-determination is that the data which are objectively prehended provide for the subject only a limited range of possibilities among which it may define its being. Such a theory is essential if Whitehead is to provide that actual entities are constituted by their relations yet at the same time causes of themselves. It is essential that every occasion have a clear identity while it is also constituted by its relations. This is a simply corollary of the principle of perspective. The issue of freedom and determination is an application of the general issue of the identity of things in relation. It is central to Whitehead's entire theory of actual entities, and is resolved most effectively by the principle of perspective.

Arbitrary self-causation cannot aid us in resolving such a complex issue. If an actual entity were "merely" a prehending agent, devoid of self-causation, would it have less of an identity? It would be *that* agent prehending *those* objects, whether or not it was free. Must we postulate a decision, an act of self-causation, or is not the sheer perspectivity of prehensive unification amidst the wealth of relevant determinants a satisfactory ground for freedom and novelty? Where being is inevitably selective and limited, a complement of determinateness and indeterminateness, no arbitrary additions are needed for freedom. Prehensiveness is perspectivity and, in the context of diverse and manifold perspectives, entails a complementarity of determinateness and indeterminateness that provides a basis for freedom and identity without arbitrariness. What is required is abandonment of the *totality* of perspectives and determinants that constitute an event, that is, abandonment of the cosmological principle in favor of an inexhaustible multiplicity of perspectives.[13]

Whitehead himself offers clues that must lead us to reject self-causation as both unnecessary and irrational. In Chapter X of *Science and the Modern World*, he claims that each eternal object has both a relational and an individual essence. Every eternal object is what it is, different from every other eternal object. If so, and if eternal objects are not subjective unities of experience or self-causation, why do we require an arbitrary principle of freedom for actual entities? Here the double status of individual and relational essences for eternal objects is either inexplicable, another irrationality, or definitive of eternal objects as themselves perspectives, subject to relational conditions yet with unique identities as well.

Two replies may be given in support of Whitehead's position. First, without self-causation no satisfactory response can be given to Bradley's critique of relations, and actualities would collapse into their relations. They would be wholly constituted by their relations. They would be nothing in themselves. Such a reply ignores the point that eternal objects are "what they are" too, needing no self-causation. I am arguing that the principle of perspective, inherent in prehensive or vectoral relations, is a sufficient answer to Bradley's critique, and may be generalized.

The second reply emphasizes the subjective aim of an actual entity and its *act* of becoming. It is based on the principle of experience. The self-causation inherent in each actual entity cannot be identified apart from the entity as a whole. Each actual entity is a drop of becoming in which data, eternal objects, and subjective aim all merge in an indivisible complex unity. In other words, there is no arbitrary but distinct step in becoming. Rather, all the determinations from outside an actual entity do not wholly determine it. It is the nature of an experience to make what is only partly determinate wholly determinate. But this determinateness is achieved in a way that cannot be entirely explained.

There are philosophers who would question Whitehead's commitment to inexplicabilities and irrationalities. I am not among them. Novelty, freedom, the contingency of things, all contain a residuum of mystery and inexplicability, what has not been explained despite our deepest explanations. What I question is whether there is an *ultimate* irrationality or mystery.[14] What I reject is that there are irrationalities utterly beyond comprehension and understanding: the primordial nature of God and the self-determination of every actual entity. The cosmological principle turns novelty into unresolvable arbitrariness, while the principle of perspective makes it a pervasive pole of every determination. To make the primordial nature of God a function of past events conjoined with the self-determination of God suggests that every determination depends on a system of relevant possibilities containing inexplicable factors: but these cannot be traced to an ultimate principle. Likewise, though each determination of an actual entity may involve inexplicable factors essential to novelty and freedom, there is no ultimate and entirely inexplicable factor of self-determination *in addition to* what is intelligible and determinate.

I formulated a principle of freedom earlier in this chapter: that *in any becoming, everything that can be determined is determined, but there is also freedom*. Whitehead analyzes freedom in each actual entity in terms of "the decision of the subject-superject of the concrescence" (PR 28). This decision, by the principle of experience, becomes an ultimate irrationality. *Something* remains wholly undetermined (though we cannot, in Whitehead's theory, say *what* this indetermination is). The alternative, based on a thoroughgoing perspectivity, is that determinateness and indeterminateness be seen as thoroughly complementary notions where neither can obtain nor be intelligible without the other. The perspectivity of Whitehead's theory, in which every actual entity is a complement of determinateness and indeterminateness, must be generalized to every other factor of existence, to every stage of concrescence, to eternal objects, and to the primordial and consequent natures of God. Here *everything* may be determined except that where there is determinateness there is always indeterminateness. Conversely, there is indeterminateness only with, and inseparable from, determinateness. This complementarity is expressed in the plurality of diverse perspectives in the absence of any total or ultimate perspective. Actual entities are indeterminate relative to their future objectifications because of the novel and unique perspectives future occasions will engender. Eternal objects are indeterminate relative to any particular ingression because every ingression is relative to a novel perspective. Neither of these forms of indeterminateness need be interpreted as a form of self-causation. But some form of in-determinateness is relevant to every determination, and nothing may be viewed as determinate (or indeterminate) in all respects. Another way of putting this is that everything is inexhaustible, but that as a consequence, it may be known inexhaustibly. Nothing is in any unqualified sense *beyond* understanding.

The irrationality of self-causation in Whitehead's theory, I am arguing, is a consequence of the principles of experience and cosmology. Self-causation is, in some ultimate sense, beyond intelligibility. I will discuss the principle of cosmology in later chapters. It is essential at this point that I consider Whitehead's theory of experience in detail, for it is one of his most remarkable achievements, yet equally one of his most profound limitations.

Notes to Chapter 3

1. The principle of perspective effectively rules out notions of "ultimacy" and "finality" where these represent unqualified modes of determination. The frequency with which such expressions appear in Whitehead's writings is an indication of the cosmological principle. Self-causation is the ultimate basis of perspective for Whitehead because of his limited perspectivity, based on the two principles of experience and cosmology expressed in the ontological principle.

2. Alfred North Whitehead, *Science and the Modern World* (New York: Macmillan, 1925), p. 149 (hereafter cited as SMW).

3. A good example of an analysis that neglects the self-determination of actual entities is the following:

> The principle that the process of an event is internally determined and externally free may be summed up as follows. Each event can be said to be internally determined by the events in its immediate past, . . . On the other hand the specific character that event will assume in the immediate future remains in the sphere of contingency. (Mays 1959, p. 189)

Mays's conclusion is incredible, perhaps the most complete misunderstanding of Whitehead's theory of freedom possible.

> Whitehead's attempt to show that either free will or determinism shall have some relevance in his philosophy is then based on a mistake. . . . Imagine what confusion would result were a little freedom injected into the general laws of physics, so that molecules from a liver cell could wander off at their own free will into some brain cell. (1959, pp. 232, 234)

Mays seems to overlook the nature of both the principle of experience and the principle of perspective.

4. This argument cannot be evaded in Whitehead's theory by making God the ground of mutual immanence of contemporaries. "Can it be without qualification true that contemporaries are causally independent? . . . Since they are all immanent in God, and he in turn immanent in them, must they not be immanent in each other?" (Hartshorne 1972, p. 87). To the extent that God is prehended *physically* by an occasion *throughout* its becoming, to that extent is self-determination undermined. Contemporary occasions can be mutually immanent only in the weak and vague sense in which their common past is projected through the present into a common future, essentially an inductive projection founded on social conditions. (See AI 198 and discussion above, pp. 45–49.) In addition, see Emmet 1966: "There cannot be 'mutual immanence' of the Consequent Nature of God in other actual entities, since this is an actual entity which has not yet become, and so cannot be in the past of other entities. When does it become and achieve 'satisfaction'? Never, as far as I can see, if it is 'everlasting' and 'with all creation!' '" (p. xxxii).

Wilcox's criticisms are well taken of "certain theists," who emphasize the direct immanence of the consequent nature of God, as holding a doctrine incompatible with the theory of relativity; but the more fundamental point is that such immanence would effectively violate the self-determination of individual occasions. These theists hold a badly weakened theory of self-causation, due to their cosmological concerns (Wilcox 1961, pp. 293–300). See further discussion below, pp. 263–64. The religious emphasis that supports interpretations like the following is a misrepresentation of Whitehead's theory: "The consequent nature acts by being concretely apprehended in feeling in such a way that God's specific response to the world becomes a constitutive function in the world. Here there is specific divine causality" (Williams 1964, p. 179) If God's consequent nature were a constitutive factor of events, it would have to be complete; moreover, it would comprise a medium whereby contemporary occasions would be immanent in each other, violating their causal independence.

5. This is also an argument against overlapping occasions, and is the basis for what Whitehead calls a "unison of becoming" (PR 124–26). Self-causation requires closure against external determination at some phase of becoming (the "decision") and is the metaphysical basis of Whitehead's rejection of the foundations of the theory of relativity. (He does not reject the coordination of geometrical and temporal relations described by the theory of relativity in our cosmic epoch.) Such interpretations as "Whitehead's actual entities include such things as tables, occasions of human sense-perception, and organs of the human body" (Wallack 1980, p. 25) are simply mistaken in their understanding of the scale of process in Whitehead's theory, overlooking the metaphysical considerations inherent in his theory of experience. I am arguing, however, that the principle of perspective carries within it a theory of alternatives and possibilities which does not require "decision," "unison of becoming," or "ultimate irrationality." Here societies as well as events, eternal objects as well as multiplicities, are all perspectival, with their own identities in perspectival relation to their constituents and determinants. Such a theory requires the sacrifice of both

of the other central principles of Whitehead's theory: the cosmological principle and the principle of experience—both implicated in the arbitrariness of the ontological principle and the doctrine of self-causation.

6. In this connection see Thompson:

> The initial aim derived from God . . . involves a determinate unification of all actual entities and moreover the envisagement of the ideal possibility relative to those actual entities. . . . The initial datum of an occasion establishes a categorical limit of what may be admitted in the way of a lure for feeling, but that what is in fact admitted to feeling up to and including this ideal limit, is determined by the actual entity in process of concrescence. God lures each actual entity toward that perfection possible for it, but each occasion "is finally responsible for the decision by which any lure for feeling is admitted to efficiency." (1971, p. 96)

Thompson does not recognize the tension between the determinateness inherent in the primordial nature of God and the self-causation and decision of individual actual occasions.

7. Victor Lowe is therefore either misleading or mistaken when he says, "I cannot agree . . . that after *Science and the Modern World* Whitehead dropped the idea that there is some fixed order among eternal objects" (1966, note, p. 101). The primordial nature of God is unchanging, but it is a system with only partial order. (See discussion of the mathematical paradigms involved, pp. 151–53.) What is at stake is the nature of freedom. The most detailed analysis of this problem is in Pols's *Whitehead's Metaphysics*. These various difficulties are produced by Whitehead's concessions to the cosmological principle and the principle of experience, for if the primordial nature of God were conditioned, as it must be by the principle of perspective, and every actual entity were another perspective for which the primordial nature was a condition, the perspectivity would guarantee alternative possibilities both within the primordial nature and within every occasion. As a consequence, however, even the primordial nature of God would be qualified by its relations. (See discussion below, pp. 231–33.)

8. This is the solution to the criticisms of Gentry and Kirkpatrick:

> To reject the idea that an experience of any sort can occur without an experient in the form of an existential condition of it violates the evidence. But . . . it is precisely this truth that Whitehead repudiates in his conception of the subject as experient. . . . The actual entity or existent (the fully actual thing) is not *given*. It arises out of its given world and is a novel focalization of this world. (Gentry 1944, p. 224)

> My objection to the Whiteheadian-Ford attempt to establish a subject prior to the completion of becoming is that it appears to me impossible to talk of a subject without presupposing a fundamental, basic notion of *a being* and that it is from such a notion that the process view has abstracted the notion of a process of unification *aiming* at a being. (Kirkpatrick 1973, p. 19)

Whitehead's theory of experience requires a process of prehensive unification which culminates in the experiencer, unified through subjective aim. Whitehead's solution, founded on the principle of experience, is the apparent source of difficulties. The principle of perspective resolves this issue entirely because it denies the priority of being over perspectival resolution.

9. This is another reason for resisting the identification of an actual entity with everyday, human, or enduring experience. ("It is human experiences that are the most important examples of actual entities since it is only through our own experiences that we can know actual entities at all. . . . a human experience is not only an exemplary actual entity but the standard by which to judge the nature of all actual entities" [Wallack, 1980, pp. 20–21]). The subjective aim can function throughout every constituent of an actual occasion, rendering that occasion a perspective upon its data, only where disruption is impossible in principle.

10. This distinction between data from a standpoint and the initial data, *for* standpoints but without a standpoint, is inherent in Whitehead's theory of experience, and is a weakening of the principle of perspective. By the latter principle, data can be such only from a perspectival standpoint.

11. Edward Pols develops a criticism closely related to mine here, though founded on the nature of subjective aim: "Without the doctrine of freedom Whitehead's doctrine becomes a God-centered determinism" (1967, p. 126). Creativity does "not appear to be the source of any (active) power to bring about the modification of subjective aim, so that this modification must seem to come about *ex nihilo*, or to result from the character of determinate components" (p. 142). "Either there is a radical finalism founded on God, or there is the appearance *ex nihilo* of an arbitrary real togetherness of abstract entities" (p. 193).

12. An interesting discussion of ultimate irrationality and arbitrariness in the context of "an ultimately satisfying explanation" can be found in Robert C. Neville's *Creativity and God*.

> There are two broad sensibilities regarding this which are so diverse as to be virtually impossible to mediate.
> On the one hand is the view that an ultimately satisfying explanation is a reduction of things to first principles. Things are explained by being shown to exhibit characters necessitated by certain determinate first principles. The first principles explain by virtue of their own character. If it is asked how the first principles themselves are to be accounted for, the answer is that they do not need to be accounted for if indeed they are "first"—the ultimate and primordial explanatory principles. . . .
> On the other hand, there is the empiricist's view that an ultimately satisfying explanation consists in locating the decisive actions from which things take their form. . . .
> The difficulty alleged against the empiricist sensibility is that there is nothing in the character of the ontologically creative act that accounts for the product of the act . . . therefore, explanation by reference to a decisive action is not an explanation at all. (1980, pp. 46–47)

Neville accepts the second alternative. I think neither alternative is satisfactory, for both are arbitrary in fundamental respects. The principle of perspective eliminates the arbitrariness. No explanation can be ultimate.

13. See my *Transition to an Ordinal Metaphysics*, especially chapter 2 (1980).

14. See my *Philosophical Mysteries* (1981).

CHAPTER FOUR

EXPERIENCE

The explicit center of Whitehead's theory of perspective is defined by his theory of experience. Yet I have argued that there are implicit notes in his theory toward a wider view of perspective. Moreover, there are difficulties inherent in the tension between the principles of experience and perspective.[1] Whitehead's theory of experience is one of his major achievements, and it is one of the primary sources of his reputation. Nevertheless, it is also the basis of a continuing confusion as to the nature of the experience and prehension of actual entities as contrasted with human experience, conscious or otherwise.[2] Some of these difficulties have been noted in earlier discussions. I will argue that Whitehead's theory of experience must be transformed into a theory of prehension in which only weak analogies hold with human experience: otherwise the consequent anthropomorphism in making inorganic elements sentient would be intolerable. I will also argue that, once this step has been taken of developing a sophisticated theory of prehension generalized to all actuality, it is unnecessary to sustain both perspective and experience as fundamental principles, and that the principle of perspective carries the full force of Whitehead's theory without concession to possible anthropomorphism.

General Considerations

Actual entities are "drops of experience" (PR 18). The concept of experience is grounded in the notion of prehension or "feeling." The application of these notions to inorganic nature may be viewed as an extended analogy.

> If we substitute the term "energy" for the concept of a quantitative emotional intensity, and the term "form of energy" for the concept of "specific form of feeling," and remember that in physics "vector" means definite transmission from elsewhere, we see that this metaphysical description of the simplest elements in the constitution of actual entities agrees absolutely with the general principles according to which the notions of modern physics are framed. (PR 116)

In human experience there is feeling transmitted from an object to the perceiving subject; in physical nature there is the vector transmission of energy from one object to another. To prevent the analogy from being abused, we need a principle emphasizing the originative elements in human experience and minimizing origination in inorganic "experience." This is the category of conceptual reversion.

Such an account of Whitehead's position omits something fundamental. He does not tell us to generalize from human experience, but "from the language of physics" (PR 116). Does he imagine that the analogy moves more easily in this direction? That would be quite implausible. Omitted in so strong an emphasis on the analogical character of Whitehead's categories are the principles upon which the analogy is based and the issues they are designed to resolve. The concept of experience is developed both to establish the interconnection of organic and inorganic nature and to resolve difficulties of explanation in the science of nature. The concept of experience embodies principles within it essential to all metaphysical explanation. In particular, it expresses the perspectivity essential to any actuality.

Why are actual entities "drops of experience"? The answer lies only partly in the properties of human experience. It lies more directly in the multivalent nature of the concept of experience.[3]

> Every prehension consists of three factors: (a) the "subject" which is prehending, namely, the actual entity in which that prehension is a concrete element; (b) the "datum" which is prehended; (c) the "subjective form" which is *how* that subject prehends that datum. (PR 23)

That an actual entity is a drop of experience entails that, inseparably and indissolubly, it (a) is a *subject* which is the ground of actuality, self-identity, and freedom; (b) possesses a *datum* which is the ground of causal inheritance and objectivity; and (c) possesses a *style* or *manner* of prehension which is the ground of novelty and the qualities of higher consciousness, such as perception, illusion, and evaluation. These factors are inseparably conjoined.

Relatedness and unification are metaphysical essentials and must be founded and expressed in fundamental principles. Whitehead's major achievement, it seems to me, is to establish such principles at the center of his theory. Both the principle of perspective and the principle of experience are intrinsically relational principles. Insofar as actual entities become by prehending, are "drops of experience," they are founded on relations. An actual entity is both an experiencer and available to be experienced. In virtue of both capacities, occasions are together in a common world, yet are also unique in their singular perspectives. They are what they are in virtue of what and how they prehend, yet the objects prehended are not wholly constitutive of a prehending occasion, for it makes its own contribution to every prehension. In conceiving of actual entities as drops of experience, Whitehead makes relatedness and perspective the fundamental categories of being, rather than self-sufficiency and fact. Put another way, he preserves both the public and private nature of every actuality.

> The theory of prehensions is founded upon the doctrine that there are no concrete facts which are merely public, or merely private. The distinction between publicity and privacy is a distinction of reason, and is not a distinction between mutually exclusive concrete facts. The sole concrete facts, in terms of which actualities can be analyzed, are prehensions; and every prehension has its public side and its private side. (PR 290)

I am arguing that actual entities are not assigned to experience from an obscure sense of analogy between human existence and the rest of the world, but to conceptually ground a principle of fundamental importance: that every actuality has a unique identity that cannot be reduced to the diversity of elements which constitute it; but these elements do constitute it.[4] "This word 'feeling' is a mere technical term; but it has been chosen to suggest that functioning through which the concrescent actuality appropriates the datum so as to make it its own" (PR 164). This is clearly a formulation of the principle of perspective, and indicates how, in Whitehead's theory, that principle is founded on the principle of experience. Nevertheless, there are some important differences between perspectives and experiences.

In particular, implicit in the view that actual entities are drops of experience is a claim that they ultimately possess an unanalyzable character, that some constituent of experience is unanalyzable. This is what is meant by saying that actual entities are *causa sui*. Whitehead generalizes Kant's argument that the subject of experience is, as subject, both unanalyzable and relational.[5] "The philosophy of organism is a cell-theory of actuality. Each ultimate unity of fact is a cell-complex, not analyzable into components with equivalent completeness of actuality" (PR 219). Nevertheless, there is a relatively concrete mode of analysis of actual entities which preserves their experiential nature. This is analysis into prehensions. In such "genetic" analysis an actuality is considered "formally," not "objectively," as subject and not as object. As shown in the last chapter, the difference between, and interrelation of, these points of view is the heart of Whitehead's conception of freedom. The notion of experience unifies the two points of view as complementary aspects of one actuality. Here may be found elements of analogy with human experience.

> The philosophy of organism attributes "feeling" throughout the actual world. It bases this doctrine upon the directly observed fact that "feeling" survives as a known element constitutive of the "formal" existence of such actual entities as we can best observe. (PR 177)

Yet the issue is not whether other actualities resemble human experience or how much, but how we are to understand the interconnection of unity with multiplicity in all modes of being. Whitehead effectively argues that only the principle of experience establishes an intelligible basis for such a complementary interrelationship. I have been arguing that the principle of perspective is sufficient and that additional features of experience beyond perspectivity create diffculties within Whitehead's theory.

Every positive prehension is

> essentially a transition effecting a concrescence. Its complex constitution is analyzable into five factors which express what that transition consists of, and effects. The factors are: (i) the "subject" which feels, (ii) the "initial data" which are to be felt, (iii) the "elimination" in virtue of negative prehensions, (iv) the "objective datum" which is felt, (v) the "subjective form" which is *how* that subject feels that objective datum. (PR 221)

It is worth commenting on these notions. Whitehead speaks of a "positive prehension" as a feeling. There are negative prehensions also, or "exclusions from feeling." While the notion of a negative prehension suggests a feeling that excludes from feeling, it is essential to perspective and must be imposed on the principle of experience. Selection and exclusion are essential to perspectives. The "initial datum" must be understood as a consequence of the principle of relativity and the second pole of perspectivity: to be is to be a potential for other becomings. All past occasions, conjoined with the complete primordial nature of God, comprise a system of potentials for the future. These potentials must be modified by selection and exclusion to constitute the diverse perspectives of the contemporary world. One principle of selection is provided by the perspective which a prehending entity takes toward its data, and is based on its unique location. The second principle of selection is that of self-causation; each occasion chooses what it will become in terms of the data provided. The modification of the initial datum by exclusion, producing negative prehensions, constitutes the objective datum.

The subject, implicit in its subjective aim, is a factor in this experiential process. What an actual entity is to become, though present only as a vague and indeterminate aim in its earliest stages, provides the ground of selection for the transition from the initial to the objective datum in which the occasion's actual world is defined and in which elements in the initial data are excluded as incompatible with the occasion's subjective aim. This portrayal of concrescence emphasizes the point of view of the occasion in imposing its selection on its initial data. It follows that the past is "objectively" determinate only from a particular point of view. "The universe is always one, since there is no surveying it except from an actual entity which unifies it" (PR 231–32). The past circumscribes the alternatives available for becoming, but is effective only in conjunction with the free choice of the occasion among its options. The way in which an occasion feels its objective datum, which has been partly determined by its own aim, is what Whitehead calls the "subjective form" of that prehension. This subjective form is clearly a consequence of the principle of experience. In particular,

Each negative prehension has its own subjective form, however trivial and faint. It adds to the emotional complex, though not to the objective data. The emotional complex is the subjective form of the final "satisfaction." (PR 41)

Yet, as I have been arguing, the essential function of the concept of experience is to establish the notion of a perspective in terms of which an occasion prehends its actual world by exclusion. The question is whether the apparent metaphor may be eliminated and the principle of perspective developed more generally. A major issue here is the role of selection and exclusion in Whitehead's theory, for perspectives depend on limitations by exclusion which are incompatible with the cosmological principle. Some tensions between perspectivity and cosmology are mitigated by the principle of experience.

Three categoreal conditions, which Whitehead says "have an air of ultimate metaphysical generality" (PR 222), hold for all occasions: the categories of subjective unity, objective identity, and objective diversity. These are sufficiently important to comprise the first three categoreal obligations of the categoreal scheme. The category of subjective unity reads: "The many feelings which belong to an incomplete phase in the process of an actual entity, though unintegrated by reason of the incompleteness of the phase, are compatible for synthesis by reason of the unity of their subject" (PR 223). Whitehead claims that this is the category of self-realization, and that "self-realization is the ultimate fact of facts. An actuality is self-realizing, and whatever is self-realizing is an actuality" (PR 222). It is the nature of an occasion to be a subject which realizes itself, which is *causa sui*, which imposes itself on the diversity of elements of its world. This Whitehead conceives as actuality: all else is derivative abstraction. The category of subjective unity establishes that the subjective aim of an occasion qualifies every incomplete phase of its becoming by determining a ground of compatibility among the diverse elements of an incomplete phase. In other words, because of the aim toward which all the feelings of an occasion tend, elements are excluded which would be incompatible with that end. Whitehead calls this category "a doctrine of pre-established harmony," and claims that it "is the reason why no feeling can be abstracted from its subject" (PR 223–24). The subject imposes its character on whatever feelings in its becoming promote the realization of its subjective aim. The harmony is *pre*-established in that it is prior to the realization of the aim, conceptually if not temporally. It is not imposed prior to the initial stages of the occasion.[6]

The category of subjective unity is a direct expression of the principle of experience. An experience can be the experience it is only if all the elements which enter it are felt within a single perspective that unifies them. This category and the last are necessary only because of the distinction between perspective and experience, for the references to incomplete phases, to lack of integration, to synthesis by a subject, are motivated by the sense of *agency* that underlies experience. That there should be phases at all is a problem in Whitehead's theory, phases largely "out of time." By the principle of perspective, an occasion is a unique perspective on its data, divisible relative to some perspectives but indivisible relative to its own point of view. The principle of subjective unity is superfluous from the standpoint of the principle of perspective.

The category of objective identity enforces the principle that becoming is a transition from indeterminateness to determinateness. In the final satisfaction, all indeterminateness is eliminated; every element plays a single role. "There can be no duplication of any element in the objective datum of the satisfaction of an actual entity, so far as concerns the function of that element in that satisfaction" (PR 225). There is no trace of "ambiguity" left in the final satisfaction: "one thing has one rôle, and cannot assume any duplicity" (PR 225). I have noted that such determinateness is only partial and from a particular point of view, for neither the actual entity nor its prehensions are entirely determinate from the standpoint of the future. Here the principle of experience departs from the principle of perspective, leading to an unqualified determinateness in the satisfaction of an occasion relative to its data. Duplicity and ambiguity are essential in every perspective, qualifying even the constituents of a perspective. *What* is relevant to a perspective is always indeterminate in certain respects.

The category of objective diversity re-enforces the sense of unqualified determinateness. "There can be no 'coalescence' of diverse elements in the objective datum of an actual entity so far as concerns the functions of those elements in that satisfaction" (PR 225). Exclusions can and must take place in defining the objective datum for an occasion, but within that datum, with its diversities, contrasts preserve themselves amid similarities. Whitehead's theory of causation requires that, in some way, each actual entity prehend what it does "as things are": objectively if perspectivally. Similarity may be emphasized in the satisfaction of an occasion that is a member of a society for which that emphasis is dominant, but the elements that are similar must also be felt as diverse, or they are not distinct elements. One of the functions of the category of objective diversity is to establish an epistemic ground of higher experience. The category entails that there cannot be "absolute" or total error. It is closely related to the cosmological character of the unqualified principle of relativity: every being is a potential for *every* becoming; *every* datum in a satisfaction functions there in a singular way. Here Whitehead departs from the exclusions and qualifications inherent in perspectives, as if the entire world—from the standpoint of the principle of relativity—or the entire actual occasion were qualified in an unqualified way, as if relation and point of view were not themselves conditioned and from a point of view. A particular point of view here is raised to predominance.

Formally speaking, the three categories together define concrescence, and thereby, creativity. The category of subjective unity defines the unification achieved amidst diversity; the categories of objective identity and diversity define the relationship between the diverse elements and the unified satisfaction. These categories together comprise the determinateness achieved by an occasion amidst its perspectival relations and conditions. It is a determinateness required by the principle of experience but incompatible, I claim, with the principle of perspective. Nevertheless, these principles lead directly to and sustain the notion of contrast.

> The real synthesis of two component elements in the objective datum of a feeling must be infected with the individual particularities of each of the relata. Thus the synthesis in its completeness expresses the joint particularities of that pair of relata, and can relate no others. A complex entity with this individual definiteness, arising out of determinateness of eternal objects, will be termed a "contrast." A contrast cannot be abstracted from the contrasted relata. (PR 228)

A contrast is a unifying relationship that preserves the elements related in accordance with the principle of objective diversity. The preservation of such diversity, especially with respect to past occasions as data, grounds Whitehead's rejection of the sensationalist principle. "The truism that we can only *conceive* in terms of universals has been stretched to mean that we can only *feel* in terms of universals. This is untrue. Our perceptual feelings feel particular existents" (PR 230). Nevertheless, a consequence of Whitehead's categories is that contrasts are not *further* perspectives in the perspectivity of an occasion, but are direct consequences of the latter. One of the limitations of Whitehead's theory, founded on the principle of experience, is that *only* actual occasions are thought to be fully perspectival. Properly speaking, contrasts are always from a point of view in which *some* elements are contrasted in *some* ways, but not all ways. Even if we emphasize the contrast of the participants of the relata with their synthesis, there is no unqualified particularity or unqualified mode of synthesis among any eternal objects.

Causal relations are understood by Whitehead to be *physical feelings*. Entities are constituents of other entities' perspectives. This perspective upon perspectives, I am arguing, is essential to the principle of perspective in its more adequate formulations. "A simple physical feeling is an act of causation. The actual entity which is the initial datum is the 'cause,' the simple physical feeling is the 'effect,' and the subject entertaining the simple physical feeling is the actual entity 'conditioned' by the effect" (PR 236). A cause is a past entity which perishes to be prehended as an object for a new occasion—the effect. The prehension is of the object's own prehensions: there is nothing else to prehend concretely. "Thus a simple feeling is one feeling which feels another feeling" (PR 236). However, the subjects of the prehensions are different. The differing subjects, by the principle of experience, comprise the basis for the different points of view on common data that is essential to the principle of perspective. Perspective here provides simultaneously and inseparably for reproduction and divergence. "In the world there is nothing static. But there is reproduction; and hence the permanence which is the result of order, and the cause of it. And yet there is always change; for time is cumulative as well as reproductive, and the cumulation of the many is not their reproduction as many" (PR 238). The emphasis on change is nevertheless misleading: there is order and variation, determinateness and indeterminateness, grounded in the principle of perspective. This applies to eternal objects as well as actual occasions, contrasts as well as prehensions.

Two other categories are necessary for understanding the transmission of feelings. These are the categories of conceptual valuation and conceptual reversion. There is also the category of subjective harmony. The latter is particularly important in defining aesthetic and teleological components of concrescence, features derived from the principle of experience that are not directly available from the principle of perspective—and which, I might mention, are not obviously plausible relative to inorganic occasions. At this point, I will not go further into these principles, for the tension between perspective and experience is clear enough, but will instead go on to consider Whitehead's theory of experience in more detailed form, with specific applications to human experience.

Mind and Body

The so-called "mind-body problem" is a question of relatedness. It is an interesting and important test of the principle of perspective to the extent that not all perspectives are experiential, not all perspectival centers are experiencing subjects. The question is whether higher forms of experience can be as naturally and plausibly derived from inorganic perspectives as they are from Whitehead's actual occasions. The place to begin this discussion is with Whitehead's own resolution of the problem. Two arguments establish the difficulty. The primary argument is that minds and bodies are so different that relations between them cannot be intelligible. The second is that if minds and bodies are connected, we can never know how. The natures of both mind and body are called into question by these arguments—not, as many philosophers have supposed, the nature of mind alone. Recognition of this point is one of Whitehead's major insights.

Various solutions have been offered, ranging from exploitation of the dualism to justify a belief in the freedom of mind (but not of body) to the extreme reductionist views of materialism and idealism. In all these cases, principles general enough to apply to both mind and body have proved difficult to delineate, while the absence of such principles creates what, prior to *Process and Reality*, Whitehead calls

> the bifurcation of nature into two systems of reality, which, in so far as they are real, are real in different senses. One reality would be the entities such as electrons which are the study of speculative physics. This would be the reality which is there for knowledge; although on this theory it is never known. For what is known is the other sort of reality, which is the byplay of the mind. Thus there would be two natures, one is the conjecture and the other is the dream.[7]

Whitehead argues that causality, time, space, and delusion all become problematic for theories that bifurcate nature. Such a theory "seeks for the cause of the knowledge of the thing known instead of seeking for the character of the thing known: secondly it assumes a knowledge of time in itself apart from events related in time: thirdly it assumes a knowledge of space in itself apart from events related in space" (CN 39). The solution, he claims, is to treat nature as a whole, containing mind and body, and to determine the principles that pervade it.

> The primary task of a philosophy of natural science is to elucidate the concept of nature, considered as one complex fact for knowledge, to exhibit the fundamental entities and the fundamental relations between entities in terms of which all laws of nature have to be stated, and to secure that the entities and relations thus exhibited are adequate for the expression of all the relations between entities which occur in nature. (CN 46)

What is required is nothing less than a complete reinterpretation of the constituents of the natural world, of all natural entities, bringing them under common principles. This is equally a problem for natural science and for philosophy, since what is at stake is the nature of natural entities and their relations.

In *The Concept of Nature*, then, Whitehead claims that he is not concerned with "metaphysical" questions, but with understanding science and nature, and what he means by nature "can be thought of as a closed system whose mutual relations do not require the expression of the fact that they are thought about" (CN 3). This may seem strange, since it denies that mind is part of nature, while in other passages, Whitehead speaks of colors as something to be explained in an adequate natural philosophy. The point, I believe, is that Whitehead is rejecting reductive materialism, the bifurcation of nature into appearance and reality: nature experienced and physical events. He is to this extent a naturalist. But he is also rejecting the extreme epistemological position that to understand nature we must understand reason. His naturalism leads him to the general principles of perspective and experience: natural events are perspectival and experiential. Human knowledge is a natural occurrence to be explained, not a fundamental premise of natural philosophy. The same approach is, I believe, maintained throughout Whitehead's later works: the theory of actual entities is a theory of natural events, not a theory about knowledge itself. The principles of perspective and experience are not primarily epistemological principles, but general principles of natural philosophy.

Whitehead's position, then, is that actual entities must be taken as "drops of experience" in order to explain the nature that is the object of scientific thought. Physical nature itself must be thought of as experience: only then can we understand causal connectedness, novelty in physical nature, relations among events, the ingression of forms, and individual identity. "An actual entity is essentially dipolar, with its physical and mental poles; and even the physical world cannot be properly understood without reference to its other side, which is the complex of mental operations" (PR 239). However, so general an approach to experience brings to prominence the contrast between lower, or physical, and higher, or conscious, experience. Knowledge and perception are to be explained in terms of categories derived from lower experience. What is central, I have been arguing, is that the concept of perspective is established as a fundamental notion throughout actuality. All relatedness is from a point of view, prehended by a subject. For the moment, I will minimize the difference between the principles of perspective and experience, treating the latter as the full foundation required by the former.

Under such general principles of perspective and experience, the issue of mind becomes one of explaining the disparity between lower or physical experience, in which primary qualities are predominant, and higher or conscious experience, in which imagination and secondary qualities are predominant. The notion of predomination is handled in both cases by the concept of a society. In the case of physical societies, the socially dominant characteristic is achieved by exclusion, a massive endurance relatively unaffected by outside elements. Such exclusion is not achieved at the expense of relatedness or prehension—that would be impossible—but by determination of environments which support endurance of a common form as a dominant element. Even massive endurance is achieved by the prehension of larger environments as supporting factors, and rests on the principle of experience.

Conscious experience, however, is the opposite of a massive endurance in which origination is fleeting and transitory and particular patterns predominate. Consciousness is origination become predominant, both in the introduction of new forms and in complex contrasts. All occasions depend on the contrast between alternatives that are selected and those that might be chosen. This contrast is inherent in the functioning of an occasion's subjective aim and is required for the transition in concrescence from indeterminateness to determinateness. However, some societies exist in environments that circumscribe the available alternatives more stringently than others. We have consciousness where alternatives are viable in great number, and where conceptual origination can be effective in promoting adaptation and adjustment. Such originative features of experience are also functions of the environment. An original mind in a paralyzed and sensorily deprived body will neither survive for long nor be effective in its decisions.

To what extent does this account of consciousness require a general principle of experience, and to what extent is the principle of perspective sufficient? The natural reply that to introduce mind only at higher levels of perspective is to restore the mind-body dualism has diminished force when we emphasize that low-grade experience is very different from conscious experience. If there is no dualism in Whitehead's theory between prehension and conscious perception, then there may be no dualism between general perspectivity and the particular perspectives of human judgment. I will argue that the uniqueness, novelty, and constitutiveness of perspectives is what is needed to break the mind-body dualism, and that subjectivity need not be introduced until advanced stages of complex processes. Before developing this notion further, however, it is worth considering those difficulties inherent in Whitehead's theory of perception and higher experience that are a consequence of too general a principle of experience.

Perception

The difficulties commonly associated with perception as a foundation for knowledge are of little interest to Whitehead. I have explained why:

natural philosophy must explain the properties of perception but need not rely on its epistemological credentials. The essential question is, "How can the other actual entities, each with its own formal existence, also enter objectively into the perceptive constitution of the actual entity in question? This is the problem of the solidarity of the universe" (PR 56). It is not an issue here of perception, but of relatedness. Indeed, despite the language of experience, it is perspectivity which is in question, passing into questions of cosmology. "The answer given by the organic philosophy is the doctrine of prehensions, involved in concrescent integrations, and terminating in a definite, complex unity of feeling" (PR 56). Perception is an instance of the togetherness shared by entities, one a prehending subject, the other its prehended object. If togetherness is not a metaphysical problem, then it provides a basis for the claim that an entity can perceive another as it is. There are real facts of togetherness among actual entities that establish a metaphysical basis for knowledge. Error arises in the additions of higher experience. Nevertheless, the importance of perspective in Whitehead's theory means that all judgment is from a point of view, and that no mode of understanding can be nonperspectival. If perspective means selection and exclusion, the problem of error becomes far more complex.

I noted in chapter 2 that recurrently where Whitehead speaks of "perception" he is not concerned with conscious perception, but with prehension. Thus, he can say that "a simple physical feeling is the most primitive type of an act of perception, devoid of consciousness" (PR 236). This perception is simply prehension, the objectification of occasions in others. There are two modes of such objectification, two ways in which occasions are prehended by others. The first is *causal objectification*, prehension in the mode of causal efficacy.

> In "causal objectification" what is felt *subjectively* by the objectified actual entity is transmitted *objectively* to the concrescent actualities which supersede it. In Locke's phraseology the objectified actual entity is then exerting "power." In this type of objectification the eternal objects, relational between object and subject, express the formal constitution of the objectified actual entity. (PR 58)

A past entity is objectified in a later occasion by being felt.

> A "simple physical feeling" entertained in one subject is a feeling for which the initial datum is another single actual entity, and the objective datum is another feeling entertained by the latter actual entity. (PR 236)

Whitehead also tells us that "the actual entity which is the initial datum is the actual entity perceived, the objective datum is the 'perspective' under which that actual entity is perceived, and the subject of the simple physical feeling is the perceiver" (PR 236).

This causal objectification is "primary"—as Whitehead calls it—in the sense of being the original phase of concrescence: inheritance of data. But it is also vague, dim, and imprecise. It

> produces percepta which are vague, not to be controlled, heavy with emotion: it produces the sense of derivation from an immediate past, and of passage to an immediate future; a sense of emotional feeling, belonging to oneself in the past, passing into oneself in the present, and passing from oneself in the present towards oneself in the future; a sense of influx of influence from other vaguer presences in the past, localized and yet evading local definition, such influence modifying, enhancing, inhibiting, diverting, the stream of feeling which we are receiving, unifying, enjoying, and transmitting. This is our general sense of existence, as one item among others, in an efficacious actual world. (PR 178)

The second mode of objectification is *presentational immediacy*. "What is ordinarily termed 'perception' is consciousness of presentational objectification" (PR 58). Whitehead's first definition is, "In 'presentational objectification' the relational eternal objects fall into two sets, one set contributed by the 'extensive' perspective of the perceived from the position of the perceiver, and the other set by the antecedent concrescent phases of the perceiver" (PR 58). This emphasizes the *position* of the perceiver. Whitehead also claims that "the contemporary world is perceived with its potentiality for extensive division, and not in its actual atomic division" (PR 62).

> Presentational immediacy illustrates the contemporary world in respect to its potentiality for extensive subdivision into atomic actualities and in respect to the scheme of perspective relationships which thereby eventuates. But it gives no information as to the actual atomization of this contemporary "real potentiality." By its limitations it exemplifies the doctrine, already stated above, that the contemporary world happens independently of the actual occasion with which it is contemporary. (PR 123)

Presentational immediacy is based on what Whitehead calls two metaphysical assumptions:

> (i) ... relatively to any actual entity, there is a "given" world of settled actual entities and a "real" potentiality, which is the datum for creativeness

beyond that standpoint. This datum, which is the primary phase in the process constituting an actual entity, is nothing else than the actual world itself in its character of a possibility for the process of being felt. This exemplifies the metaphysical principle that every "being" is a potential for a "becoming." The actual world is the "objective content" of each new creation. (PR 65)

(ii) ... the real potentialities relative to all standpoints are coordinated as diverse determinations of one extensive continuum. This extensive continuum is one relational complex in which all potential objectifications find their niche. It underlies the whole world, past, present, and future. (PR 66)

The extensive continuum provides "the solidarity of all possible standpoints throughout the whole process of the world" (PR 66). This postulated solidarity is entailed by neither the principle of experience nor the principle of perspective, but reflects the tension between the essential diversity and plurality of perspectival standpoints and the unification or solidarity of the world demanded by the cosmological principle. It is a real potentiality arising out of the world, not prior to it. "It is not a fact prior to the world; it is the first determination of order—that is, of real potentiality—arising out of the general character of the world" (PR 66). How such a potentiality can be relevant to *all* standpoints is difficult to understand, and is incompatible with perspectivity. Its obvious dependence on the primordial nature of God cannot establish its real potentiality, which must depend on the social character of some actual world.[8] For Whitehead, "extension, apart from its spatialization and temporalization, is that general scheme of relationships providing the capacity that many objects can be welded into the real unity of one experience" (PR 67). It is, here, a direct expression of the cosmological principle.

There are two largely independent issues here, one a metaphysical issue of the ground of unity among all concrescences, the other a question of conscious perception. These are conjoined by Whitehead in the notion of presentational immediacy. "The contemporary world is consciously prehended as a continuum of extensive relations" (PR 61). Relative to the first issue, the unity of all events in one universe, the character of presentational immediacy in prehension is clear: if there is an extensive continuum, and if it is required for concrescence, then it must be prehended by actual entities.[9] The status of the extensive continuum is not so clear, since it underlies all standpoints and seems not to have a standpoint itself. It both constitutes the meaning of standpoint and conjoins all standpoints into one world. It simultaneously grounds the principle of perspective and mates it with the cosmological principle. I will argue that this marriage cannot succeed.[10]

Relative to the second issue, the nature of conscious perception, extensiveness is more difficult to locate. It is even difficult to determine the relevant questions. Is Whitehead concerned primarily with the *testimony* of conscious perception as to the extensiveness of actual occasions, or is he simply concerned with the *apparent* extensiveness of everyday perception and seeking its explanation? If the latter, then further questions concerning the nonextensiveness of hearing and smell are relevant. But the fundamental issue is that of the scope of the principle of experience, expressed here in the transition from the experience of occasions to the experience of human beings. The breadth of the principle of experience raises questions from both directions: relative to the analogy in actual entities of human ends and conscious conceptions, and relative to the presence in human, social experience of elements pertinent specifically to actual occasions.

A particular point at issue, then, is that of the *purity* of the modes of perception. Granting that there are modes of prehension derived from causal inheritance and the extensive continuum, are they separable and "pure" in any intelligible sense for actual occasions, and are there corresponding modes of conscious perception in human experience? The examples Whitehead gives are remarkably implausible:

> In order to find obvious examples of the pure mode of causal efficacy we must have recourse to the viscera and to memory; and to find examples of the pure mode of presentational immediacy we must have recourse to so-called "delusive" perceptions. For example, the image of a grey stone as seen in a mirror illustrates the space behind the mirror; the visual delusions arising from some delirium, or some imaginative excitement, illustrate surrounding spatial regions; analogously for the double-vision due to maladjustment of the eyes; the sight at night, of the stars and nebulae and Milky Way, illustrates vague regions of the contemporary sky; the feelings in amputated limbs illustrate spaces beyond the actual body; a bodily pain, referred to some part not the cause of the disorder, illustrates the painful region though not the pain-giving region. All these are perfectly good examples of the pure mode of presentational immediacy. (PR 121–22)

No qualification is given: these are "perfectly" good examples of presentational immediacy.[11] Yet in every case there are the visceral bonds of causal efficacy. The mirror-image is surely related to an object, though we may be unsure which. The delusion is "pure" presentational immediacy because we do not know its cause, but it would be entirely unintelligible without reference to some cause, some historic route of occasions comprising the stone, from which the pattern assigned to the space behind the mirror is projected. In most cases, our sense of causal inheritance is dim and unclear. We do not clearly "know" what causes what. All we know is the efficacy of the past in providing data for perception. If we live in experiences of causal connection, then our most delusive perceptions of spatial regions must be inhabited by causal connections.

> When we perceive a contemporary extended shape which we term a "chair," the sense-data involved are not necessarily elements in the "real internal constitution" of this chair-image: they are elements—in some way of feeling—in the "real internal constitutions" of those antecedent organs of the human body *with* which we perceive the "chair." (PR 64–65)

Whitehead goes on to say that, "the epithet 'delusive,' which fits many, if not all, of these examples of presentational immediacy, is evidence that the mediating eternal object is not to be ascribed to the donation of the perceived region" (PR 122). True enough—but on the one hand, we may not be aware of the delusion *in* the perception, so that we perceive the region as causally efficacious even if it is not; and on the other, we certainly apprehend these spatial regions in a causal order, whether or not we know what the causes are.

As I have noted, there are epistemological concerns inherent in Whitehead's theory of perception, and they may be incompatible with his metaphysical concerns. There is a clear sense in which his metaphysical principles may be expected to address epistemological issues, providing a basis for our knowledge of the natural world. It is the inverse of this relationship that is problematical: a concern with the epistemic authority of any particular mode of experience. Whitehead's theory of prehension is metaphysically realistic: prehension preserves its object. Error is thus something to be explained, and Whitehead's official position is that "while the two pure perceptive modes are incapable of error, symbolic reference introduces this possibility. When human experience is in question, 'perception' almost always means 'perception in the mixed mode of symbolic reference' " (PR 168). The epistemological concern here with error distorts the scope of the principle of experience. If human perception is symbolic reference only—and I am arguing that it is—then it is permeated with possibilities of error, and pure modes of perception are irrelevant.[12] Human perception then is thoroughly treacherous—but not necessarily deceitful.

There appears to be a hidden agenda in Whitehead's theory of perception, a concern less with the consequences of his own theory and more with his predecessors and their views on perception.[13] The purity of the mode of presentational immediacy supports the traditional argument that perception provides no ground for knowledge of causation. Whitehead's reply is that presentational immediacy is but one mode of perception.

> ... what we want to know about, from the point of view either of curiosity or of technology, chiefly resides in those aspects of the world disclosed in causal efficacy: but that what we can distinctly register is chiefly to be found among the percepta in the mode of presentational immediacy. (PR 169)

An alternative would have been to hold that the traditional view oversimplifies perception, which has the complexity of symbolic reference.[14] Indeed, the indivisibility of occasions suggests that *only* symbolic reference is intelligible from the standpoint of an individual concrescence. Whitehead's view of pure modes of perception is a confusion as to different applications of the principle of experience.[15]

The principle of perspective effectively makes all forms of unqualified purity unintelligible, including pure modes of perception which jointly constitute human perspectives and pure modes of prehension which constitute concrescences. There is no metaphysical basis for Whitehead's division into pure modes of perception, only an epistemological basis at best, and with highly misleading results. He claims that symbolic reference is the source of perceptual error, that "the two pure perceptive modes are incapable of error" (PR 168). There is no difficulty in understanding that symbolic reference involves error—that of ascribing a spatial region to a causal route. But may one not err in the perception of a shape or color alone?[16] Are sensa incorrigible? Whitehead's metaphysical realism needs no support from incorrigible sensationalistic foundations. Indeed, any emphasis on simplicity or purity in actual occasions or eternal objects would drastically undermine the principle of perspective. Whitehead seems to borrow some aspects of sensa-data theories and their attendant incorrigibility.

> The percepta in the mode of presentational immediacy have the converse characteristics. In comparison, they are distinct, definite, controllable, apt for immediate enjoyment, and with the minimum of reference to past, or to future. We are subject to our percepta in the mode of efficacy, we adjust our percepta in the mode of immediacy. (PR 179)

Yet there can be errors in both causal efficacy and presentational immediacy, at least in higher experience.[17] Whitehead's examples of causal efficacy in conscious experience are a light flash and the agent's claim that "the flash made me blink" (PR 175). It might well have been something else, a reflex, a drug, etc.[18]

These are difficulties for Whitehead's realism—the transition from prehension, which need not be conscious, to conscious perception. They arise in the transition from a metaphysical realism of principles of connection to an epistemological realism in conscious experience. They are a result in particular of the conjoined divisibility and indivisibility of concrescences analyzed into moments, an incomplete acknowledgment of the principle of perspective. The principle of experience is the foundation of perspectivity in Whitehead's theory, but it cannot carry the weight of that principle. It makes indivisibility a persistent problem, insufficiently resolved in subjective experience. And it makes connections between lower and higher experience a continual problem, especially where epistemological issues are involved. Prehension is the ground of all metaphysical principles, the basis of Whitehead's system. It is as such neither corrigible nor incorrigible, but simply the vectoral relation in feeling among entities. It is how entities are related to other entities, thereby a full expression of the principle of perspective. It is not, however, a mode of *testimony*. Being constituted by relations and being testimony of relations may be very different to the extent that different perspectives are involved. Complexity in perspectives makes any easy transition from constitutive relations to epistemic authority quite unjustified.

Whitehead's theory of perception is a direct expression of the tension and differences between the principles of experience and perspective. The analogical and generalizing force of the principle of experience brings in epistemological and other issues that have little relevance at the so-called elementary level of experience and for the doctrine of prehension. The relationship between lower and higher experience is made problematical by the principle of experience itself, since its explanatory force and its plausibility are inseparable.

Higher Experience

I have discussed a number of ways in which the principle of experience causes difficulties in Whitehead's theory as a consequence of its conflicts with the principle of perspective. Where the principle of experience is asked to do the work of the latter principle while preserving analogies with human experience, significant confusions result. Implausible similarities exist between the experiences of actual occasions and the complex experiences of human beings, leading to questions involving the subjectivity of actual occasions and the purity of human perception. Yet there is another side to this story, for the principle of experience does permit Whitehead to develop a striking and important view of human experience that is thoroughly naturalistic without being reductionist. It must be discussed briefly here.

Every actual entity has a microcosmic dimension of process in its internal development and a macrocosmic dimension in its relation to the world.

> There are two species of process, macroscopic process, and microscopic process. The macroscopic process is the transition from attained actuality to actuality in attainment; while the microscopic process is the conversion of conditions which are merely real into determinate actuality. The former process effects the transition from the "actual" to the "merely real"; and the latter process effects the growth from the real to the actual. The former process is efficient; the latter process is teleological. . . . Thus the expansion of the universe in respect to actual things is the first meaning of "process"; and the universe in any stage of its expansion is the first meaning of "organism." In this sense, an organism is a nexus. (PR 214–15)

But human beings in particular inhabit a midway point of control and effect.

> In terms of human life, the soul is a society. . . . Beyond the soul, there are other societies, and societies of societies. There is the animal body ministering to the soul; there are families, groups of families, nations, species, groups involving different species associated in the joint enterprise of keeping alive. These various societies, each in its measure, claim loyalties and loves. In human history the various responses to these claims disclose the essential transcendence of each individual actuality beyond itself. The stubborn reality of the absolute self-attainment of each individual is bound up with a relativity which it issues from and issues into. The analysis of the various strands of relativity is the analysis of the social structure of the Universe, as in this epoch. (AI 290)

With both experience and sociality fundamental categories, there is no category required that is uniquely applicable to human life, only a heightening of awareness, a peak of intensity. Whitehead's words about God apply here with little modification: "God is not to be treated as an exception to all metaphysical principles, invoked to save their collapse.

He is their chief exemplification" (PR 343). Nor do human beings bring subjective experience and social relatedness to nature. Rather, human beings are a most intense realization of more general principles. Such a view of humanity is a natural expression of the principle of experience and a powerful expression of Whitehead's naturalism. Here the principle of experience is very important, for human life is but a version of more general principles: experience and multiple social order.

"A set of entities is a society (i) in virtue of a 'defining characteristic' shared by its members, and (ii) in virtue of the presence of the defining characteristic being due to the environment provided by the society itself" (PR 89). A *structured* society is one "which includes subordinate societies and nexūs with a definite pattern of structural inter-relations" (PR 99). Such societies have produced two major types, in response to the "problem for Nature," which "is the production of societies which are 'structured' with a high 'complexity,' and which are at the same time 'unspecialized.' In this way, intensity is mated with survival" (PR 101). There are two ways in which the intensity of specific form can be combined with endurance: (1) through massive rejection of extraneous novelty and intense reproduction of the dominant social form; and (2) through adaptation, origination, and "thought." The first kind of structured society contains the longest-lived societies known to us. The second are what Whitehead calls *living* societies. "Structured societies in which the second mode of solution has importance are termed 'living.' It is obvious that a structured society may have more or less 'life,' and that there is no absolute gap between 'living' and 'non-living' societies. For certain purposes, whatever 'life' there is in in a society may be important; and for other purposes, unimportant" (PR 102). These final remarks are thoroughly perspectival.

A further aspect of living societies is that they include inorganic nexūs within them. "A living society involves nexūs which are 'inorganic,' and nexūs which are inorganic do not need the protection of the whole 'living' society for their survival in a changing external environment" (PR 103). Animals have "inorganic" parts that endure. But the "entirely living" nexūs in organic life cannot endure by themselves. Therefore, "an 'entirely living' nexus is not a 'society' " (PR 103). The animal body is primary amidst the fitful, occasional, and dependent adventures of its mental life. Just as consciousness is a fitful condition, fading off into fringes of awareness, living nexūs are not societies, but can reproduce themselves only in conjunction with other inorganic societies, which could endure without them. The body is a society that could endure for some time without life; but its character as a living body is due to the presence of the living nexus that is conjoined with it. All of this Whitehead claims is conjectural.

A major insight is involved here that is deeply expressive of the principle of perspective. The characteristics of the things we know most commonly, including ourselves, are a function of multiple social orders in partial and complex relations and overlappings. Occasions inhabit diverse and varied environments, and what we take to be the order of nature, in its larger forms, is a function of differing environments of differing inclusiveness. This plurality of societies and subsocieties, environments and more inclusive environments, is a fundamental expression of the principle of perspective. In addition, however, the structure of ordinary objects, animals, and plants, as well as of human beings, is an extremely complex mixture of living, partially living, and structured societies. Human beings in themselves and in their environments are remarkably complex mixtures of societies and nexūs. It follows that human individuality, like human experience, is at this level of analysis no paradigm of individuality, but complexly derived from more fundamental individuals and perspectival relations. In this mode of analysis the principle of experience fades, at least in human application, and the principle of perspective takes precedence.

Human individuality is neither paradigmatic nor primary, and calls for explanation, not categorial reverence. "What needs to be explained is not dissociation of personality but unifying control, by reason of which we not only have unified behaviour, which can be observed by others, but also consciousness of a unified experience" (PR 108). Much of our existence reveals how transitory this unification can be. Our bodies can be manipulated by drugs, and we suffer loss of control over our sense of personal identity at different times when we are sleepy or ill. "This endurance of the mind is only one more example of the general principle on which the body is constructed. This route of presiding occasions probably wanders from part to part of the brain, dissociated from the physical material atoms. But central personal dominance is only partial, and in pathological cases is apt to vanish" (PR 109). The social view of humanity establishes personal identity to be a route of inheritance and dominance that may vanish if conditions are unsupportive. A unity of subjective perspective is found in each occasion; but in human beings only a social—therefore imperfect—unification is possible. Nevertheless, like all social qualities, it may be greatly enhanced by collective re-enforcement. The multiple social and environmental view of human beings provides an explanation of the fitfulness of conscious control, but also of its power where it reigns. Here the principle of experience loses its force, and human experience becomes unparadigmatic. These applications demonstrate that the principle of experience is not anthropomorphic to the extent that human experience is taken as the major exemplification of the principle.

The social character of human experience and personality in Whitehead's theory stands in marked contrast with other theories in which personal identity is made a central notion. Yet the threat to disintegration of personality in inclement environments is present for all societies, not human beings alone. Here the stability of personality is a function on the one hand of differing environments and on the other of the re-enforcement of constituent occasions comprising the relevant nexūs. Such a view of personality and human identity is thoroughly perspectival, based on the synthetic movement of creativity from many conditions to unification, and is only experiential in part. Whitehead's theory of social order is more perspectival than experiential, particularly in the wealth of overlapping perspectival environments which define the conditions for every complex society.

Subjectivity and Anthropomorphism

I have discussed some of the ramifications of Whitehead's theory of experience, particularly the power as well as the difficulties of his generalized principle of experience. The generality of this principle is essential to his theory and has its most important applications in the sphere of inorganic occasions and societies. For this reason, I am inclined to impatience with those who consider Whitehead's theory anthropomorphic.

Yet an accusation of anthropomorphism is not entirely implausible, though on balance it is unjust.[19] It is perhaps the word "experience"? Certainly the word suggests humanity and consciousness, although the category has a broader purview. Yet it is not a technical term, and is to be interpreted in terms of prehension. Nevertheless, a major element of the notion of experience that is not equally prominent in the concept of prehension is that of subjective form or "Private Matter of Fact." The question in these terms becomes whether Whitehead's theory rests on the assumption that the most elemental constituents of inorganic societies have a private, subjective existence. This question of privacy marks the fundamental difference between the principles of experience and perspective, the former committed to subjective and private forms, the latter only to vectoral, prehensive relations in which identity and multiplicity are complementarily related.

Can it be maintained that inorganic entities are prehending subjects?

As I understand Whitehead's answer, it is that no notion other than that of a drop of experience can adequately ground the following metaphysical principles: (a) Actual entities are constitutively related to each other; (b) Actual entities possess unique self-identities; (c) Causal relations are determinative and constitutive, but there is still novelty and freedom; (d) Actualities are unities of multiple constitution. Subjectivity is the basis for self-identity and self-determination; objectivity is the ground for relations and multiplicity.[20] Experience as *both* subject and object is essential. In this respect, Whitehead pursues a dominant metaphysical tradition derived from Kant and Hegel, establishing the basis for identity and relations in composites of experience.

However, I have argued against the arbitrariness of self-causation. Let us abandon this notion. It then is no longer so plausible that subjectivity (and thus feeling) be taken literally. The force of the concept of prehension is to relate a set of objects to a single, unifying subject. I have called so unified a multiplicity, from a single vantage point, a "perspective." According to the principle of perspective, every mode of being is perspectival: to be is to be a perspective and to be in perspective. Such a general principle can help us resolve some of the difficulties involving the reality of eternal objects and the primordial nature of God. They too are perspectival, and must be conditioned and restricted. In the immediate context, however, the principle of perspective achieves the force of the principle of experience without arbitrary self-causation and hidden forms of subjectivity.[21] Every being is diversely constituted by other beings, but it is also itself, a unique perspective on its constituents.

On the basis of the principle of perspective, every being is a unique composite of conditions and constituents ordered from its particular standpoint. Relations are constitutive, but they are complex and perspectival themselves, being comprised of many elements. Even the phases of an event are perspectival: phases in succession from some point of view, indistinguishable and nontemporal from another point of view. Simplicity, purity, immediacy, divisibility—all are qualified and perspectival, as are complexity, impurity, mediation, and indivisibility. Higher forms of consciousness are perspectival, comprised of other perspectival elements, events, processes, and forms, in which certain qualified features rise to prominence. The essential uniqueness of perspectives makes novelty fundamental and pervasive, therefore itself conditioned and perspectival, needing no ground in self-causation or a cosmological system of the universe. Indeed, uniqueness and novelty are functions of the diversity of perspectives intersecting in complex and partially indeterminate ways. Whitehead's cosmological principle forces him to define a specific ground for self-causation in every occasion. The principle of perspective finds uniqueness to be inherent in the very nature of the limits that define perspectives—an inexhaustible wealth of perspectives. The very conditions of perspectives—inexhaustible ramifications and relevance—provide both uniqueness and reproduction, indeterminateness and determinateness, together as complements in every perspectival being.

Notes to Chapter 4

1. The limitations of the principle of experience in relation to Whitehead's systematic concerns are nicely expressed by John B. Cobb, Jr., though he concludes that the principle can be sustained.

> Whitehead never suggested that electronic experiences are like human ones in any inclusive way. They have no sense experience, no consciousness, no imagination. If "experience" necessarily implies all these things, then surely a more general term would have to be found; but Whitehead thought the notion of experience could itself be made to serve. (1965, p. 27)

Similarly, as Christian puts it:

> It is therefore an open question whether Whitehead is a pan-psychist or not, depending on what a "psyche" is taken to be. He does not attribute consciousness to stones and electrons, or to the actual occasions that compose them. He does attribute to these occasions a kind of activity which, presystematically, he calls "experience." He means to suggest an analogy with human and animal experience, but he explains he is giving the term an extension it does not have in ordinary usage. (1959, pp. 19–20)

2. The most blatant confusion is to be found in Wallack's thorough misinterpretation of Whitehead's theory:

> It is human experiences that are the most important examples of actual entities since it is only through our own experiences that we can know actual entities at all . . . a human experience is not only an exemplary actual entity but the standard by which to judge the nature of all actual entities. (1980, pp. 20–21)

> An edible vegetable is an actual occasion. (1980, p. 226)

> Whtehead's actual entities include such things as tables, occasions of human sense-perception, and organs of the human body involved in sense-perception. (1980, pp. 25–26)

Wallack completely misrepresents Whitehead's atomism with the result that a number of technical notions in Whitehead's theory—for example, the unison of becoming, the independence of contemporary actualities—become unintelligible. The most extraordinary feature of Wallack's interpretation is the claim that there is no sharp distinction between actual entities and nexūs of actual entities: "For examples of nexūs, then, actual entities may be given, each one being composed of a nexus of other actual entities" (Wallack 1980, p. 42). This flies in the face of Whitehead's apparent view that the categories of existence do not overlap, though he does not *quite* say this:

> Every entity should be a specific instance of one category of existence, every explanation should be a specific instance of categories of explanation, and every obligation should be a specific instance of categoreal obligations. (PR 20–21)

As I have noted, he does treat actual entities and eternal objects as mutually exclusive (PR 158).

Wallack's emphasis is on the error involved in taking actual entities to be small in size. "An actual entity is not necessarily something small, short, simple, and impalpable" (1980, p. 29). "The actual entity can no more be identified solely with events of subatomic proportions than time can be identified solely with intervals of 10^{-24} seconds" (1980, p. 44). He argues that ascribing a size to actual entities is materialistic.

> Whitehead in fact made every effort to oppose this modern atomism since it is a vestige of scientific materialism. His actual occasions are atomic without being the simple, minute, indestructible bits of matter out of which everything visible and palpable is composed. (Wallack, 1980, p. 31)

Wallack is correct that, technically speaking, actual entities have no particular size. The strain locus, which assigns them a size, is a function of their social conditions. This is an ample reply to such questions as that of Rem B. Edwards:

> Whiteheadians . . . have never addressed themselves to the question of *how long the gap is between occasions. . . .* How long *between* occasions are we *not* in existence? (1975, p. 202)

and such claims as Edward Pols's:

> It is quite clear that one must go well below the order of a molecule to arrive at an actual occasion: even an electron is thought of as a "route," or "society" of actual occasions.
>
> In the realm of physics the hypothesis of such occasions is verified in so far as they help to make the experimental picture clearer, but they are inaccessible to even the indirect kind of observation that electrons can now be brought under. (1967, p. 5)

Size pertains to an occasion only relative to its strain locus, which is a social condition. Actual entities are "small" in a particular sense, but are pervasive throughout the universe in other senses. Pols never considers the singular problems involved in "observing" an actual occasion: we can observe its satisfaction, but not its concrescence. Size is not, then, an intrinsic condition of concrescence. Pols's further remarks on this subject are misleading: "an actual occasion, although it 'perishes,' neither changes nor moves; each 'enjoys' a quantum of space and time, but does not develop *in* it" (1967 p. 5). The association of an actual occasion with a spatiotemporal region is not intrinsic to it, but is a function of its social relations. (See further discussions of extension in chapter 7.)

Wallack's interpretation is thoroughly mistaken. However, it does lead him to a perspectival position concerning "the thoroughgoing relativity of his occasions, wherein each one is what it is only the virtue of its relation to and context among what others are" (1980, p. 97).

Additional confusions—perhaps more legitimate ones—stem from an over-emphasis on the principle of experience beyond the role Whitehead assigns it.

> According to the subjectivist principle, apart from the process of feeling or experience there is nothing, nothing, bare nothingness. The nature of an actual entity is to be in process. It becomes and never really is. But if process is the only actuality, actual entities as process can never be in a state of complete determination. They can never achieve a state of determinate "satisfaction." (Blyth 1941, p. 17)

A far more plausible approach to actual entities is Lango's:

> The fundamental entities of Whitehead's ontology—the actual entities—are purely hypothetical, postulated by his metaphysics, but not known in any other way. We cannot observe an actual entity with our senses. . . . We must therefore obtain an understanding of actual entities through speculation, by using metaphors derived from the *societies* of actual entities that we can observe, infer, or retrospect. (1972, p. 5)

Only such a view can make sense of all the properties Whitehead claims actual entities possess—particularly self-determination and individuality.

3. Dewey and James call "experience" a "double-barrelled" word (Dewey 1929, p. 8; James 1912, p. 10.).

4. The generalization of ordinary concepts to metaphysical significance is an extremely important procedure, but is filled with a variety of dangers.

> The procedure should now be clear for solving the linguistic paradox of using ordinary language to correct its distortions of what it tries to say. This procedure consists in retaining its concepts by intuition such as "blue" or "painful" in their ordinary meaning while also using other words in a technical way which is in part their ordinary meaning and in part a novel meaning. (Sherburne 1961, pp. xxv–xxvi)

I will argue that the concept of experience is far more precarious for metaphysical generalization than the concept of perspective, particularly in its emphasis on subjectivity.

5. This question of analyzability is a major difficulty for Whitehead's theory. He claims that actual entities are unanalyzable and indivisible, but also that there is genetic and coordinate analysis. These apparently conflicting claims can be sorted out so that they do not conflict, but only by emphasizing perspective more than experience. According to the principle of perspective, both divisibility and indivisibility are qualified notions. Everything is divisible in some

respects and indivisible in others, and neither takes unqualified precedence.

6. To the extent that the subjective aim is thought to be imposed by God upon actual occasions, to that extent is their freedom constrained. See pp. 64, 70–73, 151–53.

7. Alfred North Whitehead, *The Concept of Nature* (Cambridge: Cambridge University Press, 1964) p. 30 (hereafter citied as CN).

8. See detailed discussion in chapters 6 and 7.

9. According to Shahan, "The truly unique factor contributed by presentational immediacy apart from causal efficacy is an apprehension of the spatio-temporal or geometrical character of the contemporary world" (1950, p. 86).

10. See chapter 7. See also Blyth:

In the experience of an actual entity surveying the world from a standpoint we find only a limited continuum of entities. Such a limited continuum is relative to the standpoint from which it is experienced and does not of course include all possible standpoints. Hence any survey from the standpoint of an actual entity expresses only the unity of the world from that standpoint and does not express the solidarity of all possible standpoints. An extensive continuum which does express the solidarity of all possible standpoints cannot therefore be relative to any standpoint. It must be absolute. (1941, p. 34)

According to the subjectivist principle if actual entities are to be together in the same world, they must be together in experience. Thus in order to maintain the solidarity of the world Whitehead must somehow introduce experiential relations between contemporary actual entities. But according to the principle of relativity there can be no direct experiential relations between contemporaries. Whitehead tries to escape between the horns of this dilemma by making the assumption that all possible standpoints are united in one all-embracing scheme of extensive relations. This scheme of relations he calls the extensive continuum. (1941, p. 99)

The absolute and unconditioned nature of the extensive continuum makes it incompatible with both the principle of perspective and the principle of experience, grounded finally in the cosmological premise that the universe is solidary. Nevertheless, the cosmological character of the extensive continuum does not make it an exception to the ontological principle and the principle of experience. It can, I will argue, receive its unbounded character only from the primordial nature of God in conjunction with the social character of the actual world.

11. "It seems odd indeed that the chief examples of infallible perceptive experience should be visual delusions" (Brinkley 1961, p. 37).

12. Alan Brinkley's further comments on these matters are worth noting:

It is a fundamental doctrine of the theory of symbolic reference that each of the components involved in any symbolic reference can be grasped in the mode of immediate acquaintance or direct recognition. . . . if the infallibility of direct recognition is abandoned, this would entail the abandonment of reliable symbolic reference. (1961, p. 37)

Our judgments on causal efficacy are almost inextricably warped by the acceptance of the symbolic reference between the two modes as the completion of our direct knowledge. (P. 38)

If perception is almost always in the mixed mode of symbolic reference, the actual world would be the result of symbolic reference, but there could not be "two distinct modes of direct perception of the external world." If, however, the "two distinct modes of direct perception" be regarded as analytic moments of actual perception in the mixed mode of symbolic reference, then the contradiction could be removed. (P. 40)

13. Some of these issues were raised many years ago by John Blyth (1941). Blyth wholly misses the force of the principle of perspective and bases his interpretation of Whitehead entirely on the principle of experience (see chapter 4, note 2, p. 111). But allowing for this deficiency, Blyth reaches some important critical conclusions:

Whitehead's account of perception in the mode of presentational immediacy must be regarded as extremely inadequate when considered as a part of an integral theory. In fact, there seems to be scarcely a single notion involved in this account which is in harmony with the rest of the theory. (1941, p. 58)

Perhaps one of the most serious defects in Whitehead's theory of perception considered as a whole is his failure to coordinate the explanation of conscious perception with the two unconscious modes of perception. (P. 84)

See here also, "If prehension in the mode of presentational immediacy and conscious perception in the mode of presentational immediacy are distinguishable, why does Whitehead not distinguish them more clearly?" (Lango 1972, p. 55). Lango's position is close to mine, that the technical and central category in Whitehead's theory is *prehension* and that perception is to be understood in terms of prehension. "The concept of conscious perception in the mode of causal efficacy not only is explained by the category of prehensions (together with other relevant categories) but also secures that category's applicability" (P. 56).

14. Such a view of perception would have been much closer to such theories as Merleau-Ponty's in *The Phenomenology of Perception*. Whitehead's position is frequently not unlike Merleau-Ponty's: "The animal body is the great central ground underlying all symbolic reference" (PR 170).

15. It may also be a reflection of what I call the mechanical principle of analysis in which division is pushed to extremes. I consider this principle to be entirely incompatible with Whitehead's perspectivity, to be interpreted cautiously and with major qualifications.

16. "Presentational immediacy is not only a supplemental activity; it actually requires synthesis on the part of the observer. This factor ought to lead to the possibility of error in presentational immediacy, just as much as it does in symbolic reference" (Shahan 1950, p. 78).

17. See Paul Schmidt:

In different contexts Whitehead appears to contradict himself, for he claims that there can be no error in either of the pure modes of perception, causal efficacy or presentational immediacy, and that errors can arise in causal efficacy. The confusion arises because Whitehead fails to distinguish what we may call simple causal efficacy and complex causal efficacy, although he hints at such a distinction. (1967, pp. 126–27)

18. Compare Ewing Shahan:

A feeling can be indirect and imaginative for reasons which have to do with the responsive phase of the concrescence. This allows for the possibility of error at a very elementary level, even before the origination of conceptual feelings, and would appear to indicate that error could arise in any of the acts of experience which . . . are referred to as perception. (1950, p. 77)

19. "If Whitehead's cosmology is implicit in his psychology, then adoption of that psychology must imply adoption of that cosmology which is its consequence. . . . take issue with this theory of feelings or stand ready to reverence strange gods" (Whittemore 1961, p. 110).

20. See, however, the difficulties that arise when the principle of experience alone is made the basis for identity. Whitehead's problem, according to George Gentry, is

that of explaining *how* a novel focalization of its environment emerges from its environment and at the same stroke incorporates *it* in its own constitution in a unique synthesis. . . . It is at this point that Whitehead systematically introduces the categories of experience.

To reject the idea that an experience of any sort can occur without an experient in the form of an existential condition of it violates the evidence. But . . . it is precisely this truth that Whitehead repudiates in his conception of the subject as experient. (Gentry 1944, pp. 223, 224)

If the subject of the feelings is not a condition of the occurrence of its feelings, and consequently the actual ground of the subjective form of the feelings, then it is pure verbal anomaly to assert that feelings have subjective forms. . . . If one repudiates the notion of a subject or experient so conceived, it is meaningless to talk of a being which experiences data. (1946, p. 259)

Gentry does not fully understand the operation of the subjective aim in concrescence. Nevertheless, the difficulty is one that can be avoided entirely only by abandoning the principle of experience and replacing it by the principle of perspective.

See here also Andrew Reck, who claims that Kent "rightly saw that awareness of process or change presupposes awareness of an underlying constant or Substance."

Process, therefore, presupposes the existence of substantial entities which endure through change, and when process philosophers attempt to discard them, they undermine the foundations of their philosophy. (Reck 1958, pp. 765, 767)

21. Compare Paul Schmidt:

As regards prehensive unities we can never know the concrete being of another prehensive unity. We grasp only certain of its aspects into our own concrete being. There is then an ultimate privacy of prehensive unities. (1967, p. 98)

CHAPTER FIVE

KNOWLEDGE

The principle of experience is the center of Whitehead's theory of actual entities and the foundation of his perspectivity. Yet there are aspects of his theory of experience—especially involving the relationship between higher and lower experience—where the principles of perspective and experience are in conflict and where the principle of perspective takes precedence: certain features of Whitehead's theory involve perspectival relations that are not reducible to the principle of experience. Similarly, Whitehead's theory of knowledge is closely related to his theory of experience, yet there can be found within it perspectival features that transcend the principle of experience; and there can be found as well conflicts between the constraints of the principle of experience and the generality of the principle of perspective. Because Whitehead's theory of knowledge is tied so directly to his cosmological theory, it exhibits a striking convergence of the four principles I have been discussing as keys to his system: the principles of perspective and experience, the cosmological principle, and the mechanical version of the principle of analysis. I will trace the major features of Whitehead's theory of knowledge in relation to these principles, indicate difficulties that arise in the tension among these principles, and suggest how some of these difficulties may best be met, largely through emphasis on, and expression of, the principle of perspective.

Whitehead's theory of knowledge is not epistemological in the traditional sense, but metaphysical. With only peripheral references to purity and repetition, he is concerned not with questions of epistemic authority and testimony but with the metaphysical connections—between past and future, knower and known—that make knowledge intelligible. It is important to recognize the difference between theories that make knowledge a direct and *necessary* outcome of metaphysical principles, where error and not knowledge requires explanation—as in Whitehead's theory of perception—and theories that make knowledge *possible* but precarious. Some of the mechanisms of Whitehead's theory of experience suggest that knowledge is only conformation and repetition; but conformation and repetition are too reproductive to be plausible. From the standpoint of the principle of perspective, however, the focal point of view from which knowledge is attained, in the context of constitutive perspectival relations, allows for effective communal understanding on the one hand, where the uniqueness of the point of view may be made irrelevant, and on the other hand places all judgment in jeopardy by the novelty of interpretation.

The place to begin discussion of Whitehead's theory of knowledge is with the notion of propositions.

Propositions

Knowledge is founded on propositions: "An 'impure' prehension arises from the integration of a 'pure' conceptual prehension with a physical prehension originating in the physical role. The datum of a pure conceptual prehension is an eternal object; the datum of an impure prehension is a proposition, otherwise termed a 'theory' " (PR 184). However, propositions do not function in an epistemic capacity alone. They involve the vital metaphysical distinction between "general" potentiality, represented by the multiplicity of eternal objects, and "real" potentiality, which is conditioned by the actual world (PR 65). In addition, propositions represent the alternatives in terms of which an actual occasion establishes its becoming. This is part of what Whitehead means by calling a proposition a "lure for feeling." "The primary function of a proposition is to be relevant as a lure for feeling" (PR 25). "The 'lure for feeling' is the final cause guiding the concrescence of feelings" (PR 185). A subjective aim is the realization of some possibilities in the context of inherited conditions—thus a proposition.

Propositions express one of the fundamental conditions of events —that an occasion is a decision from a range of alternatives circumscribed by the conditions of its environment. It is from this central metaphysical category that Whitehead draws his theory of knowledge, and the wider role is predominant. "In the realization of propositions, 'judgment' is a very rare component, and so is 'consciousness' " (PR 184).[1]

Logicians only discuss the judgment of propositions. Indeed some philosophers consider propositions as merely appanages to judgments. The result is that false propositions have fared badly, thrown into the dustheap, neglected. But in the real world it is more important that a proposition be interesting than that it be true. The importance of truth is, that it adds to interest. (PR 259)

What is called "interesting" here about propositions must be interpreted very generally, for the functions of propositions cannot be understood in human terms alone.

The notion of real possibility is the fundamental one, and is interpreted by Whitehead in terms of propositions, a union of eternal objects conditioned by actual events. Yet there is an apparent disparity in function between *real alternatives* which would seem to lose their relevance, and propositions that remain eternally relevant in the guise of *facts*. Whitehead's doctrine of objective immortality is clearly involved here, but we may approach that cosmological doctrine from the standpoint of propositions.

It would appear that real possibilities become and perish with actual occasions, perishing with the passing of their actuating conditions. Whitehead's view is that propositions come into being; he does not seem to hold that they may cease to be. "New propositions come into being with the creative advance of the world" (PR 259). This is partly due to the logical function of propositions: "No actual entity can feel a proposition, if its actual world does not include the logical subjects of that proposition" (PR 259). The integration of pure possibilities and actual conditions is relevant only to occasions that can objectively prehend it.

Two principles are involved in the emergence of novel propositions. One is the ontological principle that only actual entities can be reasons. All propositions must be grounded in past occasions available for prehension. The ontological principle here functions as an expression of both the cosmological principle and the principle of experience, expressed in the unqualified formulation of the principle of relativity. The entire past remains propositionally available. A consequence is that propositions become with their actual worlds, but may not perish—not, at least, if we take objective immortality seriously. This is a direct consequence of the cosmological principle establishing the unity of all events through time. Yet even if we grant objective immortality to occasions, the eternal relevance of certain propositions for the indefinite future appears to be both incompatible with the selection and exclusion of the principle of perspective and an extreme expression of the cosmological principle. What the future excludes, from its own perspective, may be certain propositions that would thereafter be simply irrelevant for all futures.

There is, however, a second principle involved in the function of emergent propositions, and it is connected with their role in judgment. By the principle of experience, the relevance of propositions depends on the possibility of experiencing their logical subjects. "The presupposed logical subjects may not be in the actual world of some actual entity. In this case, the proposition does not exist for that actual entity" (PR 188). Experience is the constitutive ground of both these functions of propositions and defines their initiating conditions, while the unity of all experiences in the cosmic succession makes the perishing of propositions impossible. A stronger form of the principle of perspective would entail that propositions are conditioned by limitation and perspective, and that suitable conditions are necessary to both the origin of propositions and their further relevance. The central issue is clearly the cosmological impulse behind the principle of relativity—that a being is a potential for *every* becoming. A secondary issue is the preservation of propositions as facts for future cognition.

The double function of propositions is the problem here, closely analogous to the corresponding problems of the connection between lower and higher experience for prehension and perception and inorganic and human experience. This double function is closely related to the predominance of the cosmological principle and the principle of experience in Whitehead's theory. Insofar as propositions are objects of knowledge, they embody Whitehead's conviction that the remote past is permanently available for prehension, through every future. The possibility that remote events of the past might become entirely irrelevant to some future is incompatible with Whitehead's doctrine of objective immortality and the solidarity of the world through causal prehension—clearly cosmological principles. The possibility that a cosmic singularity—the "big bang" initiating our cosmic epoch—might effectively separate the details of prior events from the details of subsequent events is rejected by Whitehead as incompatible with the togetherness required for universal order.

Insofar as propositions function as lures for feeling that unify the prehensions within a concrescence, they appear to have a far more transitory relevance. Propositions define what is possible for a given occasion to become. Such possibilities may not be available within, relevant to, a later concrescence, though they were real possibilities for some occasions in the past. The lures for feeling that were not felt by a particular concrescence, because they represented only alternatives that were never realized in its satisfaction, are not available for feeling in any future prehension. In brief, real possibilities *within* concrescences cease to be relevant to future occasions and perish with changing conditions.

The function of propositions as lures for feeling must be examined in greater detail. It appears to contradict the principle of experience. "A proposition is an element in the objective lure *proposed for feeling*, and when admitted into feeling it constitutes *what is felt*" (PR 187). The function is central to the metaphysical role of propositions, for it is as lures that they define possibilities for concrescence. They embody all candidates for subjective aim. Yet the notion of unfelt possibilities seems incompatible with the ontological principle and with the principle of experience, though such possibilities are natural consequences of the principle of perspective.[2] How can a proposition which is never felt, which is only a lure for feeling, be real, have ontological status, without violating the ontological principle?

> The ... doctrine that there is a "togetherness" not derivative from experiential togetherness, leads to the disjunction of the components of subjective experience from the community of the external world. This disjunction creates the insurmountable difficulty for epistemology. For intuitive judgment is concerned with togetherness in experience, and there is no bridge between togetherness in experience, and togetherness of the non-experiential sort. (PR 190)

Any propositional theory, epistemological or teleological, must allow for *possible* objects of judgment or feeling which may not actually be entertained. This is particularly evident in deductive systems, where unknown propositions are nevertheless both relevant and true in terms of the axioms and rules of inference. In addition, there is always a greater number of alternatives for an occasion than the one it finally chooses. Unless occasions are divisible into different stages with different feelings pertinent to them—and this would be totally incompatible with Whitehead's theory of experience—occasions feel only the proposition that they select to be their subjective aim out of alternative possibilities functioning as lures.

A double sense of real possibilities is embedded in Whitehead's theory of propositions, a consequence of the conjunction of the principles of experience and perspective. Propositions represent the outcome of becoming, real possibilities for becoming, realized in the occasion's final satisfaction and not felt before. These propositions are real possibilities for becoming, turned into actualities by prehension. There are also possibilities for feeling ("lures") which may never be felt within an occasion's satisfaction, relevant only as alternatives for that occasion's becoming. In effect, propositions are both alternatives and possibilities *for* feeling and actual achievements *in* feeling. This double nature is never fully worked out by Whitehead. It may be unresolvable to the extent that experience and feeling are required by the principle of experience. The point is that propositions as possibilities comprise a far wider class than propositions as felt. Two meanings of relevance are involved, but only one is clearly defined on the basis of the principle of experience.

The primary function of a lure for feeling is the guidance it offers to concrescence. "This subjective aim is not primarily intellectual; it is the lure for feeling" (PR 85). If freedom is genuine, the subjective aim of an occasion must involve its choice among alternative possibilities. Such choices function from the very beginning of the concrescence, defining the data selected so that the proposition aimed at as final cause will be felt as the aim. This is the essential meaning of the indeterminateness inherent in earlier stages which is eliminated in the final satisfaction of an occasion: the movement from many alternatives relevant to becoming to the realization of a single subjective aim. "An incomplete phase . . . has the unity of a proposition" (PR 224). While the notion of *phases* is misleading, the selectivity inherent in every prehension is essential, a fundamental expression of the principle of perspective.

The various alternatives available as final causes cannot be felt prior to their realization. Yet they function throughout concrescence as a ground of possibilities among which the occasion chooses. We can understand this ground of possibility in part through the primordial nature of God. Complex eternal objects relevant to the actual world of an occasion through God define propositions for the becoming of that occasion as lures. But the only proposition that is actually felt is the outcome of the occasion's decision.

> If by the decision of the concrescence, the proposition has been admitted into feeling, then the proposition constitutes *what* the feeling has felt. The proposition constitutes a lure for a member of its locus by reason of the germaneness of the complex predicate to the logical subjects, having regard to forms of definiteness in the actual world of that member, and to its antecedent phases of feeling. (PR 186)

A conclusion of this discussion is that a multiplicity of pure possibilities is sufficient neither for knowledge nor for decision. Logical analysis and purposive action both depend on a multiplicity of real possibilities from which one or many are selected. Not all the theorems of a set of axioms can be thought, yet they are all possibilities defined by the axioms. Likewise, not all the possibilities for a choice can be explicitly considered, yet the choice entails their rejection or acceptance. We are committed to a multiplicity of real possibilities not actually felt by any occasion precisely as we seem committed to a multiplicity of pure possibilities. This double multiplicity seems unnecessary, and two alternatives may be proposed for avoiding redundance. One is to eliminate the entire category of pure possibilities, replacing it by real possibilities alone.[3] The other alternative is to make propositions as lures a direct consequence of the relevance of the multiplicity of eternal objects provided by the primordial nature of God. I will further explore the latter alternative as a solution to the dfficulty involved in unfelt propositions. Both of the alternatives require emphasis upon the principle of perspective at the expense of the principle of experience.

Propositions are lures for feeling for occasions that do not prehend them. But by the ontological principle, actual entities are the only reasons. Whitehead's explanation of this is "that any condition to be satisfied by one actual entity in its process expresses a fact either about the 'real internal constitutions' of some other actual entities, or about the 'subjective aim' conditioning that process" (PR 24). He tells us explicitly that propositions satisfy this condition (PR 25). It is therefore clear that "lures" are facts about prehensions—real constitutions or subjective aims—even where not felt. "A proposition has neither the particularity of a feeling, nor the reality of a nexus. It is a datum for feeling, awaiting a subject feeling it" (PR 259). Too stringent a demand imposed from the principle of experience would require that propositions be relevant only to occasions that feel them. This is clearly not an acceptable conclusion.

A solution to this difficulty must depend upon a clear understanding of the relevance defined by the primordial nature of God. What is essential is the concept of relevance. Either God's primordial nature orders eternal objects so that relevance *may* be felt by an occasion, or it defines *what is relevant* for that occasion. Either the occasion creates relevance, or it creates its decisions from what is relevant to it. Clearly the latter position is required, for if God's primordial nature offers only a multiplicity of possibilities that *may* be relevant, then we have a double sense of possibility and a double decision required of each occasion. The relevance of possibilities defined by the primordial nature of God provides the alternatives among which decision is made. Relevance thus is a notion that entails real possibilities or propositions. These are grounded in the integration of pure possibilities within an actual world by virtue of the primordial nature of God, whether or not they are felt by any occasion. God and the actual world together generate real possibilities for an occasion. Whitehead comes close to saying this, but never quite does so, because of the importance of the ontological principle and the principle of experience. "A proposition, in abstraction from any particular actual entity which may be realizing it in feeling, is a manner of germaneness of a certain set of eternal objects to a certain set of actual entities" (PR 188).

> Each entity in the universe of a given concrescence *can*, so far as its own nature is concerned, be implicated in that concrescence in one or other of many modes; but *in fact* it is implicated only in *one* mode: that the particular mode of implication is only rendered fully determinate by that concrescence, though it is conditioned by the correlate universe. This indetermination, rendered determinate in the real concrescence, is the meaning of "potentiality." It is a *conditioned* determination, and is therefore called a *"real* potentiality." (PR 23)

These formulations express an ambiguous relationship of real potentialities to concrescence and feeling, as if (1) there can be no such real potentiality without a prehending actual entity for which it is a potential, or (2) there can be no real potentiality that is not felt determinately by the prehending entity. Relative to the principle of experience and the ontological principle, two distinct modes of relevance appear required, derived respectively from the primordial nature of God and the decision of a prehending occasion. I consider this to be a weakening of the meaning of relevance inherent in the primordial nature of God and an extreme concession to the principle of experience. The principle of perspective entirely resolves this issue, since perspectival relevance may be provided by actual conditions in conjunction with available possibilities without interfering with the decision of an actual occasion, which would then further impose its own perspective on the established conditions. Nevertheless, this further perspectival selection has the consequence that some established possibilities or propositions will expire, never available for feeling again, if they are rejected by a particular subsequent occasion.

Throughout this discussion, I have emphasized the function of propositions as *lures*. It is important to emphasize that they function as lures for *feeling*, not merely for judgment. This is a straightforward consequence of the principle of experience. "The primary function of theories is as a lure for feeling, thereby providing immediacy of enjoyment and purpose" (PR 184). Propositions have a much wider role than that of objects of knowledge.

> Some propositions are the data of feelings with subjective forms such as to constitute those feelings to be the enjoyment of a joke. Other propositions are felt with feelings whose subjective forms are horror, disgust, or indignation. (PR 25)

> The primary mode of realization of a proposition in an actual entity is not by judgment, but by entertainment. A proposition is entertained when it is admitted into feeling. Horror, relief, purpose, are primarily feelings involving the entertainment of propositions. (PR 188)

In this wider role, an enduring relevance for all propositions seems an extreme and unwarranted concession to immortality. At best only those possibilities felt in the realization of an occasion's satisfaction may be objectively immortal as part of the immortality of that occasion. Nevertheless, I consider even this immortality to be incompatible with the exclusions of perspectivity. Relevance to temporal location must mean relevance to *some* times, *some* events, and *not* other events. Such restricted relevance is incompatible with the principle of relativity that to be is to be a potential for *every* becoming.

Truth

"A proposition must be true or false" (PR 256). An important difference between eternal objects and propositions is that, since pure possibilities are completely independent of any actual world, they admit of no ground of truth or falsehood. But a proposition "is a complex entity, with determinate actual entities among its components. These determinate actual entities, considered *formaliter* and not as in the abstraction of the proposition, do afford a reason determining the truth or falsehood of the proposition" (PR 257). We may recall the double function of propositions, as real possibilities and as components of judgment. It is far from obvious that possibilities and lures should be true or false. "There are two types of relationship between a proposition and the actual world of a member of its locus. The proposition may be conformal or non-conformal to the actual world, true or false" (PR 186).

There is the difficulty once again of the epistemic status of unfelt propositions. A felt proposition may well be the datum of "a special type of integration synthesizing a physical feeling with a conceptual feeling" (PR 257). The proposition here is an integration of actuality and possibility, and may well be true or false. But we are moving toward judgment—a contrast between the proposition and a physical prehension. "The term 'judgment' refers to three species among the comparative feelings with which we are concerned. In each of these feelings the datum is the generic contrast between an objectified nexus and a proposition whose logical subjects make up the nexus" (PR 270). A proposition in its function as a lure for feeling would seem to be neither true nor false until it is felt.

> The pre-established harmony is the self-consistency of this proposition, that is to say, its capacity for realization. But such abstraction from the process does violence to its nature; for the phase *is* an incident in the process. When we try to do justice to this aspect of the phase, we must say that it is a proposition seeking truth. (PR 224)

The satisfaction of an occasion may be an integration of its datum physically prehended and conceptual valuations chosen through reversion. But the lures for feeling are not true or false until one or another has been chosen. Real possibilities become true or false only after one or another alternative has been realized.

Whitehead gives propositions a double role, but he does not appear to have completely worked out the two roles. In their function as lures for feeling, propositions are neither true nor false, but relevant. They are essential constituents of perspectives, but do not become true until they enter judgment, and they do not enter judgment except within certain higher-level perspectives. A similar difficulty occurs where origination produces novelty but also falsehood. A proposition which a novel occasion feels either reproduces its actual world or does not, in which case, "a novelty has emerged into creation" (PR 187). Whitehead claims that "error is the price we pay for progress" (PR 187). This correlation of error with novelty is a consequence of a reproductive theory of truth, and is completely inappropriate to the function of propositions as alternatives for the future. Truth and falsehood are irrelevant to alternatives as such. In addition, certain truths are to be realized only through the development of novel alternatives. Reproduction is a limited basis for a theory of truth, especially in a theory like Whitehead's which so strongly emphasizes novel origination.

Whitehead explicitly denies that propositions function mainly in judgment. "The conception of propositions as merely material for judgments is fatal to any understanding of their rôle in the universe" (PR 187). He emphasizes that "in the real world it is more important that a proposition be interesting than that it be true. The importance of truth is, that it adds to interest" (PR 259). Yet propositions as real possibilities are not as such true or false, but may be *only* interesting, functioning dynamically. Conformity may be irrelevant in a lure for feeling. A biased interpretation of *Hamlet* may show it in a new and interesting light regardless of the interpretation's precise faithfulness to the text. Questions of conformity for an interesting conjunction of ideas are sometimes largely irrelevant. Propositions may then be freed from the bonds of truth and falsity, while the latter are made relevant specifically to judgment.

> This judgment is concerned with a conformity of two components within one experience. It is thus a "coherence" theory. It is also concerned with the conformity of a proposition, not restricted to that individual experience, with a nexus whose relatedness is derived from the various experiences of its own members and not from that of the judging experient. In this sense there is a "correspondence" theory. But, at this point of the argument, a distinction must be made. We shall say that a proposition can be *true* or *false*, and that a judgment can be *correct*, or *incorrect*, or *suspended*. With this distinction we see that there is a "correspondence" theory of the truth and falsehood of propositions, and a "coherence" theory of the correctness, incorrectness and suspension of judgments. (PR 191)

A consequence of emphasizing judgment in relation to truth and falsity is that two points of view become predominant: the locus of the relevant proposition and the point of view of the judge. "The 'locus' of a proposition consists of those actual occasions whose actual worlds include the logical subjects of the proposition" (PR 186). Here the principle of perspective rises to prominence. "Every proposition presupposes those actual entities which are its logical subjects. . . . The presupposed logical subjects may not be in the actual world of some actual entity. In this case, the proposition does not exist for that actual entity" (PR 188). Thus a proposition exists only for actual entities which succeed the proposition's actual subjects and which positively prehend those subjects. It follows that "propositions grow with the creative advance of the world. (PR 188).

I have discussed the limited perspectivity inherent in Whitehead's theory of emergent propositions, weakened by the cosmological principle. His doctrine of objective immortality suggests that a nexus of occasions, once relevant, is relevant to every future. This is an apparent consequence of the principle of relativity. It is also compatible with the assumption that every truth of the past, once constituted in an occasion's becoming, is eternally available for cognition. Yet those propositions that function as lures for feeling but are not felt, I have argued, seem to become irrelevant to the entire future. Moreover, the principle that all remote past events are relevant, if minimally, to future cognition is distinctly implausible. The cosmological principle may support the latter conclusion, despite its implausibility, but it cannot resolve the former difficulty. Both limitations of perspective are a consequence of an absolute past for the future, unconditioned and unperishable. Continuity through time may be achieved perspectively, by constitutive causal relations conjoined with selection, without requiring everlasting relevance.

The second point of view prominent in judgment is that of the judge.

Since each actual world is relative to standpoint, it is only some actual entities which will have the standpoints so as to include, in their actual world, the actual entities which constitute the logical subjects of the proposition. Thus every proposition defines the judging subjects for which it is a proposition. Every proposition presupposes some definite settled actual entities in the actual world of its judging subject; and thus its possible judging subjects must have these actual entities in the actual world of each of them. (PR 193)

Here we find a stronger commitment to perspective, though it too is weakened by the absolute character of the past. Nevertheless, the judge's point of view is essential: a propositional contrast requires that the logical subjects of the proposition be known to the judge. Judgment is always from a standpoint defined in terms of the prehending entity's actual world. There are no "bare facts" in judgment, only propositions tied to their logical subjects, on the one hand, and the actual world of the judging occasion, on the other. "A judgment concerns the universe in process of prehension by the judging subject. . . . The judgment is made about itself by the judging subject, and is feeling in the constitution of the judging subject" (PR 191). Judgment is always fundamentally about the subject and its actual world. Truths in judgment are always for a subject, though they may be true for other subjects as well.

A judgment is a feeling in the "process" of the judging subject, and it is correct or incorrect respecting *that* subject. It enters, as a value, into the satisfaction of that subject; and it can only be criticized by the judgments of actual entities in the future. (PR 191)

Judgment here is thoroughly perspectival: the point of view of the judge constitutes the judgment and any critical point of view on that judgment. We can see here why the notion of propositional truth is so incomplete: it is unqualified relative to any future point of view, though judgment is thoroughly qualified by such points of view. To locate propositional truth in judgment is to make it doubly perspectival: relative to its logical subjects and relative to different judges. I am arguing that propositions have functions in which truth is irrelevant and that truth is relevant to propositions only in judgment, from the judge's perspective.

Whitehead's theory of truth corresponds closely with his theory of perception, especially with respect to the relationship between higher and lower experience and the distinction between a metaphysical and an epistemological realism. Propositional truth carries the weight of reproduction. A proposition is true if there is conformation between subject and predicate by virtue of reproduction through conceptual valuation. "If the primary physical feeling involves no reversion in any stage, then the predicate of the proposition is that eternal object which constitutes the definiteness of that nexus. In this case, the proposition is, without qualification, true" (PR 262). Nevertheless, reversion is always a possibility. Thus, we have a theory of propositional truth, but no *guarantee* of the truth of any proposition. Judgment is required, with its further selections and perspectives. Every test of the truth of a proposition involves the future, and thus, "this latter test can be realized only by future occasions in the life of an enduring object, the enduring percipient" (PR 270).[4] More accurately, Whitehead claims that there are guarantees, particularly in perception, but they are not infallible.

> There are therefore two immediate guarantees of the correctness of a conscious perception: one is Hume's test of "force and vivacity," and the other is the illumination by consciousness of the various feelings involved in the process. Thus the fact, that the physical feeling has not transmuted concept into physical bond, lies open for inspection. (PR 269)

What must be avoided is the sense that guarantees suggest infallibility. "Neither of these tests is infallible" (PR 269). The word "guarantee" is misleading here. There are tests for truth and correctness, but all tests are fallible.

The theory of pure modes of prehension, which I have associated with a mechanical interpretation of the principle of analysis, is a consequence also of the conjunction of a metaphysical with an epistemological realism. It is grounded in the principle of experience to the extent that the constitution of occasions is based on their prehensions, what they feel. A consequence of this principle is that occasions feel what constitutes them, at some dim level of feeling, though pure modes of feeling and perception cannot be traced to conscious awareness in any form. Whitehead's metaphysical and constitutive realism leads to a somewhat implausible epistemological—that is, conformal—realism, in part because of the inseparability of human and inorganic feelings and prehensions. The more natural theory is that all perception is subject to error because it is a mixture of constitutive modes, and that complex methods are needed to minimize prospects of error.

Whitehead's analysis of truth and error is based on the principle of relativity with respect to causal objectification of the past. There is the reproduction of the past without reversion; there is also the synthesis of many prehensions into one unified satisfaction—the coherence in feeling necessary to human truth. Yet the entire analysis seems empiricist in the worst sense, tracing its roots back to Hume and overemphasizing feelings of the past. Consider, here, knowledge of a proposition about the future. It can be both true and known to be true, although its logical subjects may not yet exist and it cannot be felt relative to ingression in any past. It is a consequence of projections through social order into an order sustained through time, including novel propositions relevant through the primordial nature of God to the future. Knowledge of the future is based on mutually relevant and supportive nexūs through time and projected into the future.[5] We project from experienced conditions into the future, but the propositions we arrive at may have been relevant to, felt in, no past. There is projection but not reproduction. Here a far stronger principle of perspective is needed, with the consequent diminution in importance of the principle of experience.

Yet the same considerations pertain also to knowledge of the past. The ground for such knowledge lies in the mutually supportive conditions of social order, not in reproduction and its prehension without reversion. There is, in fact, reversion in every human experience. The basis for truth lies not in repetition or synthesis of feeling, but in adaptation and the invention of new propositions that express complex forms of social order. Put another way, order has metaphysical conditions. But these do not, in either repetition or feeling, define knowledge, either of the future or of the past. The capacity of the future to engender novel points of view is essential to our knowledge of the past. Here judgment becomes the test of truth as well as knowledge, based on the principle of perspective. The principle of experience severely contaminates the insights brought into

Whitehead's theory by the principle of perspective, especially where questions of truth and error are involved.

Whitehead's theory of knowledge is divided, then, into a metaphysical realism and an epistemological realism, with carryover from the metaphysical level of judgment in his theory of propositional truth and direct perception. He seems not to have recognized that the principle of perspective includes both poles of his epistemology, and that an unqualified reproductive realism is nonperspectival. Perspectives are constituted by relations—by other perspectives. But all such constitution is itself perspectival, so that conformation, reproduction, repetition, and truth are also perspectival. Not only tests of truth in judgment, but truth itself, is perspectival, from some point of view involving selection and conditions. Propositional truth and authentic perceptions are effectively unconditioned in Whitehead's theory, a consequence of too strong an emphasis on the reproductive phases of concrescence. Yet if we emphasize, as we must, that occasions are indivisible, reproduction is meaningless apart from the prehending occasion's perspective and supplementation. A proposition is always felt from a point of view, and its truth is therefore from a point of view—that is, conformation relative to particular standards or constraints. Realism, representation, and truth are all perspectival, conditioned, and qualified notions. Sheer and unconditioned reproduction produces an absolute and unqualified theory of truth, while every truth and every being is inexhaustibly incomplete. What perspectivity entails is that literal, representational truth and realism be understood perspectivally, relative to the conditions of their establishment and the limits of every perspective. Being is perspectival; as a consequence, knowledge is perspectival. Neither of these principles is incompatible with literal truth, only with an unqualified understanding of literalness and an absolute understanding of truth. The unconditioned nature of causal reproduction and propositional truth, the freedom from error of the pure modes of perception, objective immortality, and the unqualified formulation of the principle of relativity—all are cosmological absolutes and incompatible with the principle of perspective.

Philosophical Knowledge

This is an appropriate place to consider Whitehead's view of philosophy and the knowledge it provides.

Speculative Philosophy is the endeavour to frame a coherent, logical, necessary system of general ideas in terms of which every element of our experience can be interpreted. By this notion of "interpretation" I mean that everything of which we are conscious, as enjoyed, perceived, willed, or thought, shall have the character of a particular instance of the general scheme. Thus the philosophical scheme should be coherent, logical, and, in respect to its interpretation, applicable and adequate. Here "applicable" means that some items of experience are thus interpretable, and "adequate" means that there are no items incapable of such interpretation. (PR 3)

It is worth considering each of these central notions.

Coherence. " 'Coherence,' as here employed, means that the fundamental ideas, in terms of which the scheme is developed, presuppose each other so that in isolation they are meaningless" (PR 3). Whitehead has a mathematical paradigm in mind. In an axiomatic system, primitive notions singly may be given no explicit definition, but they may be defined through the axioms so that none can be eliminated in terms of the others. Where principles can be abstracted from each other, there is disconnection and, in a sense, distinct systems are intertwined. Thus,

It is the ideal of speculative philosophy that its fundamental notions shall not seem capable of abstraction from each other. In other words, it is presupposed that no entity can be conceived in complete abstraction from the system of the universe, and that it is the business of speculative philosophy to exhibit this truth. (PR 3)

Coherence is the ideal of speculative philosophy because only by means of coherence can we attain systematic unification.

It is important to recognize that Whitehead's theory of systematic philosophy can be given a cosmological and a noncosmological interpretation. Coherence among the central notions of a theory is a theoretical ideal, a recognition that complementarity and mutuality are essential to any complex notions. In this sense, coherence is compatible with perspectivity, though *complete* coherence, wherein *every* fundamental notion involved *all* the others, would be absolutistic and extreme. The complementarities and polarities of perspective, the conjunction of unity with multiplicity and conditions with uniqueness, demand a form of coherence, though not a total, unconditioned form. However, theoretical coherence is not equivalent with universal inclusiveness. That fundamental principles should apply to all beings is not equivalent with the claim that all beings belong to one universe. That speculative philosophy should define one all-inclusive universe is cosmological, not perspectival. Belonging, inclusiveness, and applicability are themselves perspectival notions.

Necessity. Closely related to the second interpretation of coherence is the notion of necessity: "This doctrine of necessity in universality means that there is an essence to the universe which forbids relationships beyond itself, as a violation of its rationality. Speculative philosophy seeks that essence" (PR 4). This is an ideal of *completeness* and, without further qualification, appears nonperspectival and cosmological. The very rhetorical force of words like "essence," "forbid," "violation" is unconditioned and cosmological. Yet the question of metaphysical generality is relevant here: a metaphysical theory must indeed be applicable to all things and must prohibit types of being to which it cannot be applied. The question is whether such generality is to be absolute or perspectival.

There are two ways of interpreting the properties of speculative philosophy: as theoretical—therefore perspectival—conditions, or as conditions imposed on the universe—essentially cosmological. Coherence and necessity may be regarded as primarily epistemological and systematic criteria applicable to metaphysical knowledge: the generality of a metaphysical theory must be sufficiently complete to include with some type of necessity every mode of being, and the first principles of that theory must be systematically interrelated. Such generality and interrelatedness need not be absolute or unconditioned, as if a metaphysical theory ideally would tell us not only the truth but the entire truth about every mode of being. It is another matter altogether to claim that, in virtue of the applicability of the criteria of coherence and necessity to a metaphysical theory, the universe itself, by some rational principles of intelligibility, must exhibit both coherence and necessity. Here a metaphysical explanation becomes the ultimate or final explanation, superseding all others, a thoroughly nonperspectival view of philosophy. The passage above appears to express not merely the coherence of metaphysical principles but the total inclusiveness of the universe: it is presupposed that no entity can be conceived in complete abstraction from the system of the universe. There is a stronger and a weaker, a cosmological and a qualified interpretation of these principles. They manifest the tension I have noted recurrently between the principle of perspective and the cosmological principle: that all beings are perpectival, to be brought under common principles of connection and qualification, does not entail a unity of the universe as a system, a unity founded in total relatedness.[6]

Adequacy, Applicability. To what extent is philosophy an empirical discipline? If it must be both applicable and adequate, is it not indistinguishable from science? Here the force of the cosmological principle is disastrous, for it would make philosophy indistinguishable in its activities and conclusions from science, except for its greater generality. Philosophy so viewed seems to war with physics and biology, generating unnecessary oppositions. The principle of perspective is far more congenial to the coexistence, but nevertheless distinctness, of philosophy and science, since each may be applicable and adequate, but from a particular point of view.

Philosophy seeks to formulate metaphysical first principles. But, Whitehead tells us, it can never hope finally to do so (PR 4). Part of the difficulty lies in the nature of metaphysics. The other part resides in the nature of philosophic language.

> Weakness of insight and deficiencies of language stand in the way inexorably. Words and phrases must be stretched towards a generality foreign to their ordinary usage; and however such elements of language be stabilized as technicalities, they remain metaphors mutely appealing for an imaginative leap. (PR 4)

This is an important claim, for it expresses the creative force of speculative philosophy. "Philosophy redesigns language" (PR 11). [7]

Language is not the only source of the limitations of metaphysics. Another difficulty lies in the generality of metaphysical principles which "never fail of exemplification" (PR 4). According to Whitehead, the sciences work by a method of difference. But metaphysical principles are always applicable. The major techniques of the sciences are therefore unavailable to metaphysics. Whitehead does not appear to consider the possibility that unqualified generality is unintelligible and that even metaphysical generality has to be selective and qualified if it is to be meaningful, that metaphysics must itself be perspectival. He distinguishes principles applicable within a particular "cosmic epoch"—laws of a particular region of time and space—from metaphysical principles applicable everywhere. "There can be no cosmic epoch for which the singular propositions derived from a metaphysical proposition differ in truth-value from those of any other cosmic epoch" (PR 197). Even an arithmetic truth is only a truth about enduring objects in a particular epoch. "We are in fact stating a truth concerning the wide societies of entities amid which our lives are placed. It is a truth concerning this *cosmos*, but not a metaphysical truth" (PR 198). There appears to be, here, an absolute distinction between restricted and un-

restricted generality, and metaphysics seems to be effectively unconditioned, absolute. Whitehead's explicit ideal of speculative philosophy
is more cosmological than perspectival, and it is indefensible for its lack
of qualification.

Yet even Whitehead's own conception of generality is limited, a particular kind of generality, but not an absolute and unqualified
generality. This is a natural consequence of the principle of perspective,
for even generality can only be in a certain respect, of a certain kind;
there can be no absolute generality over all kinds. Even if Whitehead's
principles applied to all processes, they would not apply to all *beings*,
even within his own system. He gives us very few principles applicable
to all of his categories of existence: actual entities, eternal objects, and
subjective forms alike. Relatedness among actual entities is analyzed in
terms of prehensions; relations among eternal objects cannot be. The
self-identity of actual entities is analyzed in terms of self-causation and
subjective aim; the individual essence of eternal objects cannot be.
Whitehead seeks principles applicable to all times, all epochs, all regions
of the world. He does not delineate principles applicable to all existents,
all categories, all beings. Even the principles of experience and perspective are of limited generality in his theory: eternal objects are
experienced but are not experiencing subjects; nexūs inhabit perspectives but are not perspectival centers. Such limitations, however, are a
natural consequence of the unrestrictedness of the principle of perspective in which all modes of being are perspectival in a full sense—but not
an unqualified or absolute sense. The generality of the principle of
perspective is a qualified, but thereby remarkably inclusive, generality.

We may conclude this discussion with the question of how
metaphysical knowledge, of unrestricted generality, is possible in
Whitehead's theory. A metaphysical proposition

> signifies a proposition which (i) has meaning for any actual occasion, as a
> subject entertaining it, and (ii) is "general," in the sense that its predicate
> potentially relates any and every set of actual occasions, providing the
> suitable number of logical subjects for the predicative pattern, and (iii) has
> a "uniform" truth-value. (PR 197)

Here Whitehead's commitment to the cosmological principle is very
strong. Metaphysical propositions represent the fundamental solidarity
of the universe, having reference to all occasions as logical subjects, and
as entertained by every occasion. I cannot understand the reason for the
latter, expressed as condition (i) above, and would suggest that
metaphysical propositions may not be necessarily felt or known, but may

only be lures for feeling.[8] Nevertheless, they follow from the universe as a whole, unified through the primordial nature of God. If there are metaphysical principles, they are at least potentially ingredient in every becoming. In conditioning every becoming, they are part of every datum, and can be felt via the relevance provided by God. Thus, the metaphysical principles that apply to any occasion are possibilities for the becoming of any other occasion. In this way, metaphysical principles may be discovered in human experience.

If we abandon the conviction that the universe is a single, all-encompassing system—as I am arguing we must, by the principle of perspective—then cosmology becomes far less plausible. If the world is inexhaustibly complex, and indefinitely many, then unrestricted and unqualified forms of metaphysical generality appear vain, without foundation. What is at stake is the intelligibility of the world. The principle of perspective, raised to prominence, entails a very different sense of metaphysical generality and intelligibility, and a very different conception of the relationship between metaphysical principles and the world.

Above all, we must recognize that unrestricted generality is self-contradictory and impossible if it includes *all* beings and *all* modes of being, without qualification. Such generality would be nonperspectival and absolute. Rather, unrestricted generality can be attained only in a certain respect—for example, concerning the ways in which beings are *similar*—and not in other respects—for example, concerning the ways in which beings are *different*, or different from other modes of being. This fundamental principle of limitation—that determinateness is a function of limitation—entails, by the principle of perspective, that generality is always limited, of a certain kind, and not inclusive of other kinds. No truths can be absolute and unqualified, including metaphysical propositions.

Notes to Chapter 5

1. Major confusions result from approaching Whitehead's theory of propositions from too limited an understanding of their functions, particularly with respect to subjective aim.

> Various eternal objects are not just put together. There has to be a meaningful relationship between them. Propositions exhibit this specific relationship between some specific eternal objects.... Propositions are formed or given according to the principle of determinability existing between some eternal objects as against other eternal objects. (Rotenstreich 1952, pp. 394–95)

Since the transition from potentiality to actuality is one of limitation, we might say that the first act of limitation is performed by propositions and the second one by occasions. Thus the relationship of propositions to eternal objects is similar, as it were, to the relationship of occasions to propositions. (Rotenstreich 1952, p. 398)

What is missing in this account is the role of the actual occasion in determining its own subjective aim. This is a feature of the principle of perspective. In his account, Rotenstreich is close enough to correct, except that he neglects both subjectivity and aim.

The theory of propositions tries to be an ontological theory, but there is no actual proof that the solution of the problem of the transition from the multiplicity of the eternal objects to a nexus requires an *ontological* level of existence in between. (1952, p. 400)

Rotenstreich's emphasis is Kantian and epistemological, but an epistemological analysis of propositions is simply inadequate. Rotenstreich is correct that there is a problem inherent in the independence of eternal objects from actual occasions.

If eternal objects are abstracted from actualities why need one assume that they are independent entities needing a *tertium comparationis* between themselves and actual entities? Or to put it another way: since from the outset there is no meeting ground between actual entities and eternal objects, we have to construct a meeting ground. (1952, p. 402)

Here, however, he neglects the function of the primordial nature of God. His conclusion is that "Whitehead gives an ontological status to what is only meaning" (1952, p. 404). He appears not to have appreciated C.S. Peirce's arguments concerning thirdness.

   2. Compare Blyth (1941):

On the one hand a proposition is neither a feeling nor something created by a feeling since it is a datum "awaiting a subject feeling it" and since "many subjects may feel it." And on the other hand it has no reality apart from its being felt by an actual entity, and yet it cannot be found among the data initially given to an actual entity for feeling. It can be neither a feeling nor something created by a feeling nor something given for feeling. (Pp. 69–70)

   3. See chapters 6 and 8.
   4. See Brinkley:

Whitehead admits that this is almost tantamount to saying that the "very meaning of truth is pragmatic" (PR 275; Corrected Edition 181), but he hastens to add that there must at some time be a definite determination of what is true for a particular occasion because in the absence of such a determination the pragmatic test is unable to reach a judgmental decision and must resign itself to perpetual postponement. (1961, p. 33)

   5. Some of these matters are discussed in relation to induction, in chapter 2.
   6. The foundation of Whitehead's cosmological principle may be viewed as a

religious more than a metaphysical concern, to the extent that these can be distinguished.

> The metaphysics which Whitehead drew from general experience and specifically formulated as the philosophy of organism was already theistic. . . . A new concrescence must in its process achieve a perfectly determinate novel issue of the underlying energy of creativity; it must come to stand in perfectly definite positive or negative relations to every entity (of every type) in its universe. Otherwise the finite process would achieve neither a complete individuality, nor a definite shape of value. (Lowe 1966, pp. 100–101)

7. In this context, Urban's criticisms of Whitehead's "unintelligibility" seem to me to be perverse (Urban 1938):

> The basal assumption of Whitehead's philosophy is the inability of natural language to express reality. (P. 619)

> The suggestion itself—to redesign language as pre-existing appliances in physics are redesigned—suggests an innocence as to the nature and possibilities of language which makes us gasp. (P. 620)

> The tacit assumption here—and this is the basal assumption underlying Whitehead's entire philosophy of language—is that we somehow know the fundamental nature of things apart from language and its categories and can then turn back and see that language does not correspond. (P. 622)

> When he tells us that language is not "moulded on reality" and must be redesigned, what is the "reality" and what is it that must determine the redesigning? The tacit assumption running throughout is, I think, that it is reality as determined by science, more especially physics. (P. 627)

If ordinary language were adequate, metaphysical philosophy would be far simpler than it is. Urban's position is both antitheoretical and antiscientific. Murphy's characterization of Whitehead's position is far closer to the truth.

> Modern science has held that the terms of physical analysis are both pervasive and exhaustive. We now deny that they are exhaustive but have no good reason for denying that they are pervasive and literally true *of the aspect of events with which they deal.* (Murphy 1927b, p. 299)

Urban has a legitimate criticism to offer, but it is of Whitehead's cosmology, not of his view of language.

> *Process and Reality* is made to work, it will be observed, largely by bringing God into the story. . . . I do not object to bringing God in. I object greatly to the way in which He is brought in. (Urban 1938, p. 636)

8. Otherwise there is no evading Blyth's criticisms of the unqualified nature of Whitehead's metaphysical propositions.

There can be no propositions about hypothetical entities since they are not actualities. Only actual entities can serve as the logical subjects of propositions. In the second place there can be no propositions about future entities since they are not actual. And in the third place, since further entities are not actual, there can be no universal propositions about *all*, past, present, and future entities of a given kind. (Blyth 1941, p. 75)

If there are no "universal" propositions, we can affirm no universal metaphysical truths. (1941, p. 78)

Blyth sees a conflict between the principle of experience and the cosmological principle. There is clearly a conflict with the principle of perspective. The solution is to understand metaphysical propositions perspectivally: as general, but limited and qualified in some fundamental respects.

CHAPTER SIX
ORDER

Most of the earlier discussion has emphasized the tension between the principle of perspective and the principle of experience. The concepts of order and extension, comprising the major topics of the next two chapters, manifest a far greater tension between the cosmological principle and the principle of perspective. The latter is clearly essential not only to order as the unification among nexūs of actual entities and to a perspectivity in conditions and syntheses, but also to extension in the natural sense in which space and time comprise the system of locations necessary to points of view. The two prominent senses of order of which Whitehead speaks are both perspectival: the relevance of actual occasions to other actual occasions in the future and the order of overlapping environments, that constitutes our ordinary sense of the order of nature.

> The notion of "order" is primarily applicable to the objectified data for individual actual entities. . . . But there is a derivative sense of the term "order," which is more usually in our minds when we use that word. We speak of the "order of nature," meaning thereby the order reigning in that limited portion of the universe, or even of the surface of the earth, which has come under our observation. We also speak of a man of orderly life, or of disorderly life. In any of these senses, the term "order" evidently applies to the relations among themselves enjoyed by many actual entities which thereby form a society. (PR 89)

The cosmological principle is relevant to both these forms of order insofar as they permeate the universe—insofar as an actual entity prehends all other actual entities in its past (rather than just those given by selection and exclusion), and insofar as the universe comprises the largest social environment for every occasion.

A striking set of paradigms is embedded in Whitehead's view of the universe as a system. I will take these up in the following sequence: (1) systematic order, or the order of the universe as a whole; (2) social order, or order among nexūs of occasions; (3) organic order, or order in concrescence. The cosmological principle, here, entails that multiplicity of perspective is based on a total or comprehensive perspective. I will argue that the notion of a total perspective is unintelligible to the extent that it is unconditioned.

The Order of the Universe

Whitehead was a mathematician before he was a philosopher. Several important mathematical paradigms govern his cosmology and define his understanding of system and generality.[1] As do Plato and Spinoza, Whitehead takes intelligibility to be mathematical.

> Mathematics is the most powerful technique for the understanding of pattern, and for the analysis of the relationships of patterns.... mathematics, even modern mathematics, is a science in its babyhood. If civilization continues to advance, in the next few thousand years the overwhelming novelty in human thought will be the dominance of mathematical understanding. (1951b, p. 678)

Yet his conception of mathematics is contemporary, emphasizing not measure or number but logical relations.

> We must end with my first love—Symbolic Logic. When in the distant future the subject has expanded, so as to examine patterns depending on connections other than those of space, number, and quantity—when this expansion has occurred, I suggest that Symbolic Logic, that is to say, the symbolic examination of patterns with the use of real variables, will become the foundation of aesthetics. From the stage it will proceed to conquer ethics and theology. (Whitehead 1937, p. 186)

I here emphasize the paradigmatic function of mathematics to indicate the power of mathematics to express certain complex forms of order and structure without commitment to an a priori rational system to which all events must conform. Such a system would be absolute and unqualified, a violation of the principle of perspective.[2] The principle of perspective entails qualifications that are difficult to express mathematically, yet to conclude that we can therefore dispense with mathematics in our understanding of nature is untenable. I offer the notion of paradigm to express a hypothetical force to the mathematical forms of order. Certain properties of pattern and structure can be made intelligible only through logical and mathematical systems. In particular, abstract systems define relations among their members without specifying all their properties. Such a notion makes intelligible the claim that a system can be determinately structured yet retain indeterminate alternatives. This partial determinateness, where it is complemented by indeterminateness, is essential to the concept of perspective.

Several mathematical paradigms can be found in Whitehead's system, though they are not always spelled out in detail. He defines categorial conditions in *Process and Reality* as if they were the axioms of the system (though he does not in fact deduce theorems from them). The extensive continuum is defined in terms of abstract geometrical relations. In particular, Whitehead conceives of the universe as a whole in terms of a number of mathematical paradigms. The cosmological principle is given detailed expression in these paradigms.

1. *Coherence.* One of the essential aims of speculative philosophy is the development of a coherent system of ideas. This was discussed in chapter 5 in the context of philosophic method. I am concerned here with the paradigms inherent in the concept of coherence, which

> means that the fundamental ideas, in terms of which the scheme is developed, presuppose each other so that in isolation they are meaningless. This requirement does not mean that they are definable in terms of each other; it means that what is indefinable in one such notion cannot be abstracted from its relevance to the other notions. It is the ideal of speculative philosophy that its fundamental notions shall not seem capable of abstraction from each other. In other words, it is presupposed that no entity can be conceived in complete abstraction from the system of the universe, and that it is the business of speculative philosophy to exhibit this truth. This character is its coherence. (PR 3)

Coherence is the property that defines the universe as a system.

Whitehead tells us that he has gathered this notion from mathematics. "In any branches of mathematics, the notions presuppose each other" (PR 6). In geometry, for example, lines and points presuppose each other. In number theory, based on Peano's axioms, a number is what satisfies the axioms; but on the other hand, the successor relation, which is part of the definition of number, is applicable only to what satisfies the definition. Numbers and successors entail each other.

What is involved here is the meaning of the "system of the universe."

A word like "system" cries out for a paradigm, and the most natural paradigm is mathematical. The universe comprises a unified and intelligible system only if both mathematical and coherent. However, coherence provides only a schematic unity to the universe—akin to a mathematical system. Other mathematical paradigms are needed to define the "solidarity of the universe" essential to the cosmological principle.

Coherence is an expression of complementarity in first principles and categories. It is essentially an antireductive notion denying that, of the many first principles and fundamental categories, any is to be eliminated in terms of the others. There is, here, a fundamental multiplicity of categories that by coherent interrelation define a system under a particular mode of closure. But this closure under the general applicability of the system of categories need not entail a cosmological closure based on an all-inclusive perspective toward all modes of being. Put another way, only if the metaphysical system is both coherent and absolute, unconditioned, can it express an unconditioned, inclusive perspective on the world. Coherence must be supplemented by other modes of relation if a cosmic perspective is to be established. It is not, of itself, incompatible with the principle of perspective: in fact, a systematic theory of perspective would require coherence to express its own systematic character. Coherence here is a methodological or epistemological constraint, not a metaphysical condition for the universe.

The notion of the solidarity of the universe is the central expression of the cosmological principle. To the extent that this solidarity is total and absolute, it is nonperspectival. If the universe is the name of *everything*, then we may well conceive of ascending systems and domains of interrelationship, but deny that everything comprises a single or complete order. The oneness of the universe is perspectival and conditioned—one in certain respects perhaps but not in others, closed in certain respects but not in others. This is a principle of *inexhaustibility*, closely related to the principle of perspective. Whitehead himself recognizes it:

> Fact in its totality is not an entity for cogitation, since it has no individuality by its reference to anything other than itself. I might have used the term "totality" instead of "fact"; but "fact" is shorter and gives rise to the convenient term "factor." Fact enters consciousness in a way peculiar to itself. It is not the sum of factors; it is rather the concreteness (or embeddedness) of factors, and the concreteness of an inexhaustible relatedness among inexhaustible relata.... "totality" suggests a definite aggregate which is all that there is, and which can be constructed as the sum of all subordinate aggregates. I deny this view of factuality.... Thus inexhaust-

ibleness is the prime character of factuality as disclosed in awareness. (Whitehead 1922, ch. 2)

This inexhaustibility is a direct consequence of the principle of perspective: a multiplicity of perspectives without a total perspective. The wealth of conditions and interrelations of perspectives makes them inexhaustible. This inexhaustibility is a direct expression of the complementarity of indeterminateness and determinateness in every perspective.

Inexhaustibility is not so obviously incompatible with the universe taken in totality where the latter is defined as a circumscribed domain of spatiotemporal entities that are the foundation of all other modes of being. The spatiotemporal universe appears to comprise a system unified in its becoming and its development through time. I consider this to be Whitehead's conception of the solidarity of the universe. It is founded on the ontological principle and is a direct expression of the cosmological principle. It is the only plausible conception of a unified world, under causation and process, where the principle of perspective is prominent.[3] The ground for the solidarity of the universe here lies in the interconnection of all *actualities*, and does not include imaginative possibilities, lures for feeling, or subjective forms. These are all perspectival in being potentials for becoming, but exist only in their potentiality. They are not themselves perspectival centers. Nevertheless, potentiality does not resolve this issue, for the perspectives that constitute actuality, along with whatever is relevant to such perspectives, are not subsumable under a total perspective. Were there such, it would undermine their diverse legitimacy. It follows that actual entities are together in one universe only in certain ways, and that in other ways there is no ground for togetherness—for example, in the inexhaustibility and novelty of future perspectives. Creativity and cosmology are constantly at war. There is a fundamental and unresolvable tension between the inclusiveness of the cosmic system—defined here as the supreme perspective manifested through God—and the inexhaustibility of individual perspectives in the multiplicity of actual entities. The latter cannot be simply partial, incomplete versions of God. Alternatively, even God and the universe must be perspectival, based on exclusion and irrelevance.

I am arguing that the principle of perspective is incompatible with Whitehead's notion of the solidarity of the actual universe. Precisely because no conception of the universe as a whole can be defined in which everything has a place in a unified system, the universe of spatiotemporal events cannot itself be a unified system. Nevertheless, it is Whitehead's supreme achievement to have made as plausible as can be imagined the precise sense in which inexhaustible perspectives might comprise a unified system. In this sense, he marks the apotheosis of a tradition devoted to a cosmological conception of metaphysical order amidst a multiplicity of individual beings.

2. *The Extensive Continuum.* The extensive continuum is sufficiently important to merit extended discussion in chapteer 7. My purpose here is only to discuss the mathematical paradigms inherent in the notion. There are two which are the basis of Whitehead's theory of extension, and which manifest respectively the necessity of the principle of perspective to that of experience and the influence of the cosmological principle in Whitehead's system.

Two notions require mathematical paradigms. One is that an occasion must be able to define even its initial stages so that they lead to its aim. "The feelings are inseparable from the end at which they aim; and this end is the feeler. The feelings aim at the feeler, as their final cause. The feelings are what they are in order that their subject may be what it is" (PR 222). An occasion feels as it does so that it can become what it decides to become. Even its initial phases are qualified by its subjective aim. It follows that its initial phases require something more than what is given to it by the past. For one thing, all contemporary occasions have the same gross past, yet differ from each other. There must therefore be a particular location that (a) defines each occasion as the seat or end of the feelings which flow toward it from its actual world; and (b) is different for each occasion. A geometrical paradigm is needed to define the *place* of becoming and the perspective of the prehending occasion. The principle of experience alone, grounded in the subjective aim of each occasion, cannot define the uniqueness of each occasion relative to its initial phases in which that aim becomes relevant. A distinguishing condition is needed as a ground of experience. Perspective precedes experience in relation to each concrescence.

The second consideration that calls for a mathematical paradigm is that contemporary occasions do not directly prehend each other. They are immanent in each other only through their actual worlds. A danger here is that the various actual worlds might not promote a unified contemporary world, for no principle inherent in causal inheritance entails such unification. The selectivity inherent in causal prehension can undermine the togetherness of contemporary occasions. A clear ground is needed for the cosmological principle's demand that contemporary actual entities inhabit one universe. What is required is that all perspectives form a coherent system. A natural paradigm for a multiplicity of perspectives comprising a unified system defining the contemporary world is geometrical.

I am considering here only the mathematical paradigms that constitute the model for the extensive continuum. In particular, both a nonmetric and a projective geometry are drawn upon in Whitehead's analysis. What is required is a continuum that (1) unifies the universe in its "unison of becoming," and (2) provides sufficient determinateness to each location to define uniquely the perspective from which each occasion prehends the universe.

Causation alone cannot establish the unity of the contemporary universe without contradicting the self-causation of occasions. This is the metaphysical basis of Whitehead's rejection of the theory of relativity, though he accepts its description of our epoch as the best we have. The contemporary world must be unified; yet despite this unison of becoming, contemporary occasions are causally independent. An extensive unity is required, to be interpreted in geometrical terms. However, the metric of the geometry represents spatial constants which may not be of metaphysical generality but only properties of our cosmic epoch. Analytic coordinate geometry has both a metric and, effectively, an absolute frame of reference defined by its origin.

The alternative paradigm for Whitehead's purposes is that of projective geometry, the system of geometrical relations that are preserved in projections through a specified point.[4] Certain extensive relations are well defined for any system of projections through an external point. In particular, Whitehead emphasizes the relation of "external connection": "Two regions are 'externally' connected when (i) they are connected, and (ii) they do not overlap" (PR 297). External connection is well defined for any objectification conceived as a projection from the object to the prehending subject. It is possible for causal laws to retain their properties throughout all projections or objectifications, provided that external connections are essential to such causal laws. But external connections are essential for all systems that deny action at a distance (PR 307–08). In a generalized projective geometry, all standpoints are equally legitimate; yet there are certain well-defined relations which hold for all projections. These provide a basis for the solidarity of the universe. They also constitute an interpretation of physical prehension as we know it, by straight-line projections, and explain why straight lines play so fundamental a role in Whitehead's theory of extension. In this sense projective geometry may represent the most general nonmetric geometry Whitehead could accept on the basis of uniform projections and straight lines, for the greater generality of topological relations would not provide sufficient uniformity of relation, or uniqueness, to perspectives.

Straight lines are essential to projective geometries. If mappings are allowed along any curves whatsoever, no geometrical relations will be generally maintained. Thus, the extensive continuum can serve both its unifying and locating character only if straight lines are taken as fundamental. The uniformity of the extensive continuum is required for the contemporary world to be unitary yet for contemporary events to be causally independent of each other.

The extensive continuum is required by the causal independence of contemporary occasions, demanded by the principle of experience and the self-causation of these occasions, conjoined with the cosmological principle.[5] Without the cosmological principle, there would be no need for a totality throughout contemporary occasions. Without the principle of experience and self-causation, the independence of occasions would be unnecessary. The extensive continuum is therefore the foundation of the principle of perspective in the context of the other two principles, and is unnecessary where either of these principles is rejected.

Extensive relations are not only necessary cosmologically, but necessary to the microcosmic duration of each concrescence. If freedom is possible, each occasion must possess sufficient temporal extension to accommodate its own aim and self-causation. There must be a duration that allows for genuine becoming from a phase of inheritance to a phase of completion. Otherwise, an entity will be exhausted in its inheritance and become nothing in itself. The individuality of occasions must be coordinated with the divisibility of extensive relations.

The paradigm for such coordination is provided by the method of extensive abstraction. Whitehead employs a device commonly used in the derivation of real numbers from rationals: infinite sequences of nested intervals that converge to a limit not a member of the original set. For example, we may take any positive rational number n, and choose a pair of rational numbers, one whose square lies between $2-n$ and 2, the other whose square lies between 2 and $2+n$: ($2-n < x_1^2 < 2$, $2 < x_2^2 < 2+n$). If we take an infinite sequence of numbers n_i which converge to the number 0, then sequences of numbers y_i, ($x_{1i} < y_i < x_{2i}$) will converge to the irrational number, $\sqrt{2}$. This method of convergence of intervals or regions to limits is employed by Whitehead to coordinate points of space and instants of time with occasions that are indivisibly extended in both space and time. The method rests on a clear mathematical paradigm.[6]

3. *Internal Relations*. Whitehead's doctrine of "internal relations" is

given by his theory of prehension. It is a clear manifestation of the principle of perspective. Yet there is a strong cosmological element in the doctrine, and it is this cosmological form that demands a mathematical paradigm. "An actual entity has a perfectly definite bond with each item in the universe" (PR 41). "Each actual entity includes the universe" (PR 45). (Not *its* universe.) "If we allow for degrees of relevance, and for negligible relevance, we must say that every actual entity is present in every other actual entity" (PR 50). Two metaphysical principles are involved here. One is that no occasion is, in itself, independent of other things. This is the principle of perspective. The second metaphysical principle relevant here is the cosmological principle: each occasion prehends the *entire* universe. There is some ambiguity on this subject in Whitehead's discussions. He claims that "each actual entity includes the universe" (PR 45). On the other hand, "no two actual entities originate from an identical universe" (PR 22). Moreover,

> It is not wholly true that two contemporaries A and B enjoy a common past. In the first place, even if the occasions in the past of A be identical with the occasions in the past of B, yet A and B by reason of their difference of status, enjoy that past under a difference of perspective elimination. (AI 198)

Sometimes Whitehead seems to refer to *the* universe for an occasion, meaning its actual world, and sometimes he seems to include the entire universe. The principle of relativity is clear enough: every being is a potential for *every* becoming. The totality of potentiality does not seem sufficiently qualified by the limitations of actuality, and the principle of perspective is one of exclusion and limitation. We have, here, an interaction of the cosmological principle with the principle of perspective. The latter depends on selectivity and exclusion, though it is fully based on constitutive relations: perspectives are constituted by their members—though, by the principle of perspective, these are *their* members. The cosmological principle is what demands that relevance be totalistic:

> The notion of a "common world" must find its exemplification in the constitution of each actual entity, taken by itself for analysis. For an actual entity cannot be a member of a "common world," except in the sense that the "common world" is a constituent of its own constitution. It follows that every item of the universe, including all the other actual entities, is a constituent in the constitution of any one actual entity. (PR 148)

It is worth noting that Whitehead does not propose a complete and unqualified system of internal relations. A past entity is "internal" to a future occasion, but not the converse. Nevertheless, the issue here is not of external relations, but of whether all entities in relation comprise a unified system.

> Every proposition refers to a universe exhibiting some general systematic metaphysical character. Apart from this background, the separate entities which go to form the proposition, and the proposition as a whole, are without determinate character. Nothing has been defined, because every definite entity requires a systematic universe to supply its requisite status. (PR 11)

Again, the ideal of the universe as a unified system—*one* universe —imposes a comprehensive sense of order on Whitehead's system and conflicts directly with the inherent selectivity and exclusion of the principle of perspective. It is fundamental that every occasion prehend other occasions. It is not so clear that every occasion must prehend the entire past world. Remote events, in time or space, do not appear to be relevant to each other even where the societies to which they belong are relevant. The principle of perspective is compatible with events lost in the recesses of time, having no relevance at all to the present. Whitehead's theory of experience does not permit this conclusion, for by the ontological principle, everything enters into the internal constitution of occasions.

The principle of experience and the ontological principle are relevant here, but so is the solidarity of the universe through time. If we accept a perspectival theory of relations, in which each occasion prehends only some others, under restriction, as essential to it, in what sense can we maintain that the universe is unified through time? The principle of perspective allows for only a qualified, limited unification, in certain respects and from some point of view.

The theory of internal relations, in which every occasion prehends every other item in its past universe, does not as such distinguish more and less relevant occasions prehended for a given occasion. Internal relations are not selective. What is required if the universe is to be a system, yet include selection and perspective, is a principle of relevance. Whitehead's " 'principle of intensive relevance' . . . asserts that any item of the universe, however preposterous as an abstract thought, or however remote as an actual entity, has its own gradation of relevance, as prehended, in the constitution of any one actual entity" (PR 148). This is provided by the primordial nature of God—and God here is the meeting place of the principle of perspective and the cosmological principle, providing at the same time universality and selective relevance.

4. *The Primordial Nature of God.*

The primordial created fact is the unconditioned conceptual valuation of the entire multiplicity of eternal objects. This is the "primordial nature" of God. By reason of this complete valuation, the objectification of God in each derivate actual entity results in a graduation of the relevance of eternal objects to the concrescent phases of that derivative occasion. (PR 31)

We must understand this primordial nature as a conceptual system of relations among eternal objects which defines degrees of relevance among them. A set of eternal objects ingressed in an actual world must define, through God's primordial nature, a range of relevant alternatives. The danger is that the order of relations be so conceived as to eliminate freedom by defining only a particular set of conjoint possibilities to be relevant to a given actual world, leaving no alternatives for a prehending occasion.[7] Our common conception of physical laws has this character.

What is required is a mathematical paradigm that possesses the properties assigned to God's primordial nature of imposing a partial order of relations among a multiplicity of eternal objects. I am not concerned here with the plausibility of the paradigm, but with making sense of it as a principle of limitation. The question is whether any such principle need impose total determinateness upon a system of forms of determination.

Consider an uninterpreted calculus. It defines a system of relations among uninterpreted terms, but not a completely determinate system. The same axioms that apply equally well to points on a line and the real number system define relations among the components of either system, but they do not define the precise components related. An uninterpreted or partly interpreted calculus imposes a partially determinate order on its terms. In addition, if we conceive of a partly interpreted calculus in terms of *sets* of elements, any one of which may satisfy the variables in the calculus, then we have elements related in sets, although the members are not completely determined in relation to each other. For example, any system of arithmetic laws defines relations among numbers, but leaves open the selection of particular examples. An inorganic occasion, arising in the physical prehension of a dominant society, is "determined" by the conjunction of its actual world and the primordial nature of God in its dominant characteristics, but not in the details of its subjective feelings.[8]

We may elaborate these paradigms as follows: consider a multidimensional system of relations—a set of primitive terms, perhaps infinite, and what Whitehead in *Science and the Modern World* calls an "abstractive hierarchy" constituted by complex relations among the primitive terms, ordered by ascending complexity: that is, in terms of the degree of complexity of its most complex constituent. Thus we have a, b, and c primitive terms of degree O; $R(a,b)$ of degree 1; $P(a,b,R(c,d))$ of degree 2, and so forth. (SMW 228–41). So far, we have imposed no limiting principle on the system, for we suppose each abstractive hierarchy to include all possible relations among primitive terms (sensa), and there is probably an infinite number of such relations. We now impose on this system some completely determinate relations among complex eternal objects—for example, geometrical relations among spatial patterns. However, we also include a principle of relevance such that complex eternal objects which approximate those determinately related within the system are related to each other, but less determinately or more approximately. I have in mind the difference between the definite fact that $5 > 4$ and the vaguer claim that a number *near* 5 is greater than 4. It all depends on how near.[9]

Two degrees of indeterminateness have been introduced into this system: one generated by approximations to complex configurations, the other the approximation of a complex pattern to an infinite number of other patterns. Thus, a coin is rather round, rather heavy, rather precious, rather interesting in design, and so forth. What will become of it is partly determined by all these traits; but it is indeterminate also, in not being quite a precise example of anything. Moreover, it possesses all the traits at once, and is indeterminate by virtue of their interplay. Only its decision renders it completely determinate. Its prehension by another entity is also wholly determinate, for it is based on the latter's decision. But the determinate characters are necessarily different.[10]

The paradigm here is a statistical one that defines probabilities of relations of entities with respect to a given category, but can define them no further. There are so many examples of systems with partial order that it is impossible to guess which specific system Whitehead may have had in mind for the primordial nature of God. The number system may be viewed in partial order in certain respects—there are many numbers that satisfy certain definite conditions, such as lying between 5 and 7.[11] An uninterpreted calculus possesses definite order, but an incomplete one. A statistical system imposes only a partial order on its elements.

God provides, through his primordial nature, sufficient limitation to make choices possible in concrescence, but not so great a limitation as to eliminate decision.[12] From a mathematical point of view, this is perfectly intelligible.[13]

The paradigms described here for understanding the partial order among eternal objects in the primordial nature of God affect both the individual and the relational essences of eternal objects. Neither of these essences can be regarded as entirely determinate if there is a determining role for God to play, on the one hand, and for actual occasions, on the other. This joint function of individual and relational essences among actual occasions is a prime example of their perspectivity, despite the fact that Whitehead restricts perspective explicitly to actual occasions. Indeterminateness is essential to perspective, an indeterminateness as essential to the function of eternal objects as it is to all relational modes of being.[14]

Thus, Whitehead's paradigms for the primordial nature of God manifest an incomplete but definite conformity to the principle of perspective. The system of eternal objects is ordered, from a standpoint. To define relevance for events, the system of determinations must be ordered from a standpoint. The weakness of the perspectivity is manifested in the apparent intelligibility of a mere multiplicity of eternal objects and in the unique, cosmological, and single-valued system of relevance among all eternal objects. In this latter case, there is a complete and single-valued perspective definitive of the realm of eternal objects, a total perspective consonant with the cosmological principle, but limited in relation to the principle of perspective as a principle of multiplicity. Eternal objects do not share in the multiplicity of perspectives inherent in actual entities. This is a drastic limitation of the principle of perspective.

It leads, in fact, to one of the most puzzling aspects of Whitehead's theory: the privileged role played by sensa. These are eternal objects of zero degree, in that "a sensum does not, for its own realization, require any eternal object of a lower grade" (PR 114). It is clear that Whitehead has an abstractive hierarchy in mind. Relational components may be graded in terms of their complexity. It follows that sensa are the lowest-grade eternal objects, "simple." They even appear to be incorrigible in pure presentational perceptions.

But they are not unanalyzable, for they must possess relational as well as individual essences. Whitehead assumes that there is one systematic order among all eternal objects and that sensa have a well-defined role within that order. He does not sufficiently consider the analyzable character of sensa, particularly that they may be known only through their complex relations (blue is a color, extended, etc.). Although, in general, Whitehead rejects simples as unintelligible, he allows for "lowest-grade" sensa and pure modes of perception, notions largely equivalent to simples. This is a consequence of the mechanical version of analysis which he seems to have inherited from his forebears. Insofar as this principle of analysis produces unqualified simples and pure elements, it is antithetic to the principle of perspective and is grounded in cosmological convictions. Each eternal object, since it has an individual essence, has a wealth of relations constituting its perspective on other eternal objects. The tension between the cosmological principle and the principle of perspective is repeated for eternal objects, as well as for actual occasions, without the direct contribution of the principle of experience and the ontological principle.

I have discussed several mathematical paradigms inherent in Whitehead's conception of the order of the universe. He employs a number of other paradigms to define order *in* the universe, though not *of* it. Two important notions of order are ruled by major paradigms: social order and organic interrelation.

Social Order

"A set of entities is a society (i) in virtue of a 'defining characteristic' shared by its members, and (ii) in virtue of the presence of the defining characteristic being due to the environment provided by the society itself" (PR 89). Two kinds of order are therefore intrinsic to a society: that imposed on it by its dominant characteristic and that which the society imposes on its members by the conditions it defines for them.

A society is more than a set of entities to which the same class-name applies: that is to say, it involves more than a merely mathematical conception of "order." To constitute a society, the class-name has got to apply to each member, by reason of genetic derivation from other members of that same society. The members of the society are alike because, by reason of their common character, they impose on other members of the society the conditions which lead to that likeness. (PR 89)

The second condition provides the metaphysical ground for order in our experience.

Whitehead tells us that "the point of a 'society,' as the term is here used, is that it is self-sustaining; in other words, that it is its own reason" (PR 89). The paradigm involved here is very important and one of the primary exemplifications of the principle of perspective. A nation, if powerful and successful, endures largely because of its members' actions. Each individual citizen lives his life in the society and makes his individual choices. Yet the environment provided for him is not only favorable for his own life, but encourages actions by him favorable to the state. In Whitehead's theory, a society, by definition, endures through the environment it defines for its members who, on the other hand, constitute the society by their actions. This reciprocal constitutiveness is the manifestation of perspective and is as relevant to societies as to actual entities. A society may be destroyed by external force. It may also destroy itself through inner strife. The point is that when it endures, it does so because of its success in imbuing its members with a common character—though not necessarily one ideal for everyone in the society. By so conceiving of a society, Whitehead makes the order of nature a result of communities of occasions in interaction. Once a favorable environment has been defined for a society, it will endure as long as it continues to maintain that favorable an environment.

The society-environment relation is one of the most important notions in Whitehead's theory and an example of the organic nature of his cosmology. He calls his system "the philosophy of organism." Probably the most important basis for such a description is the reciprocal part-whole relation, in which parts not only are constituted by, but also constitute, the wholes to which they belong. This is another major exemplification of the principle of perspective, for such mutual constitution needs the addition of point of view, if differentiation is to be meaningful in such a network of constitutive relations. Constituents and the organisms they belong to are intimately related, yet distinguished by point of view—by other relations, other environments. The environment of the organs of the body is the body, only indirectly the larger world. The environment of the body is composed of other bodies, only indirectly mediated by the internal organs. The mutual constitution of elements among different environments is a fundamental property of perspectives. A society can be its own reason only because organic relations are possible among organisms and their environments. Organic and social relations are fundamental for Whitehead. They manifest the principle of perspective in its most thoroughgoing form, freed from the restrictions imposed by the cosmological principle and the principle of experience.

A member of a society must reproduce the character of that society to be a member of it. A further issue is whether occasions must be members of societies. According to Whitehead:

> Every actual entity is in its nature essentially social; and this in two ways. First, the outlines of its own character are determined by the data which its environment provides for its process of feeling. Secondly, these data are not extrinsic to the entity; they constitute that display of the universe which is inherent in the entity. (PR 203)

Every actual entity, however disjoint its surroundings, is nevertheless part of some society. It inhabits many overlapping environments. By the principle of perspective, social relations and plural environments are essential to perspectivity, and sociality is a direct manifestation of the perspectivity of being. Such a paradigm of perspective is, however, not based on the principle of experience. It is conjoined with the cosmological principle in Whitehead's thought by reference to the total environment of the universe, but it need not be so conjoined if we repudiate the notion of an all-inclusive environment.

The social paradigm supports a mutuality of relevance and constitution, which I have called "organic," and which is quite different from the asymmetric character of prehensive occasions in successive becoming. An occasion's actual world is an environment for it but is also implicit in its character. In other words, every occasion prehends its environment and finds therein elements of its own character. Every occasion finds itself in its environment. In the same way, every organism in an ecologically balanced environment is at once a reflection of that environment and a contributing factor to its character. The philosophy of organism conceives of all relations of an occasion to its larger environments as organic. The principle of perspective entails that every occasion inhabits irreducibly *many* such environments, each determinative of a different perspective. The cosmological principle entails that the universe comprises the widest possible environment for all perspectives.

The organic paradigm provides a resolution of what could be a major difficulty in Whitehead's theory—the joint principles that a society "is its own reason," and that "actual entities are the only reasons." There appears to be a direct contradiction between the ontological principle based on the intersection of the principle of experience with the cosmological principle and the principle of perspective. It is clear that societies can be reasons, in Whitehead's view, only because of the characteristics of their members. This is the force of the ontological principle. Yet the members derive their characters, at least in part, from the societies to which they belong. We may note in addition that even multiplicities are such in virtue of organic and constitutive relations. It follows that what an occasion is is largely a function of the diverse environments of which it is a member, and from which it inherits, from its point of view. Here the multiple constitution of diversely overlapping environments is a major feature, manifesting the force of the principle of perspective and weakening the relevance of the principle of experience. There is a far closer analogy between the self-determination of societies and of occasions than the principle of experience can sustain. By the principle of perspective, societies as well as actual occasions are perspectival centers. As a consequence, due to the limitations of every perspective, the cosmological demand that the universe comprise a supreme social environment must be rejected. Societies, societies of societies, other multiplicities, as well as occasions, are all made perspectival in their mutual and reciprocal modes of constitution.[15]

In what sense are actual entities the only reasons, since societies are reasons too? Whitehead's position is that all explanations find their data in actual entities, even where they involve other entities as well. The reciprocity of constitution, essential to the perspectivity of societies and prehensions, is denied in relation to actual occasions, which cannot constitute each other. The ontological principle directly asserts the asymmetry: some traits of occasions—subjective forms, self-causation—have no counterparts at any other level of analysis, but all traits of societies have counterparts in the experiences of actual occasions. Such a view is cosmological to the extent that *every* trait at every complex level of inclusiveness is to be manifested at the level of individual experience, without loss or exclusion. There appears here to be a fallacy of division.

Even more important, there is the impossibility of mutual constitution for occasions as a result of their successiveness. The asymmetry of time, in Whitehead's theory, imposes an unconditional character on the past relative to the present and future. The asymmetric relation of prehension makes mutual constitution impossible. A true organic relation is impossible among actual entities, but such a relation is not impossible among environments. I consider this a drastic limitation upon the principle of perspective imposed by the ontological principle, and I conclude that the perspectivity essential to Whitehead's system is to be found more in the theory of social environments than in the relationship of societies to their constituent members. The principle of perspective is manifested at the level of social and environmental interrelations; the principles of experience and cosmology are manifested in the ontological principle. The inability of actual entities to constitute each other seems to me to be a fundamental weakness of the theory of social order, undermining the entire theory of environments and perspectives.[16]

The Philosophy of Organism

I have been discussing the order in the universe provided by Whitehead's conception of occasions as organisms. The paradigm here is biological. The theory of organism conceives of the relationship of parts to wholes in ecological terms, based on mutual re-enforcement. The concept of a society preserves the biological suggestion of a species in ecological balance with its environment. In addition, an actual entity is a prehensive creature with sensitive and originative impulses as well as reproductive capacities. Societies depend on conformation of feeling; but the organisms may not merely reproduce what is given to them. They have the capacity to engender novelties.

Another biological relation plays a central role in Whitehead's theory. It is based on the notion of "adaptation for the attainment of an end" (PR 83). "This end is concerned with the gradations of intensity in the satisfactions of actual entities (members of the nexus) in whose formal constitutions the nexus (i.e. antecedent members of the nexus) in question is objectified" (PR 83). Each occasion is an organism that strives for the realization of some aim; moreover, "God's purpose in the creative advance is the evocation of intensities" (PR 105). Each occasion defines ideals for itself which are interwoven with a quest for intensity, while on the other hand, intensity is the goal of the universe.

Intensity is discussed in chapter 2. I am concerned here with its role in defining order in the universe. Why does not all experience remain on the level of mere reproduction? Why is there not a uniform sterility of occasions devoid of social order? Whitehead's answer is "that an actual fact is a fact of aesthetic experience. All aesthetic experience is feeling arising out of the realization of contrast under identity" (PR 280). This intensity, an aim of every concrescence as well as of God, establishes a teleological order within the universe. It is a profound expression of the cosmological principle, perhaps one of its least plausible expressions to the extent that it asserts the primacy of the religious intuition—a direction to the universe founded in God's aim toward intensity. It offers an explanation of the social character of the universe in our experience:

to realize God's aim of intensification of contrast. Aesthetic experience is particularly evident in human life, for it is there that the greatest intensity can be harmonized with balance and order. Thus, man and social order are not accidents, but evidence of divine purpose. But no *particular* goal is the end of God's subjective aim except the achievement of intensity.

We find here a component of the principle of experience that cannot be easily incorporated into the principle of perspective. There is a direction of the universe toward greater social order, based on the aim of every actual entity, including God, toward subjective intensity. The principle of perspective taken alone would, I believe, entail that there is no ultimate trend toward social order, however indeterminate, only particular trends based on antecedent conditions of order. Only mankind pursues intensity and higher experience; the universe does not. The universe will some day fall apart. The principle of experience imposes a cosmic teleology on the universe that is compatible with some major religious intuitions, but that appears entirely discordant with the astrophysical awareness of the impending death of our universe. From the latter point of view, it is mankind's sublime achievement to engender intensity through invention, sublime because it is a novel contribution to the universe. We may add, however, that this intensity is a function of perspectivity: the interplay of determinateness of indeterminateness in every perspectival determination.

The Unity of the World

I have distinguished the order of the universe as a whole from order in the universe. The question here is whether the universe possesses an order. It is the question of the plausibility and intelligibility of the cosmological principle. We may recall Aristotle's criticism of Parmenides, that he treated Being absolutely. To what extent is it plausible to speak of the world, the universe, everything, totally and without qualification, in violation of the conditions demanded by the principle of perspective?

It seems reasonable to say that all things inhabit one world, belong to a single system, even a "common world." To many philosophers it has seemed a principle definitive of rationality. Our most powerful intuitions support the sense of *a* universe, if not to the extent of treating nature as a single substance, at least of resting all things on a common foundation in natural laws or first principles. We should not overlook the apparently irresistible tendency to locate all events in a single spatiotemporal or extensive system.

It is worth reviewing the ways in which Whitehead provides that the universe is one, his many concessions to the cosmological principle, despite his fundamental perspectivism and pluralism.[17] We begin with irreducible multiplicity and perspectivity: there are many actual entities; each is unique, defines a unique perspective on the world, and is *causa sui*. Each is a unique prehending subject, irreducible to any system of relations. Nevertheless, all actual entities are together in virtue of the following principles:

1. God's primordial nature provides a systematic though partial ordering of all eternal objects. Underlying actuality is one unchanging system of forms of determinateness. Many commentators have questioned the permanence of the order provided by the primordial nature of God.[18] The more fundamental question is why God in his primordial nature should not be constituted by the selective prehension of other actualities—neither complete nor permanent. How can the primordial nature of God be excluded from perspectivity?

2. God's consequent nature is the unification of all actualities as objectively prehended in one supreme becoming. Here Whitehead provides a cosmic point of view for the entire universe. We may leave aside the question of whether God's perspective, in being eternal as well as all-encompassing, does not relegate all finite perspectives to mere distortion. The more straightforward issue is whether one all-encompassing perspective toward all actuality is plausible, rather than a plurality of diverse, partly related perspectives. I have noted Whitehead's own emphasis on the inexhaustibility of the universe.

3. *Each* actual entity is all-encompassing, unifying all past occasions from its point of view. I have noted Whitehead's ambiguity here, sometimes speaking of actual entities prehending *the* universe, sometimes *their* universe. I believe he is committed to the principle that each actual entity mirrors the entire past as initial datum. Yet he is equally committed to the selection and exclusion of each occasion's perspectivity. It is not worth pursuing this controversy further here except to note that, without a complete system of causal relations, only God could provide objective unity to the world.

4. The extensive continuum provides a ground for the togetherness in one world of all contemporary occasions and establishes a ground of unity among all actual entities insofar as they inhabit a common world. Although I maintain that the extensive continuum is not antecedent to past occasions but derived from them (*with* them), the assumption that

there is one such all-inclusive extensive system is entirely unfounded. This is discussed in chapter 7.

5. The principle of coherence entails that all fundamental categories and principles involve each other and cannot be separately conceived. Such coherence manifests "the system of the universe." The ideal of a unified rational order is grounded in this notion and applied to the order of the universe.

6. The principle of relativity is all-inclusive in demanding that every being be a potential for *every* becoming. The ontological principle is hierarchical in imposing a doctrine of ontological primacy on a pluralistic system of perspectives and environments. These two principles together are the major exemplifications of the cosmological principle in its defiance of a stronger and more thorough principle of perspective.

It is to be concluded that Whitehead has provided categories for the systematic unity of the world, in conformity to the cosmological principle. Whether he has succeeded in doing so without undermining the unique self-identity of each actual entity is a difficult matter. I have been arguing that his concessions to the cosmological principle are incompatible with the principle of perspective, and that the latter is the source of Whitehead's major metaphysical insights. This discussion is continued in ensuing chapters.

Here I wish only to return to the question of the unity of the world in terms of the generality of metaphysical categories. Two conceptions of metaphysical generality are opposed in ways closely analogous to the tension between the principle of perspective and the cosmological principle.

One conception is hierarchical: there are many different modes of being, but they are all defined by the principle of relativity and the ontological principle in relation to actual entities. Generality here is defined in relation to cosmic epochs and possible worlds, but not to the modes of being themselves. The properties that are general across eternal objects, subjective forms, and actual entities are very few—perhaps reducible finally to the principle of relativity. Metaphysical generality here is permeated by the cosmological principle.

As an alternative, we may consider properties of all beings, all perspectives. Perspectivity here is a general condition of every being, and it entails that qualifications, conditions, relatedness, and uniqueness are equally relevant to every mode of being. Here the individual essence of eternal objects is pertinent, as is their relational essence; all the pure and unconditioned characteristics of Whitehead's system are muted, if not eliminated.

These two conceptions of metaphysical generality correspond to the prominence of the cosmological principle and the principle of perspective respectively. By the cosmological principle, the universe is a hierarchical system founded on actual entities. A metaphysical system can be general here only within the confines of such a hierarchy: generality relative to all possible universes. The nature of the unity of the universe is not proved, it is presupposed.

By the principle of perspective, however, hierarchy itself is perspectival and conditioned. All modes of being are in perspectives and constitute perspectives. Generality, then, is relative to all modes of being—those traits and conditions shared by any being whatsoever; but it is always qualified, a generality in certain respects only. All beings have individual and relational characteristics, both prominent in perspectivity. All beings inhabit many overlapping spheres of relatedness, and are constituted by their membership but also by their members. Constitution, identity, and relatedness are all perspectival, conditioned, and plural. Determinateness is always complemented by indeterminateness, and conversely.

I will not pursue this matter further here. In the final chapter, I will sketch a theory modelled on Whitehead's but based more thoroughly on the principle of perspective. I will also develop the consequences of extending the principle of perspective even further in the direction of generality just described. It is essential in both cases to eliminate the difficulties that are produced by the incompatibility of the principle of perspective and the cosmological principle. This can be done in two ways, one more radical than the other.

Notes to Chapter 6

1. The importance of mathematical paradigms to Whitehead's theory, their pervasiveness throughout his systematic discussions, reflect his years as a mathematician. The paradigmatic function is an expression of his respect for the powers of mathematics to express patterns and forms of order without which our conceptions of order would be vague and almost contentless. See in this connection Ralph Norman's discussion of this function of mathematics:

A close reading of his remarks upon the subject suggests that he found two uses of mathematics—the one abortive and barren, the other rich and indispensable. We shall call these the *skeptical* and the *aesthetic* use, respectively. ... Whitehead remained fascinated by the mathematical method, not in its function of building upon certainties but in its characteristically modern function of discovering and exhibiting types and modes of coherence. This is mathematics in its *aesthetic* philosophical use—i.e., in its use as the search for infinitely rich and diverse patterns of order. (1963, pp. 33–34)

In contrast, Palter claims in the same volume that " 'mathematics' has three senses in Whitehead's philosophy: mathematics as 'logic'; mathematics as 'natural knowledge'; and mathematics as 'cosmology' " (Palter 1963, p. 42).

Dewey criticizes Whitehead's overly mathematical emphasis with respect to philosophical method:

> Is it to be developed and applied with fundamental emphasis upon experimental observation (the method of the natural sciences)? Or does it point to the primacy of mathematical method? . . . I do not see how the two can be coordinate. . . . One, I think, must lead and the other follow. (Dewey 1937, p. 174)

Whitehead's reply is typical: he refuses to choose which of the "genetic-functional" or "formal-mathematical" methods should be primary.

> John Dewey asks me to decide between the "genetic-functional" interpretation of first principles and the "mathematic-formal" interpretation. . . . I must decline to make this decision. . . . The historic process of the world, which requires the genetic-functional interpretation, also requires for its understanding some insight into those ultimate principles of existence which express the necessary connections within the flux. (Whitehead 1937, p. 179)

Dewey's criticism, it seems to me, is somewhat misplaced: he is effectively arguing that Whitehead's mathematical method is absolutistic, nonperspectival, and nonfunctional. The importance of *paradigms* in Whitehead's theory is fundamental. Mathematics expresses but does not, it seems to me, *dictate* order. The question of necessity, however, is more absolutistic and cosmological. Arthur E. Murphy's criticisms are well taken to the extent that mathematical paradigms express the cosmological principle.

> [Whitehead] has none the less attributed to events, *apart from the objects which characterize them*, a spatio-temporal structure which is concrete and existential in a favored sense, which somehow *is* the occurrence itself. This structure has its basis in extension, and events themselves figure merely as terms for this ubiquitous relation. (Murphy 1928, p. 580)

> I have tried to show that absolute space-time is not involved in the theory of events and is in fact in conflict with it. The event, once more, is the object as occurring. There are no characters which *constitute* events. But there are characters which belong to events as such and others which belong to the happening of objects. These latter are the characters of events. (1928, pp. 585–86)

Whitehead does mitigate considerably the force of these criticisms, in *Process and Reality*, but not sufficiently, I will argue, to preserve his perspectivism fully.

Many of Whitehead's readers have emphasized the applicability of his mathematical paradigms to actuality, as if he remained wedded to the program of *Principia Mathematica* throughout his life, even into *Process and Reality*. "The implication of Whitehead's view is that mathematical truths are not analytic. Mathematical truths are not merely a matter of meaning; rather, they are concerned with the possible interrelations of actuality" (Lowry 1971, p. 122). The most evident difficulty with this largely accurate reading turns on the necessity of the extensive continuum to the multiplicity of actual occasions (discussed in detail in chapter 7). There must be extensive potentialities that do not ingress in actual events. For all these reasons, I emphasize the *paradigmatic* character of Whitehead's mathematical structures in his mature philosophy, as if to indicate that order can be given mathematical expression, but that the precise structures of order are a consequence of particular social conditions of occasions. Any other reading would make certain forms of order absolute and a priori, and would undermine perspectivity and functionality.

Dewey questions whether Whitehead gives priority to mathematics over experimental observation. A more fundamental question is whether Whitehead gives cosmological priority to mathematics over perspective. However, where pure mathematics is understood to be only a possibility for actuality, dependent for its applicability on actual conditions, then mathematics need not be cosmological in conflict with the principle of perspective. I will argue that Whitehead's theory of extension is based on such a view of pure geometry. There is the difficulty of the unconditioned nature of the primordial nature of God, *pure* possibilities. The principle of perspective provides a far more plausible view of the applicability of mathematics: perspectival itself, mathematical order reflects a conditioned truth about what it applies to. Such a view I am here describing as a *paradigmatic* function of mathematics: to express a hypothetical order that incompletely reflects the nature of its exemplifications.

2. To this extent, Dewey's criticisms (note 1, above) are well taken.

3. Nevertheless, there can be no such universe, even under succession, where there is an inexhaustibility of perspectives.

4. Many commentators have recognized the importance of projective geometry in Whitehead's theory of extension: "In the theory of extension, projective geometry supplies the antecedent system into which the concept of distance is introduced" (Lowe 1966, p. 83). These commentators have not, however, equally well understood the metaphysical importance of the uniform character of the extensive continuum to Whitehead's theory of atomic events. The togetherness of events, based on a strong form of the cosmological principle, leads Whitehead to a stronger demand for uniformity throughout contemporary occasions than can be supplied by the theory of relativity.

5. Even in his mature work, Whitehead often seems to base the importance of straight lines to the uniformity of extensive relations on perception in the mode of presentational immediacy.

It may be noticed in passing that, if straightness depends upon measurement, there can be no perception of straightness in the unmeasured. The notion of "straight in front" must then be meaningless. (AI 218)

I interpret Whitehead's noticing "in passing" to mean that this argument is peripheral, and I am seeking to identify the deeper reasons for Whitehead's demand for straight-line projections. The argument from presentational immediacy is an example of an illegitimate introduction, in the context of fundamental metaphysical issues of process and solidarity, of epistemological issues derived from the testimonial authority of conscious perception.

6. It will be discussed in greater detail in chapter 7.

7. See passages from Pols, chapter 3, note 11, and below, p. 241.

8. See here Wolf Mays's description of the extensive continuum.

> Whitehead thus regards the scheme as a bare logical form in which a particular type of content (i.e., events) may be fitted, just as one can assign a value (or give a determination) to a propositional function. In this connection it is interesting to note Russell's description of a propositional function as "a mere schema, a mere shell, an empty receptacle for meaning, not something already significant." (Mays 1959, pp. 57–58)

Mays regards the extensive continuum as an uninterpreted system of propositional functions (or as one complex propositional function). I am interpreting the primordial nature of God to be based on a similar paradigm. The extensive continuum is more geometrical in nature. Mays appears to blur all the different paradigms I have noted into one unclear model.

> The extensive continuum, the Receptacle, and the realm of eternal objects, all seem to refer to the same general system of undetermined relationships. (1959, p. 58)

> The general system of extensive relationships, or extensive continuum, is identical with the "Primordial Nature of God," having all its logical properties. (1959, p. 73)

Mays's insights into the mathematical structure of Whitehead's system are flawed by his failure to see that these structures are *paradigmatic* only, causing him to overlook most of the force of the principles of experience and perspective.

9. In this connection, see Mays's far too limited paradigm, which effectively neglects *degrees* of relevance:

> When he therefore states that God is the actuality of conceptual feeling at the base of things, we need to recognize that he is merely referring to the n-adic ordering relation R, the logical framework in which events are related. (1959, p. 58)

> Whitehead then in this context seems to be using the phrase "Platonic idea" to refer to the concept of an extensive pattern which has some affinity to the notion of a geometrical configuration, since it is also a set of terms ordered by a serial relation. When Whitehead speaks about "eternal objects" as in God's primordial nature, he is really referring to a system of such abstract structures. (1959, p. 59)

It is particularly important to note the force of the words "merely" and "really," limiting the richness of Whitehead's theory to the mathematical paradigms, while in truth, Whitehead employs such paradigms with limited force precisely in order not to restrict the generality and richness of his theory.

Thus, Mays actually rejects the more concrete and theological elements of Whitehead's theory of God:

> Whitehead's description [of God's primordial nature] in theological terms is much too concrete, and cloaks the abstract logical character of his whole account. . . . By "God's vision," Whitehead is here referring to the systematic complex of extensive relationships. (1959, p. 60)

10. By the principle of perspective, no being can be *completely* determinate, in all respects. Occasions and their prehensions are determinate only in certain respects.

11. This example indicates that no order can be completely determinate in all respects, since systems of partial order are included in every system with more complete order.

12. The paradigms discussed here make the primordial nature of God far more intelligible than such opaque claims as John Cobb's:

> It is extremely difficult to see how one unchanging order can provide a specific and novel aim to every new occasion.
> The solution seems to be that the eternal ordering of the eternal objects is not one simple order but an indefinite variety of orders. God's ordering of possibilities is such that every possible state of the actual world is already envisioned as possible and every possible development from that actual state of the world is already envisioned and appraised. (1965, pp. 155–56)

Indeed, Cobb approaches determinism far too closely. "God's primordial nature so orders the eternal objects that one such possibility is indeed from eternity identified as ideal given that situation" (1965, p. 156). To strengthen the role of God unduly is effectively to weaken the self-determination relevant to each occasion's perspective.

13. The partial indeterminateness of the primordial nature of God is essential to it, essential both to relations among eternal objects and their relational essences and to the freedom and self-determination of actual entities which prehend it. Lowe is therefore doubly wrong when he claims, "I cannot agree with Prof. Christian's argument . . . that after *Science and the Modern World* Whitehead dropped the idea that there is some fixed order among eternal objects" (1966, note, p. 101). Even in *Science and the Modern World*, Whitehead defines relations among eternal objects as vague and abstract. If "fixed," in Lowe's interpretation, means "unchanging," then he is correct, but not if he means "wholly determinate," without degrees of freedom.

14. Most attempts to interpret the individual and relational essences of eternal objects depend heavily on vagueness and even irrelevance.

> The relational essence of turquoise blue vis-à-vis any four-sided plane figure is not unique to turquoise blue, but is the same as that of pea green and jet black; thus the individual essence of turquoise blue is quite aloof from the relational essence of turquoise blue. . . . When included within one concrete actual occasion, several

different eternal objects exhibit a togetherness of their *individual* essences, which is the achievement of an emergent value. As together in the realm of possibility eternal objects exhibit a togetherness of their relational essences only, which, while a real and significant relatedness, preserves the isolation of eternal objects in the realm of possibility, since here individual essences stand aloof from the relational togetherness. (Sherburne 1961, p. 34)

If individual essences pertain only to ingression and relational essences pertain only to relatedness among eternal objects themselves, then, however indeterminate the latter may be, there is no obvious connection between the individual and relational essences. This is unintelligible. What is needed is an understanding that each eternal object is itself a perspective, an individual with relational essences whose individuality as well as relationality are functions of perspectival relations.

See also:

How can we speak of *an* order of eternal objects? We would seem to have rather, as many orderings of eternal objects as there are actual occasions. (Christian 1959, p. 271)

An interrelatedness between forms is as essential to the nature of form as it is that the form be what it is. Whitehead has called these two respectively the "relational essence" and the "individual essence" of forms. . . . These two essentials are not disconnected; on the contrary, the one is required by the other, so that there could be neither without the other. (Leclerc 1964, p. 135)

What an eternal object is in itself is precisely the togetherness of its relations to all other eternal objects. An individual eternal object is therefore to be conceived as the togetherness of the world of eternal objects from its perspective and its individuality as the structure of that togetherness. (Kraus 1979, p. 33)

My view, different from all of these and possibly from Whitehead's, is that each eternal object is a perspective on other eternal objects. The latter comprise its relational essence; its uniqueness of perspective comprises its individual essence. The eternal object *is* a function of both essences; each essence is a function of the other; and ingressions of eternal objects are additional functions of their relational and individual essences, but also functions of the perspectives of actual occasions. Only so thoroughly perspectival a view can bring the individual and relational essences into congruence, along with the other relations manifested in the togetherness of eternal objects in individual occasions.

15. These considerations are antithetic to the cosmological demand for an ultimate reality.

Whitehead is thus in full agreement with Aristotle as to what constitutes the ultimate metaphysical problem. To them both it is the problem of determining the nature of "that " which is the "complete existent," the "fully existing" entity. (Leclerc 1958, p. 20)

Ultimateness is also perspectival, and occasions are not ultimate in any obvious sense from the standpoint of a society complexly located within a multiplicity of other, overlapping societies.

16. Andrew Reck's argument that, without enduring substances, Whitehead's theory of atomic events is inadequate is relevant here. "Process, therefore, presupposes the existence of substantial entities which endure through change, and where process philosophers attempt to discard them, they undermine the foundations of their philosophy" (1958, p. 367). In my view, however, the difficulty is not that the notion of a durational but unchanging event is unintelligible, but that enduring objects are claimed to be less fundamental, less perspectival. Societies are their own reasons amidst constitutive perspectival relations, a consequence of a more general interpretation of the principle of perspective than Whitehead's theory can accommodate.

17. "Whitehead's universe is a *connected* pluralistic universe. No monist ever insisted more strongly than he that nothing in the world exists in independence of other things" (Lowe 1966, pp. 35–36).

18. Compare the following:

There is not one fixed and necessary order of eternal objects. There is not one and only one way in which all things *must* happen. (Christian 1959, p. 273)

It is extremely difficult to see how one unchanging order can provide a specific and novel aim to every new occasion. (Cobb 1965, p. 155)

If all the "forms of definiteness," each perfectly definite in itself, are eternally given to God, it is not altogether clear to me what actualization accomplishes. (Hartshorne 1972, p. 95)

CHAPTER SEVEN
EXTENSION

The extensive continuum is one of the two great meeting grounds of the principle of perspective and the cosmological principle. The other is God, who profoundly reflects as well the principle of experience. The relative independence of the extensive continuum from the principle of experience is a great source of confusion in Whitehead's theory, and manifests more clearly than any other feature of his theory the independence of the principles of experience and perspective. The former principle is not directly relevant to the extensive continuum, but is relevant to Whitehead's theory of presentational immediacy, producing many of the difficulties already noted. The principle of experience is indirectly involved in the grounding of the extensive continuum in the primordial nature of God through the ontological principle, but this grounding is another source of confusion since Whitehead also claims that the extensive continuum is derived from actual entities, though he never quite explains how. Whitehead's theory of extension is influenced far more by the mechanical principle of analysis than is the theory of God, and is subject to many of that principle's difficulties. The tension between divisibility and indivisibility is particularly strong in relation to extension. Most of all, however, the theory of extension is the meeting place of metaphysical with scientific principles, an intersection of different levels of generality. This makes it one of the most interesting but also one of the most difficult aspects of Whitehead's theory.

For example, there is a puzzling inconsistency in Whitehead's discussions of the relationship between continuity and becoming. In his first comments on extensiveness in *Process and Reality*, he claims that

> the extensive continuity of the physical universe has usually been construed to mean that there is a continuity of becoming. But if we admit that

169

"something becomes," it is easy, by employing Zeno's method, to prove that there can be no continuity of becoming. There is a becoming of continuity, but no continuity of becoming. The actual occasions are the creatures which become, and they constitute a continuously extensive world. In other words, extensiveness becomes, but "becoming" is not itself extensive. (PR 35)

Whitehead also asserts that "extensive continuity is a special condition arising from the society of creatures which constitute our immediate epoch" (PR 36). These remarks seem at odds with his discussion of the extensive continuum, where he asserts that "extension is the most general scheme of real potentiality, providing the background for all other organic relations" (PR 67). I have noted that the extensive continuum in its full generality is a defining condition for the perspectivity and togetherness of all occasions in one universe. It is presupposed by every becoming, and in this sense does not seem to be a consequence of becoming or a special condition of our cosmic epoch.[1] An alternative is that there are different senses of extensive continuity in Whitehead's theory, one of greater generality than the other. The earlier remarks address, not extension in general, but the special continuity of external connection in our epoch. While the extensive continuum is a necessary constituent of the universe, the continuity of most spatiotemporal relations may be only a property of our particular epoch.

So far as mere extensiveness is concerned, space might as well have three hundred and thirty-three dimensions, instead of the modest three dimensions of our present epoch. The three dimensions of space form an additional fact about the physical occasions. Indeed the sheer dimensionality of space, apart from the precise number of dimensions, is such an additional fact, not involved in the mere notion of extension. Also the seriality of time, unique or multiple, cannot be derived from the sole notion of extension. (PR 289)

I will show that the argument from the continuity of our epoch to the general conditions of extension for all occasions defines a plausible basis for the claim that extensiveness and continuity in general both are derived from occasions and constitute the ground of togetherness of occasions, and in a remarkably subtle and complex way. "Extension is a form of relationship between the actualities of a nexus. A point is a nexus of actual entities with a certain 'form'; and so is a 'segment.' Thus geometry is the investigation of the morphology of nexūs" (PR 302). The extensive continuum in its full generality cannot *antedate* actuality, for that would locate it simply in the primordial nature of God. There is a tension in Whitehead's thought between the general conditions of perspectivity and the universal togetherness required by all occasions under the cosmological principle.

A related issue is the extensiveness of space and time. Whitehead, writing in the shadow of the theory of relativity, describes space and time as comprising a single order, "the spatio-temporal continuum" (SMW 170). An event is extended in both space and time. However, he also tells us that "we must not proceed to conceive time as another form of extensiveness. Time is sheer succession of epochal durations" (SMW 177). In *Process and Reality,* he suggests that the extensive continuum is a property specifically of the contemporary world.

> Our direct perception of the contemporary world is thus reduced to exten-
> sion, defining (i) our own geometrical perspectives, and (ii) possibilities of
> mutual perspectives for other contemporary entities *inter se,* and (iii)
> possibilities of division. These possibilities of division constitute the ex-
> ternal world a continuum. (PR 61–62)

Extension here is associated with perception in the mode of presentational immediacy, thereby a property relevant specifically to the contemporary world. From this point of view, space and time are not equivalent modes of extension.[2] Geometrical perspectives are fundamental to the mode of presentational immediacy, but not to the mode of togetherness of actual entities in succession, which is based on causal prehension. There is an extensiveness which follows from the cosmological principle and which defines a togetherness of occasions above and beyond their causal relations. There is an extensiveness which is definitive of perspectivity, which defines the location of every occasion relative to other occasions, and which must involve a temporal, or successive, as well as a spatial component. There is also a geometrical extensiveness which pervades the contemporary world and which is exhibited in presentational immediacy. It would appear that the "spatio-temporal continuum," mentioned above as the extensive field in which we locate events in perception and by natural laws, is not the generalized continuum that is essential to the perspectival becoming of actual entities. Whitehead tells us that "in an organic philosophy of nature there is nothing to decide between the old hypothesis of the uniqueness of the time discrimination and the new hypothesis of its multiplicity. It is purely a matter for evidence drawn from observations" (SMW 171). The implication is that relativistic time is at a lesser degree of generality, relevant specifically to our cosmic epoch, than the successiveness and extensiveness that define the metaphysical conditions of creativity. There are different fields of extension, related as genus to species, which manifest different modes of relatedness among occasions. The extensive continuum, as a ground for concrescence, is not temporal in the same way it is spatial, though the two are closely related in relativistic physics. The connectedness of time and space in relativistic space-time is a social property of our epoch, but not an extensive condition of all epochs. In general terms, involving location, the extensive continuum is both spatial and temporal and objectifies both spatial and temporal relations; but in addition, becoming is atomically temporal or durational. The extensive continuum and temporal duration must be distinguished. Togetherness in extensive connection is essential to Whitehead's theory, since a unison of becoming is required for the self-determination and freedom of individual occasions, thereby establishing the causal independence of contemporaries. Relativistic physics cannot provide a sufficiently strong form of extensive togetherness. Simultaneity in the theory of relativity is a function of inertial frames of reference. What is at stake, I suggest, is the priority of the cosmological principle over the principle of perspective. I will take up these matters in detail.

The Extensive Continuum

The extensive continuum serves two basic functions, providing a basis for the solidarity of the universe and defining standpoints for becoming. To Whitehead, both of these functions are indispensable.[3]

> It is by means of "extension" that the bonds between prehensions take on the dual aspect of internal relations, which are yet in a sense external relations. It is evident that if the solidarity of the physical world is to be relevant to the description of its individual actualities, it can only be by reason of the fundamental internality of the relationships in question. On the other hand, if the individual discreteness of the actualities is to have its weight, there must be an aspect in these relationships from which they can be conceived as external, that is, as bonds between divided things. The extensive scheme serves this double purpose. (PR 309)

This is why the extensive continuum plays so central a role in his system.[4] In addition, extensive continuity is deeply implicated in perception in the mode of presentational immediacy.[5] It is also specifically geometrical in its structure. I will consider each of these matters. Different levels of generality are involved, producing different specifications of extension. These must be carefully distinguished.

The Solidarity of the Universe. The second of the two assumptions which Whitehead tells us are presupposed in presentational immediacy is that

> the real potentialities relative to all standpoints are coordinated as diverse determinations of one extensive continuum. This extensive continuum is one relational complex in which all potential objectifications find their niche. It underlies the whole world, past, present, and future.... This extensive continuum expresses the solidarity of all possible standpoints throughout the whole process of the world. (PR 66)

We cannot overemphasize the comprehensiveness of this statement: it is *all* objectifications, *all* standpoints, that are conjoined by the extensive continuum into one relational system. The extensive continuum is one of the primary applications of the cosmological principle's requirement that a plurality of standpoints comprise a single universe through time. It is important to consider the implications of so strong a cosmological condition for the diversity of perspectives in Whitehead's system, including that of God. God alone cannot serve as the unifying ground of all occasions, neither in his primordial nor his consequent nature. The reason for this is none other than the irreducibility of the principle of perspective: many perspectives, even on a common world, where perspectivity includes both selection and novelty, require a uniform external ground of togetherness if they are *all* to be coordinated. Put another way, perspectivity entails togetherness but not *all*-togetherness. Indeed, it is incompatible with all-inclusiveness, which is the reason for many of Whitehead's difficulties with the extensive continuum. A supreme perspective would reduce the many perspectives to partiality, incomplete manifestations of the total perspective on the world. The all-inclusiveness of the extensive continuum is so unfounded a comprehensiveness in Whitehead's system that it seems to demand a unique category of existence for extension independent of all the other categories of existence.[6] The atomicity and perspectivity of becoming determine a multiplicity of occasions which are conjoined within one world only in virtue of the extensive continuum. Reversing the entailment, the extensive continuum expresses the unity of the entire world amidst a multiplicity of occasions. If they are all within one world, that world must be a constituent of each of them.[7]

I have discussed some of the difficulties involved in the cosmological principle. Yet it is essential to Whitehead's theory. And if the universe is unitary in any respects, there must be specific principles upon which that unification rests. By the principles of experience and perspective alone, there might be entities without relation to each other or subsystems with no unified role in the universe as a whole. The statistical hypothesis applied to the entire universe defines it to be a continuum in which particles move independently of each other, occasionally colliding. Every event is independent, yet even here we have a system. Each particle inhabits a specific location within the spatiotemporal universe, and its properties are in part defined by that location in relation to the system of natural laws. The statistical hypothesis, applied to the universe as a whole, can define traits of that universe only if we presuppose that the entire system of possible spatiotemporal relations among particles is well defined. Even here we have presupposed an extensive system that defines both a unified order of spatiotemporal relations and a location for each particle. Any deterministic system of natural laws presupposes an extensive system in which all possible locations are well defined. The extensive system is both spatial and temporal in every location. It may, however, be relativistic, rather than absolute.

The primary meaning of the solidarity of the universe in Whitehead's theory refers to the unity of events through time—that is, to the bonds between the actual world of a prehending subject and its own becoming. These bonds are the basis of the extensive continuum.

> Extensive relations express the conditions laid on the actual world in its function of a medium. . . . The "extensive" scheme is nothing else than the generic morphology of the internal relations which bind the actual occasions into a nexus, and which bind the prehensions of any one actual occasion into a unity, coordinately divisible. (PR 288)

Each occasion prehends the entire world given to it as initial datum. Such prehensive relations would appear to define an adequate basis for the unity of the world. "Any item of the universe, however preposterous as an abstract thought, or however remote as an actual entity, has its own gradation of relevance, as prehended, in the constitution of any one actual entity" (PR 148). Nevertheless, causal relations alone cannot provide solidarity among contemporary occasions, for the following reasons:

1. The assumption that the immediate past consists of a multiplicity of occasions, each of which is prehended by a succeeding occasion, in no way commits us to a unified community characterizing that past. The prehension does not unify past occasions *among themselves*. All that is required for prehension is that the prehending occasion be capable of synthesizing the prehensions given to it. It is sufficient that it have the

capacity to exclude incompatible elements.[8] If we take the night sky to be composed of stars, each of which is independent of all others, though each sends light to the earth, then the universe is *ex hypothesi* disunified; yet we can unify our view by focusing on some stars and ignoring others. What is revealed here is the constituting role of perspectival relations defining a synthetic unity amidst disunity by selectivity and exclusion. Prehension here establishes unity from a point of view that is not a cosmological unity among all occasions. The latter must be established on independent grounds—in Whitehead's theory, by the extensive continuum. I must emphasize that, by the principle of perspective, there is no unqualified unity, no cosmic unity, ony qualified unifications from some point of view. The perspectivity of the agent, with its qualified unifications, is the basis from which subsequent unifications emerge.

2. The prehension of the entire past as initial datum, if unqualified, entails no principle of differentiation among contemporary occasions. Each would arise from the same world and would differ only in its choices and supplementary feelings. However, we sense the truth of the principle that contemporary occasions differ by virtue of their specific distinguishing relations to events of the past. Whitehead provides a resolution of this matter by defining a general principle of relevance. "Some principle is now required to rescue actual entities from being undifferentiated repetitions, each of the other, with mere numerical diversity. This requisite is supplied by the 'principle of intensive relevance' " (PR 148). We require an inherent principle of differentiation in occasions in terms of which they prehend the past uniquely by exclusion. This is given by the notion of *standpoint*. Too strict a principle of causal inheritance, strong enough to guarantee the immediate past to be a unified system, would also transform the present into a seamless order without differentiation. The subjective aim cannot constitute such differential relevance in itself, but presupposes it. The relevance of different aims for contemporary occasions presupposes their incipient differentiation as a basis for their respective subjective aims. The cosmological princple's demand that occasions prehend the *entire* past, without exclusion, imposes a further demand for a system of differential locations or standpoints.

3. It is essential for the freedom of actual entities that "contemporary events happen in *causal* independence of each other" (PR 61). Occasions must be closed off against further prehension, leaving room for their self-determination. If contemporary occasions prehended each other mutually, there would be an infinite regress of mutual prehension, with no room for self-causation. It follows that causal independence in the

contemporary world is a fundamental principle of Whitehead's theory. He acknowledges the theory of relativity, which accepts the causal independence of contemporary events, but his reason for maintaining the independence of contemporary occasions is far more fundamental. The essential principle is that of subjective unity, which entails that an occasion may feel another only once, taking all direct and mediated feelings into account. If the contemporary world continued to add new aspects of feeling, no final unity could be achieved.

The mechanical principle of analysis is relevant here in conjunction with the cosmological principle and principle of experience. It is necessary for the self-causation of an occasion that it be closed off from other occasions, that there be a "space" for such self-determination. The force of the metaphor leads directly to an extensive system. Self-causation entails the individuality of occasions, but self-causation plus conformation entail closure and independence. What is fundamental is selection and perspective. If actual entities were indivisible drops without stages or phases, as they should be, if coordinate division were fundamentally unintelligible, then occasions would differ from each other by exclusion and selection and could comprise no world system without an external mode of connection. It would not be necessary for contemporary occasions to be independent of *all* other contemporary occasions, but only some of them, again by qualification and exclusion. Extension has the double role of providing for the unity of the world and the incipient differentiation in location of individual occasions. In this double role, it is a meeting place of the principle of perspective and the cosmological principle, and a continual source of tension and confusion in Whitehead's theory.

If the above account is correct, then the contemporary world cannot be unified through causal relations alone. Unless there is a unifying order that defines all contemporary actual entities as part of the same world, they may bear no universal relationship to each other. By the cosmological principle, each contemporary actual entity prehends the entire past, the same past, as initial datum; but even this cannot provide inclusive unity to the contemporary world, or even to the immediate past. The alternative is to define a unifying order pertaining to both the past and the contemporary world. The natural solution to this issue is given by the extensive continuum understood as primarily a spatial—if not geometrical—system, but spatiotemporal to the extent that it includes successive as well as spatial relations.[9] This system of spatiotemporal relations is intrinsic to, and therefore constitutive of, every occasion located in that system. "It has been usual, indeed universal, to hold that spatio-temporal relationships are external. This doctrine is what is here denied" (SMW 174).[10]

Perspective. The extensive continuum is the meeting place of the cosmological principle and the principle of perspective in which the principle of experience is subordinate. The extensive continuum defines the primary or incipient meaning of standpoint or location on the basis of which prehensions and subjective aims can play their role. It is in this very important sense that the extensive continuum underlies the principle of perspective. The concept of location here—location in a perspective—is fundamental and essential. Experience cannot be a sufficient basis for understanding perspective.

Prehensions are *vectoral*, feeling transmitted from one entity to another. If the datum of a prehension is an entity of the past or God, then it is well defined by the ontological principle. The datum is constituted in part by the subjectivity of the objectified entity. The question is how the prehending subject can be well defined when it exists only by virtue of its prehensions. This is one of the major difficulties inherent in Whitehead's principle of experience, and it can be fully resolved only by making individuality fundamental to occasions, thereby emphasizing the principle of perspective.[11] An occasion becomes by prehending and is nothing until it has prehended. How then is prehension to be initiated?

Both the mechanical principle of analysis and the principle of experience are factors in this issue. If there are stages, prior to the felt subjective aim, how are they differentiated among entities with a common past? What is the basis of individuation among the initial stages of different occasions' becomings? If we reject such a question as unintelligible, as based on an illegitimate division of an occasion into stages, the question then is simply how aims can function as lures for a wealth of potential entities unless one presupposes a principle of differentiation among them. Put another way, perspectives are both coordinated and limited. If, by the cosmological principle, neither the past nor God can provide differentiating conditions for contemporary occasions, then another such differential field must be presupposed. The alternative is to abandon the totalistic cosmological principle. Perspectives would then be differentiated in every feature by selection, limitation, and exclusion. If inheritance were always qualified perspectivally by limitation and exclusion, extensive differentiation would not be needed. But then cosmological unification would be rejected, and that is the other major purpose of the extensive continuum. Location in a perspective would become the general notion required, and there would be no all-inclusive perspective—a cosmological role played by God and the extensive continuum in different ways.

Whitehead provides two elements to ground the initiation of an occasion: the initial stages of the subjective aim, which he claims are derived from God, and the unique location of the occasion. The former is a pervasive and therefore undifferentiated condition. The latter is realized through the extensive continuum. Every occasion has within it, and essential to it, an extensive location in terms of which its prehensions are constituted as vectors of differentiated feeling, and through which it is in solidary relationship with all other occasions, including those in its contemporary world.[12]

The first "metaphysical assumption" which is presupposed in any account of presentational immediacy is that

> relatively to any actual entity, there is a "given" world of settled actual entities and a "real" potentiality, which is the datum for creativeness beyond that standpoint. . . . We have always to consider two meanings of potentiality: (a) the "general" potentiality, which is the bundle of possibilities, mutually consistent or alternative, provided by the multiplicity of eternal objects, and (b) the "real" potentiality, which is conditioned by the data provided by the actual world. General potentiality is absolute, and real potentiality is relative to some actual entity. (PR 65)

The key reference here is to a standpoint or perspective. There is no actual world except from a perspective; no prehension except from a standpoint; no datum except for an occasion from its standpoint. If the extensive continuum is real as against general potentiality, then it is a function of past actual worlds. Perspectivity here is propositional, a meeting place between the pure potentiality of eternal objects and the social togetherness of the past.

The extensive continuum defines a system of extensive relations comprising both unique locations and regional relations. The problem for Whitehead is to define the minimal and most general conditions for such a continuum.[13]

> This extensive continuum expresses the solidarity of all possible standpoints throughout the whole process of the world. It is not a fact prior to the world; it is the first determination of order—that is, of real potentiality—arising out of the general character of the world, In its full generality beyond the present epoch, it does not involve shapes, dimensions,

or measurability; these are additional determinations of real potentiality arising from our cosmic epoch. (PR 66)

There is a double movement in the way Whitehead understands the extensive continuum. It is a generalized relation for all becoming—"the solidarity of all possible standpoints throughout the whole process of the world." It is also relative to and located within particular conditions in the world. Even in its full generality, it arises "out of the general character of the world." At the greatest level of generality, metrical relations are not included, for they are constants of our physical universe and arbitrary, from a metaphysical point of view.[14] They might be different for an epoch with different dominant societies. The general character of extensiveness that Whitehead is seeking to define is relevant to *all* epochs, to *all* types of social order. It is a cosmological character of the entire universe throughout space and time. It presupposes that the entire universe through time comprises one all-encompassing society. What is of general importance are the "relationships of whole to part, and of overlapping so as to possess common parts, and of contact, and of other relationships derived from these primary relationships" (PR 66). These relationships must be maintained throughout all regions of space and time. They would appear, as locating conditions, to have both geometrical and temporal, or successive, character.[15]

It is interesting that Whitehead never considers the possibility that standpoints may not all be extensive in even a generalized sense, that the limitations of metrical relations to our epoch may be an expression of the limitations of extensive relations in general. For example, numbers are located and locating, perspectival in their wealth of relational yet individualizing elements. They are not, of course, prehensive. Eternal objects are perspectival—in a generalized sense—to the extent that their individual essences are related to their relational essences. Only some perspectives are extensive—those Whitehead considers experiential and actual. There is considerable plausibility to the view that *events* can be perspectival only within a system of extensive relations (though not to the view that such a system must be all-inclusive). What is not shown by such an approach is whether extensiveness is a defining condition of perspectivity in general, or of only eventhood and prehension.[16] The question, from the standpoint of the principle of perspective, is of determining the most general conditions of perspectival location, for any and all perspectives, any and all modes of being, not events alone.

As I have shown, Whitehead's goal is to define standpoints or perspectives in connection. He does this in terms of general notions of connection, sets of connected regions, and generalized straight lines, in a cosmological context.[17] By a generalized version of projective geometry, he defines both points and lines of projection, aiming at the greatest possible generality.[18] Nevertheless, he also discusses "external connection": the specific property of regions which are connected but do not overlap. In our epoch, physical laws are represented by continuous functions—that is, properties of regions are also properties of regions connected with them. This, Whitehead tells us, is not necessarily true. What is necessary is that the relationship of external connection must be well defined in terms of general extensive relations. Two regions that are externally connected remain externally connected through all projections. Two regions externally connected from one standpoint remain externally connected from any other standpoint derived from the first by projections of straight lines. External connection is a fundamental property of our epoch, relative to the structure of natural laws, but potentially also in all epochs, a defining condition of general extensiveness. In particular, however, any property that is a function of external connection alone will define a natural law that may be referred to any prehending occasion. External connection is the property that mediates from the general conditions of perspective to those conditions definitive of extension in our understanding of natural laws. Whitehead's ability to make such connections is one of the greatest of his achievements, despite the confusions produced by his discussions of extension simultaneously at different levels of generality.

> This perceptive mode has overwhelming significance. It exhibits that complex of systematic mathematical relations which participate in all the nexūs of our cosmic epoch, in the widest meaning of that term. These relations only characterize the epoch by reason of their foundation in the immediate experience of the society of occasions dominating that epoch. Thus we find a special application of the doctrine of the interaction between societies of occasions and the laws of nature. . . .
> It is by reason of this disclosure of ultimate system that an intellectual comprehension of the physical universe is possible. There is a systematic framework permeating all relevant fact. By reference to this framework the variant, various, vagrant, evanescent details of the abundant world can have their mutual relations exhibited by their correlation to the common terms of a universal system. (PR 327)

The quest for general principles of connection is entirely compatible with the principle of perspective; the demand for "a systematic framework permeating all relevant fact" is cosmological, nonperspectival, effectively absolute, and unconditioned.

Duration

The extensive continuum is defined in terms of points and straight lines. Time also may be viewed as extensive, and instants as well as successions of time analyzed extensively. The system of locations essential to concrescence must be both spatial—quasi-geometrical—and temporal—based on a principle of succession. "The passage of the cause into the effect is the cumulative character of time. The irreversibility of time depends on this character" (PR 237). But, Whitehead tells us, we must avoid "spatializing" time. Time is *epochal*.

> The actual entity is the enjoyment of a certain quantum of physical time. But the genetic process is not the temporal succession: such a view is exactly what is denied by the epochal theory of time. Each phase in the genetic process presupposes the entire quantum, and so does each feeling in each phase. (PR 283)

Time is not actually continuous, though we may indefinitely divide actual entities coordinately, thereby moving into abstraction. I have suggested that this unqualified divisibility is a consequence of mechanical analyzability and has generated enormous confusion concerning Whitehead's meaning. Actual entities are not divided in concrescence, but their objectifications can theoretically be infinitely divided both spatially and temporally. What is suggested is that regions and divisibility do not belong to occasions *in* concrescence but only *after* concrescence, from some other standpoint, as a function of their togetherness with other occasions.[19]

> Objective identity requires integration of the many feelings of one object into the one feeling of that object. The analysis of an actual entity is only intellectual, or, to speak with a wider scope, only objective. Each actual entity is a cell with atomic unity. But in analysis it can only be understood as a process; it can only be felt as a process, that is to say, as in passage. The actual entity is divisible; but is in fact undivided. The divisibility can thus only refer to its objectifications in which it transcends itself. But such transcendence is self-revelation. (PR 227)

It follows that neither genetic nor coordinate analysis can be applied without qualification to concrescence, although the only understanding we may have of concrescence is through genetic analysis. This leads to the mechanical principle of analysis. Yet the qualifications profoundly reflect the principle of perspective.

We may return to the passages with which this chapter began: "There can be no continuity of becoming" (PR 35), but "extensive continuity is a special condition arising from the society of creatures which constitute our immediate epoch" (PR 36). Grave difficulties are posed by these remarks unless we interpret the continuity involved in different senses and do not equate "extensive continuity" with the extensive continuum. This last distinction seems perverse. But how else are we to understand Whitehead's claim that extensive continuity is a special condition of our epoch? The extensive continuum is a general condition necessary to all occasions. There are different kinds, or levels, of extensive continuity, of differing generality, and there is a continuity throughout *all* becoming as well as a continuity produced by social conditions in a particular epoch. It is essential that we be able to connect these notions intelligibly. A perspectival solution is natural: occasions are divisible in some respects and indivisible in others; becoming is continuous from some standpoints and discontinuous from other standpoints. However, this is not the solution Whitehead seems to accept.

He speaks of the "extensive continuity of the physical universe" (PR 35). This refers in part to the infinite divisibility of events, but it refers to a much stronger condition. Infinite divisibility can be provided by a continuum of rational numbers. In fact, the continuum we employ in physics is one of real numbers, a "dense" continuum. Whitehead's theory of events is atomistic—primarily to allow for self-determination. Yet the space and time of physics are infinitely and densely divisible. Even the indivisibility of quantum-mechanical events must be compatible with an infinitely divisible mathematical continuum.

Whitehead gives several arguments for the epochal theory of time, two of which are, I think, most important. One argument is derived from Zeno's paradox of the arrow in flight.

The argument, so far as it is valid, elicits a contradiction from the two premises: (i) that in a becoming something (*res vera*) becomes, and (ii) that every act of becoming is divisible into earlier and later sections which are themselves acts of becoming. Consider, for example, an act of becoming during one second. The act is divisible into two acts, one during the earlier half of the second, the other during the later half of the second. Thus that which becomes during the whole second presupposes that which becomes during the first half-second. Analogously, that which becomes during the first half-second presupposes that which becomes during the first quarter-second, and so on indefinitely. Thus if we consider the process of becoming up to the beginning of the second in question, and ask what then becomes, no answer can be given. For, whatever creature we indicate presupposes an earlier creature which became after the beginning of the second and antecedently to the indicated creature. Therefore there is nothing which becomes, so as to effect a transition into the second in question. (PR 68)

Whitehead fully agrees that an infinite number of acts of becoming may take place in a finite time if each subsequent act is smaller in a convergent series. There is no fallacy involved in the conception of acts of becoming that diminish in duration in a convergent series. There is no intrinsic or minimal size to events. But to Whitehead, there is a fallacy involved in conceiving of *one* act of becoming as divisible into an *infinite number* of smaller acts: the need to specify *what* becomes makes such an act unintelligible. If the process of an arrow flying through the air is to be subdivided into smaller and smaller intervals, each of which involves the arrow in flight, then we cannot connect the motion at the end of one second with the motion at the beginning of the next. What is needed is a clear criterion of *succession*. Moreover, "the difficulty is not evaded by assuming that something becomes at each non-extensive instant of time. For at the beginning of the second of time there is no next instant at which something can become" (PR 68). Either becoming is not infinitely divisible and the measurement of time is impaired, or becoming is so divisible, but not into *acts* or *events*.

Whitehead's solution is that "in every act of becoming there is the becoming of something with temporal extension; but that the act itself is not extensive, in the sense that it is divisible into earlier and later acts of becoming which correspond to the extensive divisibility of what has become" (PR 69). Actual entities may be divided, but their further division produces no smaller acts of becoming. An actual occasion is irreducible in this sense.

The second argument is based on causal inheritance. An event can either inherit from an earlier event by reproduction or it can change by deviation. But it is impossible to understand *both* causal inheritance and freedom in the same event unless it occupies a duration.[20]

I have explained Whitehead's claim that "if we admit that 'something becomes,' it is easy, by employing Zeno's method, to prove that there can be no continuity of becoming" (PR 35). What requires closer examination is the claim that "there is a becoming of continuity." It is surely not true that the extensive continuum becomes, for it is a general precondition of every becoming and appears to undergo no modifications. Furthermore, it is not true that the extensive continuum as such "is a special condition arising from the society of creatures which constitute our immediate epoch" (PR 36). The extensive continuum defines every standpoint for every becoming, in all epochs. Nevertheless, it cannot be unconditioned by becoming, for it would then be a pure, not a real, potentiality.

As I have noted, there are two senses of extensive continuity, which correspond respectively, I believe, to extensiveness as a *potentiality* for division and the world as *actually* an extensive continuity. The sense of "potentiality" here is that of eternal objects on the one hand—"pure" potentiality—and of propositions on the other—the "real" potentiality. (note quotation on p. 178.) The geometrical patterns exemplified in extensive connection are first of all complex eternal objects in the primordial nature of God. "The quantum is that standpoint in the extensive continuum which is consonant with the subjective aim in its original derivation from God" (PR 283). They are eternal objects of the "objective species."

> An eternal object of the objective species . . . is always, in its unrestricted realization, an element in the definiteness of an actual entity, or a nexus, which is the datum of a feeling belonging to the subject in question. . . . Eternal objects of the objective species are the mathematical Platonic forms. They concern the world as a medium. (PR 291)

They are relevant to particular actual worlds by propositional relevance: hybrids of physical prehension and conceptual valuation. Put another way, nexūs and social order in the past actual world constitute a basis for the ingression of certain specific extensive patterns, including those particular geometrical and spatiotemporal patterns found in our cosmic epoch. But more generally, Whitehead holds, the social order of the universe as a whole, for *any* actual world, must be based on general potentials of definiteness, geometrical but not metrical, topological or algebraic perhaps, which define the general conditions of extensive connection. In this sense, the extensive continuum is a condition of all becoming, but it is a real potential expressive of a general condition of actuality, not a mere, or pure, potential found in the primordial nature of God alone. The principle of perspective here is prominent: extensiveness is conditioned by occasions in their social relations, in actual worlds.

> When we divide the satisfaction coordinately, we do not find feelings which *are* separate, but feelings which *might be* separate. In the same way, the divisions of the region are not divisions which *are*: they are divisions which *might be*. . . .
> The notion has reference to three allied doctrines. First, there is the doctrine of "the actual world" as receiving its definition from the immediate

concrescent actuality in question. Each actual entity arises out of its own peculiar actual world. Secondly, there is the doctrine of each actual world as a "medium." ...

Thirdly, it is to be noticed that "decided" conditions are never such as to banish freedom.... There are alternatives as to ... determination, which are left over for immediate decision. ... These alternatives are represented by the indecision as to the particular quantum of extension to be chosen for the basis of the novel concrescence. (PR 284)

This extensive divisibility is the meeting place of the principle of perspective and the cosmological principle. Every possible location in both space and time has to be included in some way in the extensiveness of becoming if perspectivity throughout the universe is to be well defined.

The order of nature, prevalent in the cosmic epoch in question, exhibits itself as a morphological scheme involving eternal objects of the objective species.... These eternal objects express the theory of extension in its most general aspect. In this theory the notion of the atomicity of actual entities, each with its concrescent privacy, has been entirely eliminated. We are left with the theory of extensive connection. (PR 292)

There are two different levels of generality, with two distinct types of extensiveness, involved in Whitehead's analysis. They are closely related, since the particularity of one is but the manifestation of the other with respect to the social conditions of our epoch, while the second is a manifestation of the first at a cosmological level of generality. Perspectivity permeates both levels and is the basis of their connection. Nevertheless, one manifests specific conditions of our physical laws, the other manifests conditions essential to the social togetherness of all occasions through time.[21]

It is in this connection the morphological scheme of extensiveness attains its importance. In this way we obtain an analysis of the dative phase in terms of the "satisfactions" of the past world. These satisfactions are systematically disposed in their relative status, according as *one* is, or is not, in the actual world of *another*. Also they are divisible into prehensions which can be treated as quasi-actualities with the same morphological system of relative status. This morphological system gains special order from the defining characteristic of the present cosmic epoch. The extensive continuum is the specialized ordering of the concrete occasions and the prehensions into which they are divisible. (PR 293)

Extension here defines the most general properties of events in prehensive causal relation. In effect, Whitehead is seeking to demonstrate the *necessity* of extensive relations to prehensive succession. The goal is, of course, cosmological. It involves a proof that a pure geometry can be applicable to all actual conditions. The demonstration and the premise are questionable. More important, the most general properties of *perspectives*, in a more general sense than that of successive events, are by no means obviously extensive, even in a generalized sense. The two levels of generality are thoroughly confused.

In discussing mediate and direct causal inheritance, Whitehead claims that, "provided that physical science maintains its denial of 'action at a distance,' the safer guess is that direct objectification is practically negligible except for contiguous occasions; but that this practical negligibility is a characteristic of the present cosmic epoch, without any metaphysical generality" (PR 308). Causal inheritance as we know it is direct only between connected regions; disconnected regions are related indirectly, mediated by the regions between them. There is then a special sense of continuity involved in direct objectification. Events in contiguous regions are directly objectified in each other, and they influence each other more than regions remote from each other. This principle is inherent in all physical laws defined by continuous functions of position. It manifests the particular importance I have noted of extensive connection in the physical laws of our epoch. It cannot, however, be of metaphysical generality in a system in which events prehend the entire past universe directly, or even the entire immediate past. Geometrical connectedness in the narrow sense might be of scientific importance only in our epoch. The continuity in our natural laws is not of metaphysical generality.[22]

The close connection between the two levels of generality of extension, and the difficulties of mathematical generalization, make the determination of the extensive relationships that are of metaphysical generality extremely difficult, if not impossible. "It is difficult to draw the line distinguishing characteristics so general that we cannot conceive any alternatives, from characteristics so special that we imagine them to belong merely to our cosmic epoch" (PR 288).[23] The necessity of the extensive continuum to becoming does not determine which features of extensive connection are of metaphysical generality, only that some must be.[24] Whitehead is convinced that "extensive relations do not make determinate *what* is transmitted; but they do determine conditions to which all transmission must conform. They represent the systematic scheme which is involved in the real potentiality from which every actual occasion *arises*" (PR 288). But the most that could be concluded from his analysis of extensive relations is that "some general character of coordinate divisibility is probably an ultimate metaphysical character, persistent in every cosmic epoch of physical occasions. Thus some of the simpler characteristics of extensive connection, as here stated, are probably such ultimate metaphysical necessities" (PR 288). The word "probably" is to be taken quite seriously.[25]

> For our epoch, extensive connection with its various characteristics is the fundamental organic relationship whereby the physical world is properly described as a community. There are no important physical relationships outside the extensive scheme. To be an actual occasion in the physical world means that the entity in question is a relatum in this scheme of extensive connection. In this epoch, the scheme defines what is physically actual.
>
> The more ultimate side of this scheme, perhaps that side which is metaphysically necessary, is at once evident by the consideration of the mutual implication of extensive whole and extensive part. If you abolish the whole, you abolish its part; and if you abolish any part, then *that* whole is abolished. (PR 288)

We may consider the possibility that no *extensive* relations are of such metaphysical generality, since they presuppose what they would establish: the generality of extensiveness throughout all perspectives and standpoints. A generalization of the principle of perspective entails the limitation of all perspectives based on extension, even in its most general forms. At the metaphysical level of generality, setting extension aside, the whole-part relation, as described above by Whitehead, comes very close to a principle of perspective, but its geometrical character is no longer prominent. Moreover, at this level of generality, relevant to all perspectives, it does not provide conditions for the cosmological unification of all perspectives into one all-encompassing universe.

The extensive continuum, though it defines perspectives essential to becoming, does not include within it the notion of becoming.

> The notion of nature as an organic extensive community omits the equally essential point of view that nature is never complete. It is always passing beyond itself. This is the creative advance of nature. Here we come to the problem of time. (PR 289)

Time is problematical in that, on the one hand, it has reference to the extensive continuum which defines spatial and temporal perspectives for becoming, and on the other, it refers to becoming itself and the transcendence of the scheme of real potentiality. This doubling, especially involving transcendence, is perspectival. The permanence of the extensive continuum is unfathomable, given its dependence on events, and thoroughly nonperspectival.

Becoming is atomic; but it must be possible for what becomes to be analyzed within a continuum of extensive relations. Whitehead represents this distinction in terms of "physical time" and concrescence. "Every actual entity is 'in time' so far as its physical pole is concerned, and is 'out of time' so far as its mental pole is concerned" (PR 248). Each occasion is actually—during the process of concrescence—a "quantum" of physical and spatial extension. But each occasion is potentially divisible indefinitely in coordinate analysis after the fact. Time has a double meaning in Whitehead's system: that given by succession and transcendence, a fundamental expression of creativity; and that inherent in the extensiveness necessary to concrescence, a system of locations.[26] Time is thus thoroughly perspectival, located and locating, but also transcendent.

Whitehead's conception of the extensive continuum is of a scheme of *real potentiality*. The world is actually atomic but potentially a continuum. I have explained what sense of potentiality is involved here, relating it to the potentiality of eternal objects and propositions, not to possible operations or sense-perception.[27] "Potentiality" in Whitehead is relative to actual entities: something is potential and not actual relative to acts of concrescence, a factor in concrescence but not the concrescence itself.[28] What is actual is the concrescence in becoming, in particular its subjective unity.

> The concrescence presupposes its basic region, and not the region its concrescence. Thus the subjective unity of the concrescence is irrelevant to the divisibility of the region. In dividing the region we are ignoring the subjective unity which is inconsistent with such division. But the region is, after all, divisible, although in the genetic growth it is undivided. (PR 283–84)[29]

This joint divisibility and indivisibility seems self-contradictory. I am arguing that it reflects a partial understanding of the multiple nature of perspectivity, a notion only weakly captured by the distinction between actuality and potentiality. "When we divide the satisfaction coordinately, we do not find feelings which *are* separate, but feelings which *might be* separate. In the same way, the divisions of the region are not divisions which *are*; they are divisions which *might be*" (PR 284). I have interpreted this duality perspectivally: actual entities are divisible in some respects and indivisible in others, and they are indivisible relative to their self-determination, concrescence, and subjective experience. Nevertheless, we must be told how to coordinate atomic and undivided regions with the continuum that is potentially realizable within them in relation to particular social conditions. This is one of the functions of the method of extensive abstraction.

Many of the confusing passages in Whitehead's discussion concerning the divisibility of concrescence into stages stem from his mechanical view of analyzability, so that he is led to phases that are both separable and inseparable. The subjective aim is a factor in every constituent of a concrescence, thereby unifying all phases inseparably, from the occasion's point of view. Yet this subjective aim does not unify what *was* separate, but constitutes unity as an irreducible element of concrescence. Even the self-causation of every occasion is treated as a phase or stage, subsequent to causal prehension and part of reversion. Yet it is clearly a component of the subjective aim and a factor in its unity. By the principle of perspective, the interpenetration of multiplicity and unity is an irreducible element in every being, a defining characteristic of perspectivity. The principle of experience, when coupled with the principle of analysis, erroneously suggests stages in experience. There are no stages in concrescence, for it occurs completely, all at once, its synthesis and its multiplicity complementary and coordinate. The epochal theory of time is a perspectival, not an absolute, theory of time. The analysis of occasions into multiplicity is an analysis of perspective from one side only, the constitutive side. It cannot accommodate the full force of the principle of perspective.

The Presented Duration

Whitehead defines three nexūs of occasions for an actual entity as follows:

(i) The nexus of *M*'s contemporaries, defined by the characteristic that *M* and any one of its contemporaries happen in causal independence of each other.

(ii) Durations including *M*; any such duration is defined by the characteristic that any two of its members are contemporaries. (It follows that any member of such a duration is contemporary with *M*, and thence that such durations are all included in the locus (i). The characteristic property of a duration is termed "unison of becoming.")

(iii) *M*'s presented locus, which is the contemporary nexus perceived in the mode of presentational immediacy, with its regions defined by sensa. (PR 125–26)

Nexūs (i) and (ii) are defined in causal terms. The first is comprised of all the contemporaries of a given occasion. A duration, however, consists of occasions that are *mutually* contemporary, so that none can influence any of the others. They occur together. This is necessary if there is to be a creative advance that allows for freedom.[30] "No occasion can be both in the past and in the future of a duration. Thus a duration forms a barrier in the world between its past and its future" (PR 322). In classical physics, nexūs (i) and (ii) are identical: contemporaneity is a transitive relation. It is not transitive in relativistic physics, however, where the velocity of light represents a maximal rate of causal influence. Two events may be unable to influence a third (if distant enough) but be themselves in causal relation. (I am neglecting the different accelerations and velocities of the relevant systems.) Nexus (ii) has a fundamental metaphysical significance in Whitehead's theory; nexus (i) does not, but it is important for distinguishing classical from relativistic theories.

In addition to the first two nexūs, defined in causal terms, there must be another mode of relation among contemporary occasions, if they are to comprise a single system. Extension is the ground of unification of contemporary entities that are both perspectival and causally independent. We have, then, two distinct loci—(ii) and (iii)—one defined in terms of causal independence, the other defined in terms of geometrical relations to the percipient body.

> Perception in the mode of presentational immediacy solely depends upon the "withness" of the "body," and only exhibits the external contemporary world in respect to its systematic geometrical relationship to the "body." (PR 333)

> A strain-locus is defined by the "projectors" which penetrate any one finite region within it. Such a locus is a systematic whole, independently of the actualities which may atomize it. In this it is to be distinguished from a "duration" which does depend on its *physical content*. A strain-locus depends merely upon its *geometrical content*. This geometrical content is expressed by any adequate set of "axioms" from which the systematic interconnections of its included straight lines and points can be deduced. (PR 330)

We have a temporal duration, or unison of becoming, associated with any individual occasion. We also have a geometrical locus of elements related by straight-line projections to a region associated with individual occasions. One of these is based on causal relations, the other

directly on the extensive continuum. Each is also grounded on a particular mode of prehension: causal objectification or presentational
immediacy. The separation of these loci, a unison of becoming from
geometrical relations, is nonperspectival, required by the absolute independence of contemporary occasions demanded by Whitehead's
theory of self-causation, on the one hand, and the absolute unification of
contemporary occasions by the cosmological principle, on the other.

In part IV of *Process and Reality*, Whitehead identifies the presented
locus of an occasion with its "strain-locus." It, and the durations which
include that occasion as a member, are defined independently. The nexus
of contemporary occasions, defined by causal independence, and the
nexus of occasions related geometrically by straight lines projected
through all points in the region of an occasion, do not in general coincide.
It is, however, a common conception of our cosmic epoch that the
presented locus is associated with a particular duration. "It is an
empirical fact that mankind invariably conceives the presented world as
consisting of such a duration. This is the contemporary world as
immediately perceived by the senses. But close association does not
necessarily involve unqualified identification" (PR 323). Duration and
geometrical extension rest on distinct principles, in Whitehead's theory,
though they are unified through the cosmological principle as part of one
extensive system inclusive of all events. Duration is based on causation
and succession; the presented locus is based on geometrical projection.
The two are coordinated into one system of extensive divisibility,
definitive of our cosmic epoch. The defining conditions of perspectival
standpoints are transformed by local conditions into a metric system of
extensive relations. This identification is an example of the limited
conditions of extension associated with the natural laws of our epoch, in
contrast with the more general conditions of extension for all epochs.[31]
Nevertheless, the identification of contemporaneity, in both perception
and scientific explanation, with geometrical elements in our epoch
requires an explanation based on more general principles. This is one of
Whitehead's reasons for rejecting the generality of the theory of
relativity. The entire dispute is a reflection of the limitations of
Whitehead's understanding of perspective, for according to that
principle, the identification of duration and geometrical extension must
be limited and qualified, relevant to certain perspectives and not others.

The distinctness of duration and the presented locus, in Whitehead's
theory, is in part due to his desire to provide a theory of perception
explanatory of the salient features of classical empiricism—the
impression and sense-data theories of Locke and Hume, for example. Yet

the distinction is also based on metaphysical principles, as I have indicated, and is the reason for Whitehead's rejection of relativistic
physics, which systematically associates the presented locus with a particular duration.[32] Einstein's association of space and time is effectively
nonperspectival; Whitehead's alternative, however, is equally nonperspectival.

Whitehead concedes that empirical evidence suggests the legitimacy
of identifying a set of mutually contemporary occasions with the locus
defined by straight-line projections through points within a region—in
effect, coordinating spatial perspectives and temporal location.[33] But
he claims that such evidence is not of metaphysical generality.[34]
Duration—the unity and succession of concrescence—and extension are
distinct principles. Duration, unlike connection, is indivisible.[35] What
Whitehead must show is that the presented locus can be defined entirely
in terms of geometrical elements, and without reference to a duration.
He must separate succession and duration from the continuum of extension that constitutes the togetherness of contemporaries and the
ground of presentational immediacy.

> The objection to this doctrine of "presentational immediacy"—that it pre-
> supposes a definition of straight lines, freed from dependence on external
> actualities—has been removed by the production of such a definition in Ch.
> III. Of course the point of the definition is to demonstrate that the extensive
> continuum apart from the particular actualities into which it is atomized,
> includes in its systematic structure the relationships of regions expressed
> by straight lines. These relationships are *there* for perception. (PR 325)[36]

This leads to the method of extensive abstraction. In the present context,
it is simply a question of the conceptual independence of mathematics
from physics. The independence of contemporary occasions demands, by
the cosmological principle, that the presented locus be in principle
independent of causal relations.[37]

> In so far as straight lines can only be defined in terms of measurements,
> requiring particular actual occasions for their performance, the theory of
> geometry lacks the requisite disengagement from particular physical fact.
> The requisite geometrical forms can then only be introduced after
> examination of the particular actual occasions required for measurement.
> But the theory of "projection," explained above, requires that the definition
> of a complete straight line be logically prior to the particular actualities in
> the extensive environment. (PR 324)

It is worth emphasizing that, although the presented locus as defined by geometrical events alone is conceptually distinct from a duration defined by mutually contemporary occasions, the association of a presented locus and a particular duration (the "presented duration") follows from the nature of societies within our cosmic epoch. In this respect, Whitehead's theory is entirely perspectival. The properties of extensive connection are social patterns of togetherness at all levels of generality. Presented durations are real facts of experience for conscious percipients; this is the foundation of perception in the mode of presentational immediacy.[38] More generally, a presented duration is a real fact in the physical constitution of members of enduring objects. This explanation of the coordination of the presented locus with a particular duration in our experience is a manifestation of the principle of perspective in general, and of the particular type of perspective I consider most important in Whitehead's theory, that which lends itself to the most significant generalizations. The properties of our experienced world are a consequence of the general perspectival features embodied in social order, conjoined with the particular societies present in our cosmic epoch. The pervasiveness and importance of measurement in the physical sciences is a consequence of the prominence of presentational immediacy in giving information about contemporary events in a duration.

Whitehead argues that the strain locus of an occasion, if well-defined, is a locus within which the occasion is "at rest."

> The meaning of the term "rest" is the relation of an occasion to its strain-locus, if there be one. An occasion with no unified strain-locus has no dominating locus with which it can have the relationship of "rest." An occasion "rests" in its strain-locus. This is why it is nonsense to ask of an occasion in empty space whether it be "at rest" in reference to some locus. For, since such occasions have no strain-loci, the relationship of "rest" does not apply to them. (PR 319)

An occasion can be at rest only with respect to a locus that conveys no sense of change, unified through the various regions of the contemporary world.

> The regions, geometricized by the various strains in such an organism, not only lie in the contemporary world, but they coalesce so as to emphasize one unified locus in the contemporary world. This selected locus is penetrated by the straight lines, the planes, and the three-dimensional flat loci

associated with the strains. This is the "strain-locus" belonging to an occasion in the history of an enduring object. This occasion is the immediate percipient subject under consideration. Each such occasion has its one strain-locus which serves for all its strains. The focal regions of the various strains all lie within this strain-locus, and are in general distinct. But the strain-locus as a whole is common to all the strains. Each occasion lies in its own strain-locus. (PR 319)

All enduring objects possess such a locus—the presented duration —which defines what "at rest" means for them. The strain-locus is therefore a manifestation of social order. An occasion that is part of no enduring object has no unified character in reference to which to be at rest. Whitehead concludes that

spatialization is a real factor in the physical constitution of every actual occasion belonging to the life-history of an enduring object. For actual occasions in so-called "empty space," there is no reason to believe that any duration has been singled out for spatialization; that is to say, that physical perception in the mode of presentational immediacy is negligible for such occasions. (PR 321)

The strain-loci provide the systematic geometry with its homology of relations throughout all its regions; the duration share in the deficiency of homology characteristic of the physical field which arises from the peculiarities of the actual events. (PR 128)

One of the conclusions of this discussion is that occasions which are not members of enduring objects are not easily associated in durations via perception in the mode of presentational immediacy. The region of an occasion is not unequivocal and, in the clearest cases, is a function of social nexūs, not individual concrescences alone. This analysis provides, among other things, an explanation of why occasions are perceived by us only through the societies to which they belong.[39] It manifests the important principle inherent in perspectivity that the conditions which constitute perspectives—in this case, enduring objects—have pervasive and important ramifications, and that the pervasiveness of such conditions is what makes perspectives the foundation of natural order.

Extensive Abstraction

The method of extensive abstraction followed Whitehead throughout his career, improving with each volume he wrote. Yet it remains an enigma in his philosophy. It is closely related to the extensive continuum and to the different levels of generality of extensiveness to which Whitehead frequently refers in his discussions of space and time, but its peculiar application to these issues is never made entirely clear. This has led to remarkable confusion.[40] The method simply cannot fill some of the roles that have been proposed for it.[41] It is fundamentally a method of *abstraction*, to be interpreted in terms of role played by such abstraction in Whitehead's theory. It exhibits extensiveness as potentiality rather than actuality in the specific sense given to such terms in Whitehead's theory.

The method seems to aim at the definition of points and lines from regions. Whitehead tells us that "we have not defined either points, or lines, or areas; and that we propose to define them in terms of abstractive sets" (PR 298). The issue, however, is whether he can define points as he asserts he intends to, and just what he is defining them in terms of. This can be made clear only by considering the method in detail.

In Part IV of *Process and Reality*, Whitehead defines an "abstractive set" to be a set of regions such that, "(i) any two members of the set are such that one of them includes the other non-tangentially, and (ii) there is no region included in every member of the set" (PR 297–98). The second condition is required to establish convergence. He then defines sets that are *equivalent* (when they cover each other), and defines a *geometrical element* to be "a complete group of abstractive sets equivalent to each other, and not equivalent to any abstractive set outside the group" (PR 298–99). Geometrical elements—in particular, points and lines—are then defined as (or associated with) a system of equivalent abstractive sets. It is essential that there always be a smaller region included nontangentially in every given region of an abstractive set. The question is how Whitehead can ensure that there is no limit to the size of relevant regions and how he can ensure that the method of extensive abstraction produces a continuum, rather than merely a denumerably infinite system of points.[42]

The method is similar to one common in the foundations of mathematics for defining the real numbers in terms of the rationals. However, one cannot establish that sets of nested intervals converge without points to which they may converge. In other mathematical applications, nested intervals with well-defined point boundaries are assumed. Convergence may be postulated in terms of numbers or points already established in order to define other points or numbers. Whitehead presumably has no points at all in his system until he defines them.[43]

Much more important, Whitehead seems to be defining a point in terms of an infinite set of regions which contain each other. What do these regions represent—the regions associated with actual entities? [44] If so, then occasions include a given quantum of spatial and temporal extension, and cannot be further divided. Yet it is essential to Whitehead's method that abstractive sets contain members as small as desired. The method therefore cannot be used to derive the indefinite, dense divisibility of the continuum from the atomic actuality of the world. But if Whitehead is not trying to show that points or instants can be defined in terms of quanta of becoming, what is he doing?

I have touched on one fundamental purpose of extensive abstraction: to define geometrical points without reference to durations or time.

> The "method of extensive abstraction" developed in those [early] works was unable to define a "point" without the intervention of the theory of "duration." Thus what should have been a *property* of "durations" became the definition of a point. By this mode of approach the extensive relations of actual entities mutually external to each other were pushed into the background; though they are equally fundamental. (PR 287)

The method is an exercise in pure geometry. Whitehead separates the extensive continuum of the presented locus from the continuum of duration. The geometrical continuum represents the spatial perspectives within the contemporary world, at least for this epoch. This is a cosmological condition demanded by the causal independence of contemporary occasions in the context of unity imposed by the cosmological principle.[45] This geometrical continuum is distinct from the durations associated with acts of becoming. Whitehead argues that the relationship of extensive connection can serve to define a geometry, thus that a spatial geometry does not entail a theory of time as suggested by the theory of relativity. His view is that the theory of relativity—special and general—is too restricted in relating space and time. In addition, the general theory is arbitrary in its coordination of geometrical relations with paths of light.

There is a way to understand Whitehead's method of extensive abstraction that resolves most of the difficulties posed for it and that sharply clarifies its functions. I have mentioned the approach several times, and believe it gives the meaning and function of extensive abstraction Whitehead arrives at in his mature work as he moves away from an overemphasis on sense-perception and toward a greater concern with acts of becoming. I have been arguing that extensiveness is a real potentiality for all becoming, therefore that it is propositional in nature and derivative, on the one hand, from the primordial nature of God and, on the other, from the social character of actual worlds of actual occasions. Relative to eternal objects and the primordial nature of God, the geometrical patterns definitive of extension are complex eternal objects defining potential conditions of togetherness. These are comprised of what Whitehead calls eternal objects of the objective species—mathematical forms. These forms are the basis for a pure mathematics, independent of actual events.

> The order of nature, prevalent in the cosmic epoch in question, exhibits itself as a morphological scheme involving eternal objects of the objective species. The most fundamental elements in this scheme are those eternal objects in terms of which the general principles of coordinate division itself are expressed. These eternal objects express the theory of extension in its most general aspect. In this theory the notion of the atomicity of actual entities, each with its concrescent privacy, has been entirely eliminated. We are left with the theory of extensive connection, of whole and part, of points, lines, and surfaces, and of straightness and flatness. (PR 292)

These pure potentials become real potentials in conjunction with the social conditions in a given actual world grounded in the real experience of particular occasions.[46] We have here an answer to the ontological status of the extensive continuum: it is grounded in the first instance in the primordial nature of God and in the second instance in the experiences of actual occasions which comprise a common world.[47] This interpretation bridges the two different levels of generality of extensiveness: within a particular cosmic epoch and for all epochs comprising one world. The force of the cosmological principle in the second level is paramount.

A consequence of this analysis is that size does not pertain intrinsically to actual entities. It is rather a function of their social relations—a thoroughly perspectival point of view. This is why Whitehead never assigns even a theoretical size to occasions.[48] Nevertheless, in any actual world, an actual entity is associated particularly with a region defining its strain locus—a function of its social conditions.[49] Associated with any particular extensiveness in an actual world are two infinite, or continuous, patterns of extensiveness—one an infinite potentiality of diverse patterns of extension through the primordial nature of God, those forms of extension that *might* be relevant, and the other a particular but abstract extensive pattern that is a condition of all actual worlds, belonging to them by common inheritance. This interpretation gives a legitimate meaning to Whitehead's claim that becoming is actually atomic, but potentially divisible. The potentiality here is one of an infinite range of possibilities in the primordial nature of God, which is given real status by the actual world—but still a potential status, one of real potentiality. Divisibility is a function of actual entities in the aggregate, comprising nexūs; atomicity is a function of individual concrescence.

What this means in Whitehead's theory, it seems to me, is that the actual world is *not* infinitely *divided*, but is infinitely *divisible* into geometrical elements, based on the conditions that promote division. The method of extensive abstraction *exhibits* the nature of this divisibility; it does not create the divisions. The fact that actual entities have no particular size means that regions of any size can in principle be put in correspondence with actual occasions, in some actual world, though in no particular actual world will more than a relatively few sizes of regions be exemplified in the becoming of occasions. Sense-perception is of no particular importance here, except to manifest some of the most paramount extensive features of our cosmic epoch. Rather, the associated regions relative to particular occasions in our epoch are members of potential aggregates of regions, with no smallest member corresponding to patterns in the primordial nature of God. The method of extensive abstraction effectively coordinates infinite patterns in the primordial nature of God that have a fundamentally mathematical character with particular events and their social conditions. The method indicates the overlapping of geometrical regions—but not the overlapping of actual entities.[50] Another way of putting this is that very small regions, relative to our cosmic epoch, represent *lures* for feeling, but are not in fact to be felt in this epoch. This interpretation effectively explains Whitehead's claim that

> the loci of "unison of becoming" are only determinable in terms of the actual happenings of the world. But the conditions which they satisfy are expressed in terms of measurements derived from the qualification of actualities by the systematic character of the extensive continuum. (PR 128)[51]

The method of extensive abstraction serves, in *Process and Reality*, not to derive geometrical elements from sense-perception, but to coordinate the regions associated with acts of becoming, which may have *any* size but always have *some* size, with a dense geometrical continuum in which points and lines of nondenumerable density are exemplified as potentials in the primordial nature of God. Whitehead is, in effect, explaining how a potentially pure mathematics can have powerful applications in experience and becoming. Both points and regions are real, but the existence of one is a function of a complex abstractive pattern, while the other is a social condition of events. The method of extensive abstraction coordinates members of one pattern with members of the other actual conditions, and defines a method for exhibiting relations among different members of the mathematical pattern. The exact definition of a point is not fundamental. What is required, according to Whitehead, is a way of avoiding the assumption that points are actual—that is, that they correspond to something essential in a concrescence—while also avoiding the alternative assumption that they are unreal. The reality of potentiality is one of Whitehead's ways of expressing perspectivity.

The method of extensive abstraction is fundamentally a method of *abstraction*, in the sense in which eternal objects are abstract. It is motivated by Whitehead's requirement that actualities be drops of becoming, although points and lines are entirely *real*. The potentiality of extensive divisibility is a mathematical pattern inherent in the primordial nature of God and only incompletely exemplified in any particular nexus. Here the cosmological principle generates the difficulty of a totality requiring unconditioned resolution, and the principle of experience generates the need for a special method of coordination. Whitehead can never in fact demonstrate that some extensive conditions are unchanging throughout all epochs: the very notion that some such conditions obtain is cosmological. The suggestion I will offer is that a more plausible theory is given by making the primordial nature of God a function of actual conditions. As a consequence, the extensive continuum would not be timeless, but would fulfill its functions quite satisfactorily as exemplified in particular actual worlds and changing with them.

Similarly, if points and lines are taken to be real, and we relinquish the ontological and cosmological principles, so that this reality is not of a subordinate ontological status, then the method of extensive abstraction can be given a relatively straightforward interpretation. It simply provides coordinating definitions between a system of events and a system with a geometrical continuum.[52] It is straightforward to define regions in terms of points and lines—but such a geometrical definition cannot provide room for undivided becomings. What is specifically required is the reverse step: to assume a beginning in extended regions and to derive points from them—or better, to analyze points in terms of systems of regions. More accurately, what is required is to indicate the *complexity* of points in a system of complex events.[53] This complexity is a natural consequence of perspectivity, for simple and unextended points appear unconditioned and nonperspectival, effectively absolute. Both points and events are assumed here, though they are of very different ontological kinds. What is needed is a way of understanding how they are related. The construction of points from events and their associated regions is not a proof or definition of the existence of points, but a clue to their identity—to the conditions that constitute them. This kind of construction is a natural consequence of a functional and perspectival theory of identity.

Nevertheless this last interpretation is symmetric with respect to events and geometrical elements, and does not explain how the latter are more abstract. This question of abstractness is fundamental in Whitehead's theory, and must be examined in detail.

Notes to Chapter 7

1. The generality of the extensive continuum is so great that it appears to define a mode of relation independent of all other modes, based on cosmological principles of world unity. In their complex and intricate discussion of regional inclusion, John B. Cobb, Jr., and Donald Sherburne correctly recognize that the question of the uniqueness and necessity of the extensive continuum plays a pivotal role in their respective views on the necessity of God to Whitehead's theory (Sherburne 1971a, pp. 305–28; Cobb 1971; Sherburne 1971b; Cobb and Sherburne 1972). I hold that extensiveness is a double function of eternal objects of the objective species and the social character of the past universe, agreeing with Sherburne in this particular controversy. Whitehead's own language is indicative.

> In these general properties of extensive connection, we discuss the defining characteristic of a vast nexus extending far beyond our immediate cosmic epoch. It contains in itself other epochs, with more particular characteristics incompatible with each other. Then from the standpoint of our present epoch, the fundamental society in so far as it transcends our own epoch seems a vast confusion mitigated by the few, faint elements of order contained in its own defining characteristic of "extensive connection."

> Our logical analysis, in company with immediate intuition (*inspectio*), enables us to discern a more special society within the society of pure extension. This is the "geometrical" society. In this society those specialized relationships hold, in virtue of which straight lines are defined. (PR 97)

I mention the controversy as a prime example of the moving spirit behind much contemporary Whiteheadian scholarship, that of establishing and grounding adequate cosmological conditions (in God or space-time) rather than perspectival and selective conditions, including extension, which express functional relationships among different types and categories of beings.

2. According to Palter,

> Whitehead's basic assumption is that "time is a stratification of nature." Now, although the temporal stratification of nature in each individual experience may be unique, there is good reason to believe that this uniqueness does not extend to different experiences generally. (1960, p. 41)

Both the stratification of time and the variability Palter describes are, in relation to different occasions' experiences, to be distinguished from the homogeneity of geometrical relations that define togetherness among contemporary entities.

3. In Whitehead's earlier work, the locations of events are made fundamental to their eventhood, distinguishing them from objects (or later, eternal objects).

> The uniqueness of an event is constituted by its occupancy of a certain internally related spatio-temporal position with respect to all other events. It is this factor which places an event "in nature." Remove this factor of position and you have an object. (Shahan 1950, p. 15)

4. Yet, as indispensable as it is, it is not one of the categories of existence. One of the great gaps in Whitehead's theory is his failure to relate the extensive continuum precisely to the categories of existence relevant to it. I will indicate such relationships as precisely as I can, in particular, to certain patterns among complex eternal objects in the primordial nature of God as exemplified in nexūs of actual occasions comprising the actual world of an occasion, comprising complex geometrical propositions relevant to its becoming.

5. Confusing these two functions—ground of concrescence and element of presentational immediacy—has led to a variety of misunderstandings of the nature of Whitehead's theory of extension.

> Whitehead holds that we experience space-time as a continuum of potentialities. We perceive an actual spaciousness not as an infinity of individual existents, but as a potentiality of *heres* and *theres* unlimited in number. (Lowe 1966, pp. 81–82)

Presentational immediacy requires the extensive continuum, but it does not *display* it in all its generality. *Actual space* is always divided atomistically into becomings; *potential* extension is infinitely divisible, a continuum. "Continuity concerns what is potential; whereas actuality is incurably atomic" (PR 61). These matters are very difficult and are complicated by nonperspectivity.

6. Most of John Blyth's criticisms of Whitehead are obstinate and unfounded. Those related to the extensive continuum, however, are well taken,

largely because of the arbitrariness introduced into Whitehead's system by the cosmological principle.

> An extensive continuum which does express the solidarity of all possible standpoints cannot therefore be relative to any standpoint. It must be absolute. (Blyth 1941, p. 34) (See above, note 10, p. 112.)

However, Blyth confuses standpoints with experiences, the principle of perspective with the principle of experience, greatly weakening his criticisms, since absoluteness might be provided by God. By the principle of perspective, it is the *unconditioned* nature of the extensive continuum that is problematic—though in Whitehead's system that continuum is also essential as a ground of perspective (but not *total* perspectivity).

7. It is important to understand that the relevance of a common world to every actual standpoint is a type of *multiple location*. William Alston is correct when he suggests that

> The doctrine of simple location does not express an absolute, as opposed to a relativist, theory of space-time. It asserts, not that a natural entity occupies a spatio-temporal region independently of any relations it might have to other regions or the occupants thereof, but rather that it occupies this spatio-temporal region to the exclusion of *occupying* any other. (1951, p. 716)

More accurately, a particular location (and a particular size) belongs to occasions only in virtue of particular *social* relations. Nathaniel Lawrence is misleading when he claims that

> the denial of simple location is the assertion of neither multiple nor complex location; it is the assertion of complex ingression, of which *location* is one single feature. (1954, p. 236)

> The difficulty of simple location, then, lies in the error of supposing that in specifying the location of something we have concretely and adequately accounted for its presence in space-time. (1954, p. 235)

> For Whitehead there is nothing fallacious about saying that a bit of matter is simply located, provided that you recognize the limitations of not talking about something concrete. (1954, p. 238)

The fallacy of simple location is, as Lawrence notes, a form of the fallacy of misplaced concreteness. But as a consequence, location is not one of the actual and determinative properties of concrescence. More accurately, perspectivity entails multiple relevance in relation to a standpoint: *there* as relevant to *here*. The continuum is a system of standpoints. Location is therefore not only a deficient property, it is a complex one.

> Every actual entity in its relationship to other actual entities is in this sense somewhere in the continuum, and arises out of the data provided by this standpoint. But in another sense it is everywhere throughout the continuum; for its constitution

includes the objectifications of the actual world and thereby includes the continuum; also the potential objectifications of itself contribute to the real potentialities whose solidarity the continuum expresses. Thus the continuum is present in each actual entity, and each actual entity pervades the continuum. (PR 67)

8. See Kraus:

If it is the case that each actual occasion arises out of an actual world unique to it, how can actual worlds enter into subsequent concrescences as subordinate nexuses in the actual worlds of those entities? ... How can the atomic regions actualized in a superject be connected with other such regions? (1979, p. 135)

In other words, if each actual entity establishes a unique perspective on the past through selective causal prehension, how are these different perspectives unified? As Kraus points out, the extensive continuum is Whitehead's answer to this question.

9. Yet the naturalness of extensive relations in providing the most general conditions for the togetherness of actual entities is gainsaid by the presence of God, who is not extensively located. The principle of perspective entails that some general conditions of location and relation are necessary to perspectives, but these are not obviously extensive nor must they relate all perspectives. Indeed, the generality of the relations Whitehead is seeking makes their extensiveness quite implausible.

10. I am using passages from *Science and the Modern World* to support my interpretation of Whitehead's theory in *Process and Reality*, where they seem to me to do so. There are unquestionably important changes between *Science and the Modern World* and *Process and Reality*, but to go into them here would distract from my primary purpose, which is to indicate the importance and character of the principle of perspective in Whitehead's later theory, an importance that increases throughout his later thought.

11. See the detailed discussion above, in chapter 4, particularly the criticisms of Whitehead's theory by Gentry, Reck, and Whittemore, pp. 114.

12. This unique location of an occasion is itself perspectival, for it is neither unconditioned nor unqualified. An occasion is in one sense multiply located to the extent that many different locations are prehended by it, and that many different occasions in other locations prehend it. Locatedness is a necessary but extremely difficult property for Whitehead, and is one of the reasons for his variable views on the generality of the extensive continuum. (See discussion, above, of the views of Alston and Lawrence.) I will argue that the most effective interpretation of the method of extensive abstraction in *Process and Reality* depends on relinquishing the notion of a unique region associated with each occasion, a notion thoroughly incompatible with the principle that regions are derived from actual entities, not given to them.

13. "Extensive connection—the public interlocking of regions and subregions revealed in coordinate division—is the primary relationship among physical occasions and makes all other relations, both internal and external, possible." (Kraus 1979, p. 131)

14. Compare Palter:

The most general characteristics of the extensive continuum ... include indefinite divisibility and unbounded extension (either finite or infinite) but not shape or dimensionality or straightness or measurability; in our own particular epoch, on the other hand, the extensive continuum is a four-dimensional metrical manifold with three spatial dimensions and one temporal dimension. (1960, p. 110) (See also note 34, below)

15. "Extension is the most general complex of possible relatedness; it is the most general structure exhibited in common by actual entities" (Plamondon 1979, p. 31).

The physical world is bound together by a general type of relatedness which constitutes it into an extensive continuum. When we analyse the properties of this continuum we discover that they fall into two classes, of which one—the more special—presupposes the other—the more general. The more general type of properties expresses the mere fact of "extensive connection," of "whole and part," of various types of "geometrical elements" derivable by "extensive abstraction"; but excluding the introduction of more special properties by which straight lines are definable and measurability thereby introduced. (PR 96–97)

16. A trace of this insight is shown in Shahan's comments on the extensive continuum: "Surely the dreams and ambitions of a human being, which are inherited in causal efficacy, do not involve a geometrical structure in the inheritance itself" (1950, p. 95).

17. This emphasis on extension and perspective is to be found in Whitehead's work largely from the beginning.

Whitehead's limited view of experience exhibits these characteristics: (1) Experience is understood in objective terms, almost to the complete exclusion of subjective conditions. (2) As a consequence of this, the factors of "meaning," "significance," or "interpretation," in experience, are "given." (3) Because of the character of the extension analysis, this element of meaning, understood objectively, is reduced to the apprehension of spatio-temporal relations, which tend to be directly perceivable apart from objects. (4) The spatio-temporal relations between nature and the percipient are of greater importance, invariably entering into experience, and, to a marked extent, control the character of experience. (Shahan 1950, p. 34)

18. Such generality cannot avoid limitation, for determinateness is limitation. This is a fundamental principle of perspectivity. Shahan is therefore simply wrong when he makes the following claim:

There is a passage in Part IV of *Process and Reality* ... in which the extensive continuum is discussed in terms of the conditions it lays on the world.... The general conclusion of the discussion, however, is that the extensive continuum probably does not possess any formal properties which are such to limit the world. (1950, p. 116)

What Whitehead says is:

These extensive relations do not make determinate *what* is transmitted; but they do determine conditions to which all transmission must conform. . . . Some general character of coordinate divisibility is probably an ultimate metaphysical character, persistent in every cosmic epoch of physical occasions. Thus some of the simpler characteristics of extensive connection, as here stated, are probably such ultimate metaphysical necessities. (PR 288)

19. According to Sherburne:

The extensive continuum, the region correlated with an entity, actually *originates* with its entity—it is not a Newtonian receptacle there already waiting for its occupying entity to come along. . . . The actual being of space is a function of the emergence of entities which have in the depths of their being and as an integral part of their "subjective unity" an indivisible extensive unity. (1971, p. 102)

As accurate as I think Sherburne's comments are, I must add that extensiveness is not "intrinsic" to an actual entity in its private depths, but in its social relations with other actual entities.

20. The epochal theory of time has been criticized by many commentators on the basis of the apparent contradiction between the temporality of the continuum in relation to physical events and the atomicity of concrescence.

Actual occasions, Whitehead says, are temporally extended, but their acts of becoming, which is to say their happenings, are not. But if an occasion is its happening, if it exists by happening, then Whitehead's doctrine ends in a contradiction: one self-same thing both is and is not extensive. (Chappell 1963, p. 75)

Concrescences, or acts of microscopic becoming, *take* no time in Whitehead's view; they could not do so and still be nonextensive. But they must occur *in* time; they must have dates even if they are without duration. But the events or occasions that are the products of such acts are also located in time. . . . But if both the act and the product of the act of becoming are in time, there must be some temporal relation between them. (Chappell 1963, p. 74)

This double nature, which Chappell finds self-contradictory, is fundamental in Whitehead's theory. Actual occasions are divisible objectively and indivisible in concrescence. Put another way, there are perspectives (or respects) in which occasions are divisible, but other perspectives in which they are not. This perspectivity is essentially what Whitehead means, though he does not fully recognize it as perspectivity, when he claims that occasions are divisible, genetically and coordinately, but that as concrescences they are undivided. "The actual world is atomic; but in some senses it is indefinitely divisible" (PR 286). "But it is only the physical pole of the actual entity which is thus divisible. The mental pole is incurably one" (PR 285). What must be shown is how the division and the concrescence are related, if not temporally, as Chappell demands, then in some other ways.

The possibility of finite truths depends on the fact that the satisfaction of an actual entity is divisible into a variety of determinate operations. (PR 220)

Physical time makes its appearance in the "coordinate" analysis of the "satisfaction." The actual entity is the enjoyment of a certain quantum of physical time. But the genetic process is not the temporal succession: such a view is exactly what is denied by the epochal theory of time. Each phase in the genetic process presupposes the entire quantum, and so does each feeling in each phase. The subjective unity dominating the process forbids the division of that extensive quantum which originates with the primary phase of the subjective aim. The problem dominating the concrescence is the actualization of the quantum *in solido*. (PR 283)

21. "Our four-dimensional space-time is the special form that the universal extensive continuum takes in our world.... Some kind of extensiveness, Whitehead believes, is a function of relatedness as such." (Cobb 1965, p. 69) See also:

Whereas the extensive scheme, owing to its complete generality, defines an infinite range of possible types of order, the spatio-temporal continuum may be described as a selective limitation, since it has certain definite characteristics, e.g. three dimensions of space and one of time. (Mays 1959, pp. 78–79)

22. "The universe does not have an ultimate spatio-temporal character at all in *Process and Reality*. Spatio-temporal relations are derived from organic patterns and prehensive relations" (Shahan 1950, p. 59).

23. This is one of the reasons why no size can be assigned unequivocally to actual entities, though we may be confident that they are small to the extent that every ordinary object is a nexus of many occasions. "Whitehead does not say what the time-span of an actual occasion is, even in the cosmic epoch in which we live" (Lowe 1966, p. 55). Whitehead does not say what size an actual entity has, in duration or geometrical extension, because size is not an intrinsic or general property of occasions. (See discussion of extensive abstraction.) The size of the region associated by strains with an actual entity may vary from epoch to epoch, even from society to society. This is the profound and important consequence of the principle that extension is derived from occasions and not conversely: the size of an occasion is a property of its social conditions. There is no *intrinsic* size of an actual entity, since its regions are always from a standpoint. There is no absolute size relative to concrescence. In one sense, an actual entity is as large as the extended universe. This is the fundamental answer to Wallack's point that too many commentators seem to think, as does Lowe, that a size of occasions could be determined in principle.

The actual entity can no more be identified solely with events of subatomic proportions than time can be identified solely with intervals of 10^{-24} seconds. (Wallack 1980, p. 44)

An actual entity is not necessarily something small, short, simple, and impalpable. (Wallack 1980, p. 29) (See also above, pp. 109–11.)

Wallack is misled by Whitehead's claim that size can be variable with social context, essentially a perspectival view.

Just as, for some purposes, one atomic actuality can be treated as though it were many coordinate actualities, in the same way, for other purposes, a nexus of many actualities can be treated as though it were one actuality. This is what we habitually do in the case of the span of life of a molecule, or of a piece of rock, or of a human body. (PR 287)

24. Some must be, that is, by the cosmological principle. Abandoning the cosmological ground of togetherness of all occasions would entail a far simpler theory in which extensive continuity would be a variable property of social conditions. This would correspond closely to the suggestion below that the primordial nature of God should be regarded as dependent on actual conditions (pp. 231–33).

25. This is the appropriate reply to Schmidt's claim that "Whitehead's use of the term 'extensive continuum' is ambiguous, for in some contexts it refers to the most general conditions of extensiveness holding for any cosmic epoch, . . . and in other contexts it refers to the particular conditions of extensiveness holding in our cosmic epoch" (Schmidt 1967, p. 140). The ambiguity is unavoidable because the two meanings of extensiveness are both logically and empirically insepar-able.

26. Confusion as to these two meanings, and the primacy of creativity, has led some commentators to question lapses of time that have no meaning in Whitehead's system—for example, between successive occasions.

Whiteheadians have never addressed themselves to the question of *how long the gap is between occasions.* . . . How long *between* occasions are we *not* in existence? (Edwards 1975, p. 203)

My position is that genetic phases are earlier and later than one another in exactly the same sense that successive occasions are earlier and later. (Ford 1971, p. 201)

I contend that the succession of actual entities and the succession of phases of prehensions are both successions of becomings. (Lango 1972, p. 97)

Such views, including Christian's puzzlement over the role of the past in the present (see above, pp. 32–33), all manifest the same confusion involving the indivisibility of actual occasions and the divisibility of time. Actual entities are not divisible in concrescence—this includes God: they are divisible *analytically.* *Before* and *after* in concrescence refer to the role of conditions for different stages; but the stages occur at once, together, under the domination of the sub-jective aim. Any other view would place concrescence absolutely *in time* and would completely sacrifice Whitehead's emphasis on the self-determination of actual entities. "Edwards' 'gap theory' criticism rests upon a surreptitious return to Newtonian time and to the fallacy of simple location" (Fancher 1971, p. 40).

A corollary of this interpretation is that God's satisfaction must be viewed as equally nontemporal, a function of all other becomings but not temporally related to them—for it would otherwise be in time and would change through time. This conception of the atemporality of God is as mysterious as the unconditioned nature of his primordial envisagement of all actual entities, and it manifests the confusions that follow from the cosmological principle in relation to the closure afforded by God: for example, "God, an actual entity, can prehend himself" (Lango 1972, p. 75).

Not only are all these confusions violations of perspectivity, but they ignore the epochal nature of actual occasions. They are natural conclusions from Whitehead's description of *stages* of concrescence, resulting from his mechanical interpretation of analyzability, but they are nevertheless quite mistaken.

> Whitehead did not sufficiently analyze the problem of the relation between the continuous and the discrete. To say that potentiality is continuous and actuality is discrete does not solve the problem. . . . Whitehead seems to insist on having it both ways. His emphasis on the atomicity of actual entities gives them discrete characteristics, but they are continuous too, as they are extensive. (Lee 1961, p. 70)

Whitehead's perspectivity not only permits him to, it demands that he have it both ways; but there is little doubt that perspectivity is obscured in connection with the extensive continuum and often muted in the context of cosmological considerations.

27. See Palter:

> In the method of extensive abstraction . . . one is concerned with *perceived* events and with indefinitely prolonged sequences of these events (abstractive classes of events). Neither the events . . . nor the indefinitely prolonged sequences of events are susceptible of precise definition because of the inherent limitations of sense-perception. However, *some* of the events in an abstractive class are perceived through the senses as extending over one another; and the general concepts of events and of extension between events are clear enough to make the search for congruence to simplicity an "instinctive procedure of habitual experience." (1960, p. 100)

Here Palter's emphasis is on sense-perception and on operational procedures projecting out of sense-experience. Yet he also recognizes that the relations of the extensive continuum are not *pure* potentials but rather real potentials arising directly out of the immediately preceding actual world but indirectly out of the entire past world, and referring indirectly to the entire future world. (1960, p. 112)

See also:

> In coordinate division one confronts an achieved, fully determinate, static occasion of experience and examines the *possible* divisions of the region occasioned by this occasion and the *possible* relations of these divisions to other regions. In this way one attempts to find the most universal set of extensive (i.e., spatio-temporal) relations which coordinate in a homogeneous way the divisions *within* one actual entity and the divisions *among* all actual entities. The theory of extension is thus essentially mathematical and, in particular, geometrical in character. (1960, p. 5)

28. "Whitehead maintains that extensive continuity is real. But its reality is the reality of a relation and not of actuality as such" (Leclerc 1963, p. 121). The

problem is to show that the reality of the extensive continuum is not a violation of the ontological principle. This is one of the functions of the method of extensive abstraction, though it is a profoundly problematical one. See here also, "when Whitehead speaks of the extensive continuum, it is clear that he is simply referring to a system of logical relations. In that case, we may ask, how can it be a constituent of actual fact, as he claims?" (Mays, 1959, p. 103). My explanation of the grounding of the extensive continuum in the general social conditions of all actual worlds resolves all questions but one: How can the *necessity* of such conditions be demonstrated? I think they cannot, and I think that Mays's overly logical reading must therefore be considered logically deficient.

29. One interpretation is that "extensiveness involves a general scheme of relationships beyond mere space and time, but this scheme is merely a matrix of possibilities. Actual entities 'atomize' the extensive continuum. *It* is infinitely divisible, and it is precisely *they* who divide it." (Levi 1964, p. 150) How the extensive continuum can be "merely" a matrix of possibilities (and whatever "merely" means) is the difficulty. Levi overlooks the *reality* of the potentiality of extensive relations.

Another interpretation is that

> there is no possibility of *existentially* separating the incomplete phases from each other or from the whole. There is no existential time in which an occasion's incomplete parts exist without the whole. The division of an occasion into phases is an abstraction made from the whole, and only the whole is a *res vera*. (Neville 1980, p. 16)

Such an account is true enough as far as it goes, but it does not go far enough. It effectively separates parts and wholes absolutely, giving unqualified primacy to the latter. It is far more plausible, I maintain, that divisibility be regarded as a genuine and real property of occasions, but a perspectival property, and that from the standpoint of the occasion as a whole, it is undivided.

30. See Christian:

> The real reason that, in Whitehead's system, the independence of contemporaries is necessary is the categorical obligation of internal unity and completeness. If the concrescence is to eventuate in a complete integration of its feelings, if it is to achieve subjective unity, then there must be a duration in which the concrescence is closed to further contributions of data from other individual actual entities. (1959, p. 60)

31. "One may raise the question why this cosmic epoch has just the existent, necessary relationships prescribed by the extensive continuum. The ontological principle provides part of the answer, for according to this principle, the present character of the world must be causally dependent upon its past character." (Ballard 1961, p. 14) The dependence on past conditions is perspectival; the question, however, is why *extensive* relationships are universal and necessary.

32. In the "general theory of relativity . . . it is no longer possible to speak of synchronous clocks at a finite distance apart, but this is precisely one of the grounds upon which Whitehead rejects the general theory of relativity." (Palter 1960, p. 39)

In *The Concept of Nature,*

cogredience . . . leads to a theory of absolute position, since a percipient event possesses within its associated duration a unique standpoint, one which is different from the standpoint of any other event which is a component of that duration. On the other hand, Whitehead holds that there may well be alternative definitions of absolute position, corresponding to different meanings of simultaneity for different percipient events. (Palter 1960, p. 40)

Palter's emphasis on the scientific elements in Whitehead's theory seems to make him unaware of the *metaphysical* need for a ground of togetherness among contemporary occasions.

Whitehead's separation of geometry and physics precludes any appeal to Einstein's principle of equivalence, which, in Whitehead's view, is essentially a way of illegitimately identifying a genuine physical phenomenon, gravitation, with purely geometric properties of space-time. (Palter 1960, p. 189)

Whitehead *defines* geometry as the study of the "uniform relatedness" of nature. (Palter 1960, p. 190)

The metaphysical issue is one of self-determination and identity.
33. See Kraus:

Immediate objectification (i.e., the direct physical feeling of the physical feeling of another actual entity) can come about only between an emerging occasion and past occasions whose spatiotemporal quantum of extension is contiguous—externally connected—with the standpoint in the extensive continuum which is in the process of actualization by the emerging occasion. (1979, p. 149)

34. "It is inherent in my theory to maintain the old division between physics and geometry. Physics is the science of the contingent relations of nature and geometry expresses its uniform relatedness." (Whitehead 1922, pp. v–vi) In Palter's words:

geometry concerns itself with the *possible* types of uniformly curved space—with what is common to all of them (projective geometry) and with what is peculiar to each of them (the three definitions of congruence or distance); physics decides among the three metrical geometries. (Palter 1960, p. 138)

35. The most detailed technical discussions of Whitehead's theory of time and extension—found in Grünbaum, Palter, and Mays—fail, it seems to me, to grasp in Whitehead's metaphysical theory the importance of a unison of becoming to the self-determination of actual occasions, with a consequent emphasis on the separability of geometry from time. In his *Whitehead's Philosophy of Science and Metaphysics* (1977), Mays makes this very clear. Discussing both Northrop's and Grünbaum's criticisms of Whitehead's theory of simultaneity (Northrop 1951, esp. pp. 200–201; Grünbaum 1962, pp. 222–3; see also Grünbaum, 1963), Mays concludes that

Whitehead is not primarily concerned with the causes of our knowledge. He is engaged in an epistemological rather than a causal enquiry. Whitehead would say that the congruence judgments of physicists, biologists, and psychologists, ultimately depend on their recognition of self-identities in their experience of matching, etc. . . . Grünbaum would seem to be appealing to something like a materialistic theory of perception as evidence for the falsity of Whitehead's views. But such a theory for Whitehead gives what he considers to be abstract scientific notions a greater reality than the perceptually given. (1977, p. 76)

The entire discussion neglects the metaphysical issues. Emphasis on sense perception can certainly be found in Whitehead's writings, especially the early ones, but it undergoes a major transformation in *Process and Reality* and later. In his theory of actual occasions, Whitehead needs a unison of becoming correlated with the extensiveness of the contemporary world. This coordination is displayed in particular in presentational immediacy. A relativistic theory of simultaneity is incompatible with durational self-determination. We may view this as a limitation of Whitehead's perspectivism, produced by the absolute character of his theory of self-causation and freedom.

36. However, see Palter's criticisms of the success of the method of extensive abstraction in relation to sense-perception:

We are forced to ask the seemingly unanswerable question: how can the *topological* and *projective* properties of Whitehead's flat geometrical elements serve adequately to account for the general *metrical* features of sense-perception (e.g. the recognition of an object moving in approximately a "straight line"). (1960, p. 140)

there is considerable doubt as to whether the non-metrical straight lines of Whitehead's theory of extension can serve meaningfully to define what Whitehead calls the "projective" properties of sense-perception. (Palter 1960, p. 143)

I consider sense-perception not to be essential within the method of extensive abstraction, but to be a consequence of more fundamental principles of concrescence.

37. An interesting interpretation of Whitehead's theory of extension that emphasizes the principle of perspective beyond the perspectivity of the theory of relativity is found in Jordan.

Whitehead's universe, as extended in space and time, is ultimately relativistic, but not under the same mode as Einstein's. The continuum of Einstein is relative to the field, system or state of motion in which the observer happens to be. Whitehead's continuum is relative to the viewpoint of the one particular atomistic occasion in which it is being felt. The Whiteheadian universe is never the same for any two occasions. It cannot be understood (except as an example of *potentiality*) apart from the viewpoint of a particular occasion. (Jordan 1968, p. 107)

However, this interpretation is intelligible only where perspectivity is qualified and selective, with consequent implications for the limitations of extension.

38. Confusion as to the logical relations between the independence of geometry and the nature of conscious perception is what underlies many of the

criticisms of Whitehead's theory of extension. Grünbaum, for example, criticizes Whitehead's theory of simultaneity for its sensationalist principles: "In opposition to the GTR's spatially and temporally *variable* geometry, Whitehead affirms the *uniformity* of the world's geometry" (1963, p. 426). Whitehead's error, according to Grünbaum, is rooted in "the contention that the unique spatial and temporal congruences provided by our *sensory* contents are such as to require the spatial and temporal *uniformity* of the world's geometry" (1963, p. 427) Grünbaum concludes that he has demonstrated that "the complete failure of A. N. Whitehead's attempt to ground the concept of distant simultaneity of physical theory on the sensed coincidences experienced by sentient observers" (1963, p. 344). (See also Northrop's criticisms [1951].) Northrop and Grünbaum do not recognize the major changes in Whitehead's theory of extension in *Process and Reality*, where the togetherness of contemporary occasions in causal independence is fundamental, not our conscious perception of geometrical projections and simultaneity. See, in this connection:

> Whitehead himself in *Process and Reality* rejected his earlier point of view. Instead of an alternative theory of relativity, Whitehead offered an alternative interpretation of the "orthodox" theory. This change was consequent upon Whitehead's new belief that creativity was atomic rather than continuous. (Seaman 1955, p. 222)

> In his writings published between 1919 and 1924 . . . he argued that space was an abstraction from events and expressive of the relations between events; that space was uniform; and most important (which he later gave up) that space-in-process is continuous. . . .
> Since space is, so to speak, constitutive and uniformly extending, it must not be affected by such factors as mass and electromagnetism. Whatever exists besides space-time, must react *apart from* and *along side of* that extensive continuum. This put Whitehead at odds with the orthodox theory of relativity. The latter considered space as being more or less non-homogeneous in the presence of mass. . . .
> Although he accepts the mathematical description of the world as given by relativity [in *Process and Reality*], Whitehead reinterprets the orthodox views in a most novel and exciting manner. (Seaman 1955, p. 223)

> It is true that in one sense Whitehead did not give up his early view, for in *Process and Reality*, the physical factors concrese in independence of the spatio-temporal. (Seaman 1955, p. 225)

> The spatio-temporal standpoint as such cannot effect that togetherness (stratification of nature), for the general theory of perspectives or of stratifications of nature rests upon the assumption that the spatio-temporal factors in the world of events are commensurable. (Miller 1936, p. 279)

> Whitehead was unable to account for stratification without introducing an act of prehension as an integral part of his system. . . . A prehending subject is that which effects the togetherness of events, thereby giving them a definite spatio-temporal order. . . . Unless there is a subject, there will be no qualitative differences between one stratification of nature and another, for spatial and temporal intervals are homogeneous and commensurable. (Miller 1936, p. 280)

Whitehead's acceptance of most of the tenets of the theory of relativity, expressed in his distinction between the nexus of an occasion's contemporaries and its duration, raises some fundamental difficulties for the cosmological principle. This is, on the surface, a problem for the immanence of the consequent nature of God (see Wilcox 1961). It is, however, also a problem for the totality of relations among contemporary occasions realized through the extensive continuum.

39. "Whitehead has to explain why on his view we perceive not a series of events having electronic or molecular characteristics, but perceptual objects" (Mays 1959, p. 121). Mays's solution fails to acknowledge adequately the role of contemporary societies in transmutation and presentational immediacy.

In sense-perception this change is brought about by a process of simplification (or transmutation), as a result of which the characters illustrating the many individual events are fused into one sensory quality. (1959, p. 161)

40. See Harry Wells:

What Whitehead wants to arrive at is nature without passage. To accomplish this he applies the method of extensive abstraction to space and time (1950, p. 44)

The method of extensive abstraction is in fact impaled on the horns of a dilemma. One horn is the logical procedure to nothing, the extrinsic character of ideal simplicity, in which the world is lost, but abstract certainty is achieved. ... The other horn is to avoid the convergence to pure abstraction. ... This is accomplished in the form of events as the situations for self-identical objects. But if events are such situations for objects, then there is no essential need for the method of extensive abstraction, for they are already defined by the objects for which they furnish the locus of ingression. (Wells 1950, p. 47)

Whitehead does derive the extensive continuum from actual entities, but his acknowledgment of the power of mathematics in expressing pattern makes his account of this dependence unclear. Wells would sacrifice mathematical expression and the precision of the physical sciences to a fuller theory of process. The principle of perspective resolves the issue without difficulty: applied both to events and to mathematics, it cannot make process ontologically primary, for both events and patterns are perspectival and condition each other. On the other hand, to the extent that objects are related to events, to that extent are they constituted by temporal relations. Perspectivity emphasizes the qualifications and conditions of both process and mathematical order. Conversely, of course, eternal objects can be timeless only in certain respects (see the next chapter). But it is clear from Whitehead's own account that extensiveness is a function of actual conditions, and is neither timeless nor pure.

41. Compare Lowe:

Many persons (we may call them, philosophically, intuitionists) think that Whitehead assumed exact points—otherwise he would not have been able to construct his abstractive sets. ... The assumed idea is the idea of "being precisely *there*." That is what we intend to talk about when we talk about a point: we imagine the possibility of perfect precision. But—how possible? This is the idea of an undefined superlative not exemplified in experience. . . . The definition and realization of the ideal, the super-lative, can be achieved only by an unending series of comparatives. (1966, pp. 68–69)

42. See in this connection Grünbaum's criticisms of the method of extensive abstraction (1953, pp. 215–26), discussed in Mays (1959) and Palter (1960). Grünbaum argues that points cannot be defined unambiguously from regions, nor can a densely infinite continuum of points be so defined. His criticisms are:

(i) that the Method is vitiated by Zeno's paradox of plurality because of an important violation of the two conditions stated by Broad; (ii) that the convergence of the Method's abstractive classes is fatally ambiguous; (iii) that Whitehead's modification of the Method in *Process and Reality* does not remove the crucial ambiguity; (iv) that the abstractive classes do not belong to the domain of self-awareness; and (v) that Professor A. P. Ushenko's recent defense of the Method is unsatisfactory. (1953, p. 216)

In detail,

An interval *can* be consistently regarded as an aggregate of points only if this aggregate is *super-denumerably* infinite. . . . Can Whitehead establish the existence in sensed nature of the super-denumerable infinity of abstractive sets required? . . . The answer could be in the affirmative only if a super-denumerable infinity of objects could be among what Whitehead calls "the termini of sense-awareness." (1953, p. 217)

Sense-perception itself provides no means for distinguishing from one another the abstractive classes which Whitehead needs to confer a separate identity upon such points as $X = 0$ and $X = 10^{-1000}$. (1953, p. 219)

How then do Whitehead and the exponents of his Method propose to overcome the difficulty that the infinitudes of regions needed by the Method do not belong to the domain of sense-awareness? (1953, p. 223)

[If] mere objects of thought are to propagate the infinite sets required by the axiom [of infinity], then we find again that on Whitehead's premises, as interpreted by Broad, there is no reason for saying that point-events occur or *exist*. (1953, p. 226)

Nevertheless, Grünbaum does acknowledge certain "baffling" changes in *Process and Reality*:

In *PR*, Whitehead no longer requires the members of abstractive classes to be *sensed* regions. Hence, my criticisms are not aimed at the rather baffling treatment in *PR*. But they *are* directed against conceptions of the Method which (a) require with Broad that the Method rest on *sensationist* foundations. (1953, p. 220)

Grünbaum criticisms are particularly effective against Palter's and Lawrence's interpretations of Whitehead's method, which emphasize its early sensationalist commitments (Palter 1960; Lawrence 1956). *Process and Reality*, with its emphasis on concrescences and associated regions, is not susceptible to Grün-baum's particular criticisms.

Mays's interpretation is that

the interpretation of the method which seems to agree best with Whitehead's general position is that he was not trying to construct a geometry from sense-experience, but rather using a mathematical model to make clear certain relations appearing in perception. (1959, p. 117)

Mays concludes that "there still remain the difficulties arising from the nature of the mathematical continuum" (1959, p. 117). Palter takes the argument from sense-perception by analogy more seriously (See above, note 27.)

43. Palter and Lowe both emphasize that, in *Process and Reality*, Whitehead defines points and lines as sets of convergent regions, therefore without assuming the existence of such geometrical elements in the definition of the regions, which they take to be primitive elements in sense-perception and the becoming of actual entities.

Whitehead sees as a fundamental problem of philosophy of science the explanation of *how* points (and other similar entities) are related to events and objects and *why* such entities are important in natural science. (Palter 1964, p. 61)

Why not, then, make a virtue of necessity and define a point, not as a specific sort of infinitely small spatial region but as a class of finite spatial regions? ... Of course, in the formal definition of a point any reference to the point must be avoided; otherwise the definition would be circular. It should be noted that Whitehead denies that points are real in the sense in which events are real; hence, as far as we know, there is literally *nothing* to which the convergent classes of regions could converge. Instead, a point is to be identified completely with a class of regions. (Palter 1964, p. 62)

He introduced the idea of regions in exact contact only as a case to be *excluded* from his definition of an abstractive set, which was then made in terms of non-temporal enclosure. Thus Whitehead uses the fact that perfect accuracy in the determination of relative position, though definable only by a process of approximation, nonetheless has at every stage a perfectly definite negative; thereby he avoided assuming that any region actually has just one unextended point or breadthless line in common with another. (Lowe 1966, p. 81)

In Whitehead's early work,

only finite spatial regions are revealed in sense-awareness. Hence it is to finite spatial regions that Whitehead turns in order to arrive at an understanding of a point. In particular Whitehead attempts to define a point (and elucidate the notion of an "ideal limit") by the conception of a class or series of finite spatial regions. (Plamondon 1979, p. 15)

In Whitehead's later theory:

Whitehead's meaning is not that a point or straight line is the smallest member of a particular abstractive class of events. Indeed Whitehead explicitly maintains that an abstractive class does not converge to a limiting event which is not a member of the class. (Plamondon 1979, p. 17)

I am by no means sure that Lowe's solution is plausible, for the elimination of a tangential point does not solve the problem of the nature of the regions which may or may not be infinitely divisible without points or lines, thereby comprising a convergent set. What is needed is an interpretation of how it can be meaningful to presuppose an infinitely, densely divisible extensive continuum that does not actually divide the becoming of actual entities.

> The method of extensive abstraction does not account for the existence of points and segments independently of the infinitely diminishing regions which define them. Whitehead still is maintaining that the diminishing series has no limiting region. (Plamondon 197, pp. 22–23)

The method of extensive abstraction, it seems to me, coordinates the undivided quantum of becoming of actual occasions with an infinitely divisible extensive continuum. The indivisibility of acts of becoming is what is at stake, and the coordination of contemporary occasions, not the definition of points and lines. Nevertheless, this view presupposes the unconditioned nature of the primordial nature of God.

A major advantage to my interpretation is that it explains the peculiar ambiguity of Whitehead's claims that the extensive continuum is *derivable* from actual entities. I have argued that actual entities may have *any* size (in principle), that the primary regions (the strain locus) to be associated with actual occasions may in principle have any size as the foundation of the abstractive sets converging to points and lines. Here the potentiality of convergence cannot be matched by the conditions in any particular cosmic epoch, for social conditions inevitably determine a particular regional scale associated with becomings in that epoch. The generalization from particular epochs to extensive conditions of *all* epochs is inevitably dubious and overly cosmological.

44. Alternatively, the regions are consciously perceivable fields out of which points are to be constructed.

> The method of extensive abstraction, as later developed, grows out of two purposes: to define meanings for "point," "line," "instant," etc., thus giving the relational theory of space and time the exact mathematical formulation which its adherents had previously neglected to provide; and to answer the epistemological question ... "how is the space of physics based upon experience?" (Lowe 1966, pp. 163–64)

Here the limitations of sense-perception relative to infinitely convergent sets appear disastrous. (See discussion of Grünbaum's criticisms, note 42.)

45. David Miller has an interesting expression of the cosmological imperative in Whitehead's theory of extension, in which the *potentiality* of the continuum defines a comprehensive togetherness of occasions:

> The atomic element in the extensive continuum is that which limits, divides, and places special emphasis on satisfaction of subjective aim. Hence the atomic merely places special emphasis on one limited phase of the continuum and asks us to look at it from a limited point of view. The organic, on the other hand, stresses the continuum as a whole and asks us to see it, not in a divided, limited fashion, but as a whole in which the parts are thoroughly interrelated. ... from a purely organic point of view all differences, both quantitative and qualitative, are ignored and we have a parmenidean world which just *is*. (Miller 1946, p. 148)

46. Compare Schmidt:

The character of the unity derived from the past is projected upon an extensive region as characterizing contemporary entities which for that subject are potential, not actual, and are called an "image" in contrast to an "object" in causal efficacy. (1967, p. 136)

Regions are a special kind of nexus. . . . This interpretation of the status of a region renders it a derivative notion derived from the basic extensiveness (an eternal object) of actual entities and from the category of transmutation. (1967, pp. 137–38)

47. See passage from Palter (1960, p. 112) quoted in note 27.

48. Compare Lawrence:

It is a curious thing that Whitehead never asks himself, "How big is an actual occasion?" If the actual occasion be an electronic one, its temporal extent will be measured in terms of microseconds. But what of the actual occasions of the human sort? (1961, p. 157)

Lawrence overlooks the unison of becoming, which prevents actual occasions of different types in the same cosmic epoch from being of different sizes. In fact, actual entities have no definite size, and the regions associated with them are functions of the social types to which they belong. It follows that actual entities have neither a particular size nor a particular gap between them, and any question concerning these is unintelligible. This is part of the reason for Whitehead's claim that extensiveness is derivative from concrescence, but not the converse: whatever extensiveness means specifically is a function of social conditions. Nevertheless, because of the importance of a unison of becoming in Whitehead's theory, size seems to me to be a function of the general social conditions throughout an epoch, one of its essential conditions.

49. The importance of the strain locus and relevant social conditions testifies to the misunderstanding in Christian's remarks:

The region of an actual occasion is definite in the sense of having a definitely limited extent with definable boundaries. (Christian 1959, p. 86, Christian's italics)

No two regions of actual occasions are separated by "empty space." . . . "something is always going on everywhere, even so-called empty space" (CN 78). (Christian, p. 91).

Christian makes the region and location intrinsic to the occasion, rather than a function of its environments. "Empty space" is as social a condition as is matter.

50. In this respect, Shahan is simply wrong, for actual entities cannot overlap, although their strain-loci may. "The extensive continuum concept of the process analysis merely requires, with respect to causal efficacy, that actual entities overlap" (Shahan 1950, p. 93) The possibility that actual entities may have any size is the equivalent, for Shahan's purposes, of overlapping.

51. See Kraus:

Congruence in its most general sense consists in "a certain analogy (between the functions of two segments) in a systematic pattern of straight lines, which includes both of them" (PR 505; Corrected Edition p. 331). The further definition of that analogy is performed by the dominant society in a cosmic epoch, and hence, on Whitehead's assumption, is discoverable in nature through presentational immediacy. With the dominant congruence definition established, physical measurement is possible to the scientist. (1979, p. 157)

52. According to Thomas O'Keefe, Whitehead's

problem is rather this: In the science of nature we have perfectly exact concepts and forms are employed to express what is in itself essentially lacking in exactitude; how then are we to reconcile the exactitude of the scientific expression with the essential inexactitude of the nature which science claims to be expressing? . . .

To dissolve this paradox Whitehead devised the system of abstractive elements, a system of one-to-one correspondences between exact mathematical entities and inexact sense-perceivable natural entities. (1951, p. 278)

Whitehead's system of abstractive sets may be fairly described as an attempt to set up an analogous one-to-one correspondence between mathematical elements of a four-dimensional geometry on the one side and natural entities on the other. (1951, p. 279)

O'Keefe's account is weakened by his emphasis on sense-perception.

For an abstractive set, then, to have no smallest member (duration) and still to qualify as a natural entity requires the assumption that there is *no* duration so small that the senses cannot distinguish it. . . . Though the assumption mentioned is necessary to Whitehead's argument, it is one that cannot be defended even theoretically. (1951, pp. 281, 282)

Once we realize that occasions, in *Process and Reality*, have no particular size, the method of geometrical construction in Part IV becomes far more intelligible as a foundation of geometrical elements in perception from potential patterns in the primordial nature of God than as a coordinating construction in terms of perceptual elements.

53. See Palter:

Whitehead's justification is that if points, for example, are really complex entities—as he thinks they must be on the relativistic view of space—then it is incumbent on the philosophy of science to exhibit this complexity and not to conceal it. (1964, p. 63)

CHAPTER EIGHT
REALITY

There are eight modes of existence in Whitehead's theory: actual entities, prehensions, nexūs, subjective forms, eternal objects, propositions, multiplicities, and contrasts. All are quite real. By the principle of relativity, their reality is determined by their potentiality for becoming. This emphasis on becoming is an expression of the ontological principle. The emphasis in the principle on *every* becoming is an expression of the cosmological principle. I have suggested that a more powerful understanding of what is involved here is given by the principle of perspective: to be is to be in perspective; what is real is a constituent of perspectives.

Quite at odds with this perspectivity of being is Whitehead's emphasis on *final reality* and *concreteness:* " 'Actual entities'—also termed 'actual occasions'—are the final real things of which the world is made up" (PR 18). "The explanatory purpose of philosophy is often misunderstood. Its business is to explain the emergence of the more abstract things from the more concrete things" (PR 20). The notions of concreteness and abstractness define the major meeting place, in Whitehead's theory, of the cosmological principle with the principle of experience: what is concrete is metaphysically primary in relation to what is abstract, and what is concrete is an act of experience, a concrescence. To the extent that the principle of perspective is founded on the principle of experience, an extraordinary relationship between concrete actuality and perspectivity is found in Whitehead's theory: actual entities are the only modes of being that are both *in* perspective and *centers* of perspective, both locat*ed* and locat*ing* perspectives. All other modes of being are located in perspectives by the ontological principle, but are not themselves perspectival centers. By the principle of experience, then, concreteness imposes a systematic constraint upon perspective, in

Whitehead's theory. This constraint must be examined in detail.

In *Science and the Modern World*, Whitehead speaks of the *fallacy of misplaced concreteness*: we must avoid the errors that arise when "we have mistaken our abstractions for concrete realities" (SMW 78). He argues that substances and qualities, though entities, "are of a high degree of abstraction" (SMW 74). Far too many of the notions we employ are abstract: "The only question is, how concretely are we thinking when we consider nature under these conceptions? " (SMW 74). "Philosophy is explanatory of abstraction, and not of concreteness" (PR 20).

> The "fallacy of misplaced concreteness" . . . consists in neglecting the degree of abstraction involved when an actual entity is considered merely so far as it exemplifies certain categories of thought. There are aspects of actualities which are simply ignored so long as we restrict thought to these categories. (PR 7–8)

> Philosophical thought has made for itself difficulties by dealing exclusively in very abstract notions, such as those of mere awareness, mere private sensation, mere emotion, mere purpose, mere appearance, mere causation. These are the ghosts of the old "faculties," banished from psychology, but still haunting metaphysics. There can be no "mere" togetherness of such abstractions. The result is that philosophical discussion is enmeshed in the fallacy of "misplaced concreteness." In the three notions—actual entity, prehension, nexus—an endeavour has been made to base philosophical thought upon the most concrete elements in our experience. (PR 18)

It is worth noting that the mark of abstractness in these passages is given by the word "mere": mere awareness, mere appearance. Here Whitehead explicitly rejects the mechanical version of the principle of analysis and seems to approach a major element of the principle of perspective: no mode of being is unconditioned. Purity and simplicity are signs of abstractness or oversimplification, the absence of conditions. It is a long way from such a notion to the abstractness of prehensions and societies, neither of which could be conceived without limits and conditions.

Actuality is the center of Whitehead's theory. Actual entities are the final realities. But eternal objects pervade the world (as do propositions, contrasts, and subjective forms). The ontological principle demands that all explanation lead to actual entities, yet eternal objects are the "forms of determinateness" inherent in all actuality. There is a complementary relationship between eternal objects and actual entities that is incongruent with the ontological principle, yet closely related to the principle of perspective: eternal objects and actual entities are complementary and mutual conditions ingredient in all events and states. This complementary relationship of actuality and possibility must be explored further before returning to the hierarchical elements of Whitehead's system based on the ontological and cosmological principles and inherent in the notion of abstraction.[1]

Actuality

Actuality is Whitehead's fundamental category: actual entities "are the final real things of which the world is made up" (PR 18). However, these occasions are not unanalyzable: though fundamental, they are not "simple." Perspectivity entails that being is relational and plural: actual entities are constituted by their prehensive relations, prehensions of past occasions and their ingredient eternal objects and subjective forms, prehension of eternal objects in the primordial nature of God, and so forth. One pole of perspective is relational; the other is the focal point of view to which the prehensions point. Reality here is perspectivity, and is restricted by the ontological principle in virtue of its emphasis on concrescent experience and actuality, through the principle of experience and the cosmological principle.

In one sense, an actual entity is analyzable in terms of all the categories—other occasions, its own prehensions, subjective forms, the extensive continuum, and so forth. "Each actual entity is analysable in an indefinite number of ways" (PR 19). It is analyzable by the principle of relativity into all its constituents and conditions. In another sense, an actual entity is not analyzable at all—that sense which emphasizes its unitariness and point of view. Analysis distorts the singularity of the entity. In yet a third sense, however, all modes of analysis specifically involve the mediation of eternal objects, since they represent the "forms of definiteness."

> One rôle of the eternal objects is that they are those elements which express how any one actual entity is constituted by its synthesis of other actual entities, and how that actual entity develops from the primary dative phase into its own individual actual existence, involving its individual enjoyments and appetitions. (PR 50–51)

On the one hand, actual entities "are the final real things of which the world is made up." On the other hand, "among these eight categories of existence, actual entities and eternal objects stand out with a certain extreme finality" (PR 22). A third consideration is that "the analysis of an actual entity into 'prehensions' is that mode of analysis which exhibits the most concrete elements in the nature of actual entities" (PR 19). Actual entities are first in all respects, but they are constituted by the other modes of existence. Prehensions are second in some respects; eternal objects are second in other respects. Societies, it should be noted, are primary in ordinary experience, though abstract. In addition, eternal objects and actual entities are mutually related, necessary to each other. Even "pure" possibilities are possibilities *for* actualities. "An eternal object is always a potentiality for actual entities" (PR 44). In return, " 'actuality' is the decision amid 'potentiality.' It represents stubborn fact which cannot be evaded. The real internal constitution of an actual entity progressively constitutes a decision conditioning the creativity which transcends that actuality" (PR 43). Possibilities represent the alternatives for actuality; actualities represent the decision amidst possibilities. By the principle of perspective, alternatives and selections, indeterminateness and determinateness, are complementary factors in every perspective, every being. An important question in Whitehead's theory is how a pure or unconditioned possibility can play a constitutive role in actual entities, how an actual entity can prehend an unconditioned form.

Whitehead takes the principle of experience to define a solution. The term "decision" is crucial. " 'Decision' . . . constitutes the very meaning of actuality. An actual entity arises from decisions *for* it, and by its very existence provides decisions *for* other actual entities which supersede it" (PR 43). In relationship to possibility, actuality is a decision among alternatives. Without the notion of decision, actuality and possibility would not be distinguishable. "Just as 'potentiality for process' is the meaning of the more general term 'entity,' or 'thing'; so 'decision' is the additional meaning imported by the word 'actual' into the phrase 'actual entity' " (PR 43). Possibilities represent ranges of alternatives, thus some degree of indeterminateness; actuality is a definite decision that renders determinate what had some degree of indeterminateness. At least one alternative for interpreting the meaning of actuality, then, is as *determinateness*.[2]

However, the past is determinate, but it is no longer actual.[3] Moreover, prehensions are said to be *wholly* determinate. "A feeling is in all respects determinate, with a determinate subject, determinate initial data, determinate negative prehensions, a determinate objective datum, and a determinate subjective form" (PR 221). It is not determinateness that is actual, but the *process of becoming determinate.* "The 'formal' constitution of an actual entity is a process of transition from in-determination towards terminal determination. But the indetermin-ation is referent to determinate data" (PR 45). Actuality is the move-ment from indeterminateness to determinateness. "Every explanatory fact refers to the decision and to the efficacy of an actual thing" (PR 46). Only occasions are effective; and their effectiveness is realized in the transition from indeterminateness to determinateness. Never-theless, eternal objects also are essential to transitions and determination, but are not actual. Past actual entities and ingressed eternal objects are, relative to any present, quite determinate and set-tled, but are not fully concrete and real, and suffer from abstraction. The principle of experience here is fundamental: eternal objects are never subjects; past actual entities are no longer subjects. The key to actuality lies in satisfaction, subjective form, decision, and self-causation. Agency and actuality are equivalent: occasions are actual because they act, because they are self-caused experiencers. "An entity is actual, when it has significance for itself. By this it is meant that an actual entity functions in respect to its own determination. Thus an actual entity combines self-identity with self-diversity" (PR 25).

This equation of experience, actuality, and concrescence as a pro-gressive movement toward decision justifies Whitehead's view of occasions as *processes*—at the expense, however, of undercutting their completeness and indivisibility. If they *progress* toward determinate-ness, the progression should have stages. If they *are* fully determinate, there is no progression. Either actual entities are *drops* of experience or drops of *experience.* Self-causation is lost within the indivisibility of the occasion, along with decision. No stage can be that in which self-causation and decision transpire.

I have noted the tension, in Whitehead's theory of experience, between the wholeness and indivisibility of actual occasions and the mechanical principle of analysis which suggests stages of becoming in every occasion. Devoid of temporal transition, an occasion is both whole and determinate, yet a function of many prehensions in virtue of the per-spectival character of prehensions. "Any characteristic of an actual entity is reproduced in a prehension. It might have been a complete actuality; but, by reason of a certain incomplete partiality, a prehension is only a subordinate element in an actual entity" (PR 19). A prehension is almost concrete, but makes reference to the whole experiencing occasion that is fully concrete. "A reference to the complete actuality is required to give the reason why such a prehension is what it is in respect to its subjective form" (PR 19). There is a reference within a prehension to the occasion that is the prehending subject. Thus the occasion is the minimal element that is "complete," possessing self-reference and self-creativity. Here, however, Whitehead appears to overlook the *double* character of prehension. A prehension requires reference to the entire occasion—especially its subjective aim—to be intelligible. But it also requires reference to the object prehended. A prehension is indeterminate because of its transcendent reference; but so, then, is every occasion transcendent in reference, and doubly so—to its past and to its future. The final basis for actuality lies in self-causation, in its determining, but also its unintelligible, arbitrary nature.

What is involved here is a sharp conflict between the principle of perspective and the cosmological elements of the principle of experience and the ontological principle. By the former, all being is qualified and perspectival, including actuality and possibility. By the latter, an absolute, unqualified, and nonperspectival distinction is needed between actual entities and eternal objects. Actual entities act, prehend, and experience; eternal objects do not, are only *pure* possibilities. Yet even in Whitehead's own theory, actual entities are both actualities and potentialities—for the future. Eternal objects ingressed in the past are in some respects settled—actual in that sense—though potentials for the future. The absolute and unconditioned nature of actuality, in Whitehead's theory, is a consequence of the cosmological principle, and is incompatible with the principle of perspective, including even the perspectivity of his own theory. The ultimate criterion of actuality lies in self-causation, the foundation of self-significance and experience. It is an arbitrary and unintelligible foundation in relation to the principle of experience, and is incompatible with the principle of perspective.

It has been a common complaint in the history of philosophy that philosophers lose the concrete in the abstract. This is expressed by Whitehead in the fallacy of misplaced concreteness. The question, then, is where to find a category that is unambiguously concrete, unambiguously primary.[4] For Whitehead, the answer lies in the concept of *experience*—in particular, the experiencing subject and its prehensions. He offers a generalized Kantian answer to the Aristotelian question of what mode of being is primary: the subject of experience is prior to its perceptions and relations.[5] Whitehead devotes almost half of Part III of *Process and Reality* to establish that the meaning of actuality rests upon the subjective nature of an actual entity's experience. "In a real complex unity each particular component imposes its own particularity on its status. No entity can have an abstract status in a real unity. Its status must be such that only it can fill and only that actuality can supply" (PR 225). The categories of subjective unity, objective identity, and objective diversity exhibit the determinateness of elements that define actuality as an act of experience. The priority of experience over perspective as the determinant of actuality is closely related to the ontological principle and the primacy of actual entities. The circularity of the equation of actuality with experience and with ontological priority is very tight.[6]

The truth, however, is that eternal objects are just what they are, as are prehensions, data, and especially societies, which are "their own reasons." The general principle is that everything is what it is, actual or not, and everything is related to other beings. By the principle of perspective, every being is perspectival, relational, and unique. It is as determinate as its nature and conditions permit it to be, and nothing is wholly determinate, including actual occasions. Eternal objects in particular are determinate and indeterminate in many ways, possessing both individual and relational essences. The number 3 is just what it is, though it is called abstract. In the last analysis, saying that an occasion is actual and concrete because it is self-creative, self-significant, is not an explanation or reason for its actuality, but its criterion. As Whitehead says, his aim is not to *explain* actuality, but to determine its essential properties: "Philosophy is explanatory of abstraction, and not of concreteness" (PR 20).

In relation to possibilities (eternal objects), actualities (actual entities) are determinate in certain ways. "Actual occasions in their 'formal' constitutions are devoid of all indetermination. Potentiality has passed into realization. They are complete and determinate matter of fact, devoid of all indecision" (PR 29). But they are not and cannot be determinate in all ways—with respect to other actual entities, for example, especially those in the future—and eternal objects cannot be wholly indeterminate.

> Each actual entity, although complete so far as concerns its microscopic process, is yet incomplete by reason of its objective inclusion of the macroscopic process. It really experiences a future which must be actual, although the completed actualities of that future are undetermined. In this sense, each actual occasion experiences its own objective immortality. (PR 215)

Every mode of existence is perspectival in being determinate and indeterminate in different respects, settled and open in various ways. In this sense, there is a wider meaning of potentiality pertinent to every mode of existence—alternatives for the future—and correspondingly, a meaning of actuality relative to every mode of existence to the extent that alternatives are irrelevant. Unqualified determinateness cannot be a distinguishing property of actuality, for determinateness and indeterminateness always qualify each other. Whitehead assumes he is forced, by the cosmological principle and by the metaphysical tradition, to define a *primary* reality, and develops a criterion grounded in the principle of experience. The premise that there is a primary reality is an expression of the arbitrariness of the cosmological principle. The inexhaustible complexity of modes of being requires a hierarchical principle of ontological priority in order to establish a unified and all-encompassing order of the universe. Only relative to such a universe can a mode of being be primary, without qualification. The ontological principle can be adopted as a premise, but can be neither explained nor justified, nor can it be made compatible with the qualifications demanded by the principle of perspective. Eternal objects permeate Whitehead's universe and can be relegated to secondary status only on arbitrary grounds. These grounds are defined by Whitehead in terms of the principle of experience. Actual entities are primary because they are experiencing subjects. The final criterion of primary reality and actuality in Whitehead's theory is the decision or self-determination of actual entities. The arbitrariness and unintelligibility of this notion undermines his entire metaphysical theory. Any doctrine of ontological primacy is arbitrary in being unconditioned, absolute, and thereby incompatible with the principle of perspective. The cosmological principle and the principle of experience are given unqualified primacy over the principle of perspective. By the latter principle, every mode of being is perspectival, as real as any other, as determinate (and indeterminate) in its own ways as any other. Differences of modality and kind are not differences of reality, but are functions of establishing conditions. Reality, relationality, determinateness, and indeterminateness admit of distinctions of kind, but not of degree.

Possibility

Acknowledging that in this respect the philosophy of organism follows Plato, Whitehead asserts that

in such a philosophy the actualities constituting the process of the world are conceived as exemplifying the ingression (or "participation") of other things which constitute the potentialities of definiteness for any actual existence.

The things which are temporal arise by their participation in the things which are eternal. (PR 39–40)

These eternal objects have occasioned a great deal of comment, much of it critical.[7] We have a repetition of the controversy Platonism has occasioned through the years over the status and meaning of things that are eternal, particularly over entities "whose conceptual recognition does not involve a necessary reference to any definite actual entities of the temporal world" (PR 44). The definition seems to violate the ontological principle. It certainly violates the principle of perspective to the extent that eternal objects are *pure* possibilities, unconditioned by their ingressions in actuality. Moreover, the location of eternal objects in the primordial nature of God is a second violation to the extent that this valuation is also "unconditioned."

The question, then, is Why eternal objects? Why *pure* possibilities? If it is not too naive, we may begin with a prior question, Why possibilities at all? The suggestion I made in discussing actualities was that, generalized, actualities are to be taken as settled and determinate in particular ways while possibilities are to be taken as alternatives, unsettled in certain ways. In this sense, possibilities manifest perspectival plurality: indeterminateness in the being of actualities for each other. Here, then, beings are actual with respect to their individuality and uniqueness, their being for themselves, and are possibilities with respect to their being for others. This is a far more general perspectival, and functional view than Whitehead's, but as I will show, it is not alien to his view of possibilities. However, possibilities here cannot be *pure*.

It is essential to emphasize the ambiguity inherent in the notion of possibility, for there is an important difference between an entity that represents the *definiteness* of an actuality and one that represents a possibility *for* or *in* an actuality. Eternal objects are both forms of definiteness, inherent wherever determinateness is involved, and possibilities inherent in conditions directly relevant to events and becomings. Rather different conceptions of both the purity and the eternity of eternal objects follow from whichever role is emphasized. Forms of definiteness are required for determination, and in this sense suggest the priority of eternal objects—a logical priority founded, in Whitehead's system, on God and directly at odds with the ontological principle. Such forms of determination have three functions exhibiting their character.

An eternal object can only function in the concrescence of an actual entity in one of three ways: (i) it can be an element in the definiteness of some

objectified nexus, or of some single actual entity, which is the datum of a
feeling; (ii) it can be an element in the definiteness of the subjective form of
some feeling; or (iii) it can be an element in the datum of a conceptual, or
propositional, feeling. All other modes of ingression arise from integrations
which presuppose these modes. (PR 290)

Possibilities as alternatives for events, resident in conditions and succession, are subsequent to decisions by the principle of experience, but
are not then pure.

An eternal object considered in reference to the privacy of things is a
"quality" or "characteristic"; namely, in its own nature, as exemplified in
any actuality, it constitutes an element in the private definiteness of that
actuality. It refers itself publicly; but it is enjoyed privately. (PR 290)

These two roles of eternal objects—as modes of determination and as
possibilities for the future—are quite different, and exhibit quite
different properties. The former are determinate among themselves and
in their individual and relational essences, but indeterminate relative to
particular ingressions; the latter are determinate as alternatives relative
to a particular actuality, but indeterminate in certain respects for that
actuality, since many alternatives are corelevant. Forms of definiteness
are essential to any metaphysical theory—though we have not settled
whether these must be *pure*. Alternatives for becoming are also essential,
even in a deterministic system.

The question is whether we need *both* pure and real possibilities, and
whether they can be intelligible together. Given actualities as data, and
possibilities for those actualities, do we also need forms of definiteness
that bear no relation to particular actualities? What is inadequate about
a system that includes actualities of the past as well as their actual
properties, elements, and aspects, and the real possibilities for what may
come to pass from them?[8] Several reasons may be proposed for
preserving a notion of pure possibility. First, and least important, we
frequently speak of properties in abstraction from actualities, not so
much as if we believe such properties to exist wholly independently of
the actualities they *might* qualify, but insofar as we have no particular
actuality in mind which they *do* qualify. Thus, a man may speak of a
particular look of a woman he has imagined but never seen. If
imagination is at all free, we can entertain traits apart from the actualities in which they participate. Such traits would appear to be "pure" in
their abstraction from particular actualities. Conceptual reversion
seems to depend upon such a notion of pure conception.

A second and more important example is given by mathematics. Relations among concepts in a mathematical system may be understood as relations among pure modes of determination, even if the system is both interpreted and applied. Despite the uses to which such systems may be put, they are valid and meaningful as deductive systems based on uninterpreted axioms. A calculus has a definite relational meaning despite its inapplicability until interpreted. We may even maintain that such a system was devised *for* application and interpretation. But it is what it is, independent of such application. It is a relational system of conceptual determinations.

Nevertheless, neither of these considerations is persuasive. Moreover, the mathematical paradigm does not support the notion of *eternal* determinations related to no actualities, but rather suggests changing and impermanent prospects of mathematical order where certain real possibilities take on a remarkable generality. "Abstract" possibilities need not be "eternal." The purity of conception in both of the above cases is effectively self-contradictory. A wholly free imagination would have no application to events. Indeed, neither example suggests a *wholly* free or pure determination, for conceptual relations are presupposed. Determinations must be thought to be relevant to other determinations, or imagination would be unintelligible. Nevertheless, conceptual relations alone are equally unintelligible. The look of a person never seen must be related to persons seen (or experienced in some other way); mathematical systems are derived from norms established in lived experience. Purity of determinate form is equivalent to *privacy* of language and thought, and is unintelligible.[9] The applicability of conception to experience is dependent on conditions that effectively undermine the eternality of those conditions. A pure system of geometry would be no system, and certainly not geometry. It can be nothing without establishing conditions. The principle of perspective demands not only that being be conditioned, but that the relevance of a mode of being to another establishes a reciprocal, if very different kind, of relevance. Purity and eternity are unintelligible separate from the changing world. The analogical character of conception under the principle of experience cannot solve this difficulty. If we can entertain a concept, it is because that concept is conditioned by our lived experience, therefore neither pure nor eternal in relevant respects. We need an expanded and effective theory of real possibilities, conditioned by their relations and rooted in established conditions from which they emerge, not an unintelligible theory of unconditioned forms.

The third reason, then, is the crucial one. Pure forms of determinate-

ness are necessary to explain novelty. Creativity is "the principle of
novelty" (PR 21). The question is whether real possibilities
alone—possibilities conditioned by actualities—can provide a satisfactory basis for novelty. On Whitehead's account, the primordial nature of
God is required for novelty. "By reason of the actuality of this primordial valuation of pure potentials, each eternal object has a definite,
effective relevance to each concrescent process. Apart from such orderings, there would be a complete disjunction of eternal objects unrealized
in the temporal world. Novelty would be meaningless, and inconceivable" (PR 40). Without God, novel possibilities would bear no relevance
to actuality. And without pure possibilities, there would be no source
from which novelties could emerge.

> Transcendent decision includes God's decision. He is the actual entity in
> virtue of which the *entire* multiplicity of eternal objects obtains its graded
> relevance to each stage of concrescence. Apart from God, there could be no
> relevant novelty. (PR 164)

It is worth noting that the system of relevance among eternal objects
with respect to any actual conditions is neither pure nor eternal, but
continually changing with the changing world. This is what Whitehead
means in saying that "where there is no decision involving exclusion,
there is no givenness. For example, the total multiplicity of Platonic
forms is not 'given.' But in respect of each actual entity, there is givenness of such forms" (PR 43). Givenness, here, is thoroughly perspectival,
for it emphasizes exclusion and selection. The question is whether we
must postulate an unchanging, eternal, and complete system of
determinations as the basis of the varying systems of perspectival
relevance for different actualities. Whitehead clearly thinks we must.
Yet such a system is effectively absolute, unconditioned in God. The
alternative is to bring the primordial nature of God under conditions
provided by the actual world, thereby changing with them. Whitehead
denies that eternal objects can be so conditioned, emphasizing their
eternity and purity.[10] "In the becoming of an actual entity, novel
prehensions, nexūs, subjective forms, propositions, multiplicities, and
contrasts, also become; but there are no novel eternal objects" (PR 22). It
is worth noting, however, that even if eternal objects could never be
novel, they could not be eternal in all respects. Their ingressions are both
novel and unique.

The principle of perspective, generalized to include forms of
determination as perspectival, entails that determinations must be con-

ditioned by what they apply to, by their relations. Determinations
emerge from, and are transformed by, their applications. The principle
of perspective also entails that uniqueness—and therefore novelty—is a
generic condition of all being, all perspectives, therefore not explainable
by any nonperspectival conditions. Eternal objects are in many ways
nonperspectival in Whitehead's theory: in their purity, unaffected by
actual events, in the unconditioned nature of the primordial nature of
God, and in their individual essences. All of these are inexplicable because of their unconditioned nonperspectivity. It follows that we have
gained nothing in trying to explain novelty and uniqueness by unintelligible and arbitrary principles, especially those in which novelty is
meaningless and conditions are irrelevant. Rather, to the extent that
being is perspectival, uniqueness and novelty are conditions relevant to
all being. Whitehead generalizes emergence and creativity to include all
actualities. He fails to generalize novelty far enough to include all modes
of being under the principle of perspective.

One of the most remarkable limitations of Whitehead's theory is that
he has no explanation of the uniqueness of God's primordial nature, or of
the individual essences of eternal objects. Novelty in actual entities is to
be explained, but in terms of conditions that admit no novelty and have
no explanation. A related defect in Whitehead's theory is that he effectively makes process specious by explaining novelty in terms of something unchanging and eternal. Novelty is explained away in the sense
that it rests on static and unqualified conditions to which novelty is
irrelevant. A simpler view, far closer to the principle of perspective, is
that novelty is part of perspectivity, but perspectives are always
qualified. Perspectivity includes both conditions and uniqueness as
conjoint determinants of every being, complementarily and functionally
interrelated.

I have criticized self-causation in actual entities as unintelligible
because it is unqualified. The primordial nature of God is equally unqualified and equally unintelligible. And it is introduced as an additional principle beyond the self-creative decision of individual
occasions. Two principles of novelty are required in Whitehead's theory,
one grounded in actual occasions, the other in God.

> He is the unconditioned actuality of conceptual feeling at the base of
> things; so that, by reason of this primordial actuality, there is an order in
> the relevance of eternal objects to the process of creation. His unity of
> conceptual operations is a free creative act, untrammelled by reference to
> any particular course of things. (PR 344)

An alternative would be to make God an entity fully dependent on the world, fully consequent to the succession of occasions, thereby eliminating the unconditioned nature of his primordial envisagement. No eternal essences would be required in this case, for God's self-causation would serve as the basis of all relevant determinations. One principle of novelty would be required, that of self-determination in every actual entity, subject to the conditions inherent in its concrescence. The ordering of possibilities, changing with the changing world, would be neither unqualified, timeless, nor primordial, and all possibilities would become functions of established conditions. While the changing order of relevance of possibilities to actualities would in some sense be inexplicable, since it would be the outcome of self-causation in God, it would be dependent on actual past conditions, to whatever extent such conditions were relevant.[11]

The birth of a person is a novel event, but it requires no basis in eternity, only in the conditions that brought the parents together and made conception possible. The actual conditions of the past produce the real possibilities of marriage, conception, and birth. Novel actualities are to be explained in terms of settled or persistent actualities and their real possibilities. For novel actualities to become, in this case, novel possibilities must become relevant. But such novel possibilities can be understood only in terms of the settled actualities and real possibilities of the prior world.[12] No further understanding is possible; appeal to "ultimate" conditions is unintelligible.

By the principle of perspective, unconditioned absolutes are unintelligible, but there is a uniqueness in every perspective that is not reducible to its multiplicity of constituents. Its point of view is unique and irreducible, but conditioned. Whitehead's notion of self-causation expresses this truth about actual entities, though it is limited by the principle of experience and the mechanical principle of analysis. It dissolves into arbitrariness. Generalizing, however, we may emphasize the perspectivity of all beings, their uniqueness, and their relational conditions. Novelty is no more unintelligible than being.

This position, in relationship to events, is far closer to a full process theory in making no commitment to anything eternal.[13] Moreover, it accommodates our powerful intuitions that only a limited range of possibilities prevail within a given state of affairs, and that these possibilities change with the circumstances in which we find ourselves. Possibilities here are the alternatives relevant in circumstances—and alternatives are always relevant. Possibilities and actualities are functional complements conjointly expressive of perspectivity. The conception of possibilities that arise and perish due to their relations with actualities and other possibilities, and the repudiation of all timeless possibilities that bear no relationship to actualities, entail an open-ended universe. The principle of perspective forbids closure of perspectives by any unqualified conditions. Here, of course, the principle of perspective transcends the limitations of process. Every being is both unique and conditioned, but not all beings may be conditioned by process and succession. In any case, there is no permanent and complete realm of possibilities to serve as the ground of all definiteness. Whitehead's conception of the primordial nature of God, especially in its timeless encompassment of all determinations, is an extreme concession to the cosmological principle and leaves no room for novelty in possibility or actuality. In the conviction that there are formal determinants that govern all becoming, Whitehead again capitulates to the cosmological intuition that the world is a unified system, here unified under unconditioned, and therefore atemporal, determinants.

Abstraction

Whitehead's theory of actuality and possibility is permeated by conflicts among the principles of experience and perspective and the cosmological principle. I have suggested that a thoroughgoing and powerful resolution of these conflicts can be achieved by raising the principle of perspective to prominence at the expense of the other two principles. The same conflicts, in an even more intense form, can be discerned in Whitehead's notions of concreteness and abstractness. Here, the doctrine of ontological primacy is predominant, and we must consider the possibility that it is both unintelligible and unfounded. With respect to one strain in Whitehead's theory, actuality and possibility are complementary categories: actuality is the ingression of possibilities; possibilities are potentials for ingression. By the principle of perspective, each is a perspectival determinant and a result of conditions involving the other. What is the justification for Whitehead's further claim that actualities are more concrete or, in terms of the ontological principle, that they are the only reasons—since they are intelligible only in terms of the possibilities inherent within them?

The issue is whether one category of a metaphysical system can be regarded without qualification as "more final," "more real," or "ultimate." Such a notion of primacy is unqualified and unperspectival. It is a direct application of the cosmological principle and incompatible with perspectivity. It is worth noting that the notion of creativity is characterized by Whitehead as the "ultimate metaphysical principle" (PR 21). Both actual entities and eternal objects have "extreme finality," but " 'Creativity,' 'many,' 'one' are the ultimate notions involved in the meaning of the synonymous terms 'thing,' 'being,' 'entity.' These three notions complete the Category of the Ultimate and are presupposed in all the more special categories" (PR 21). There appears to be a confusion in Whitehead's formulations as to what is "really" fundamental, even what fundamentality is. The question is whether this confusion is due to the unwarranted assumption that anything at all is metaphysically more fundamental or ultimate in an unqualified sense.[14]

Whitehead defines Speculative Philosophy as "the endeavour to frame a coherent, logical, necessary system of general ideas in terms of which every element of our experience can be interpreted" (PR 3). This definition has no implication of ontological or epistemological priority. We require a philosophical scheme that is "coherent, logical, and, in respect to its interpretation, applicable and adequate" (PR 3). But Whitehead also tells us that "our datum is the actual world, including ourselves; and this actual world spreads itself for observation in the guise of the topic of our immediate experience" (PR 4). I have been arguing that there are three major strains in Whitehead's theory, expressed through the cosmological principle and the principles of perspective and experience. The first two, however, are particularly relevant, here, in the interdependence of fundamental categories expressing mutual constitution and uniqueness of point of view inherent in perspectivity, and in the hierarchy generated by the ontological priority founded on the cosmological principle.

One way of formulating the issue is whether the fallacy of misplaced concreteness should instead have been considered the fallacy of concreteness: whether the errors of traditional systems have been due (a) to their failure to discern what is *truly* concrete or (b) to their willingness to consider any category at all as "more real" or "more concrete." Concreteness is a type of ontological priority that, along with other forms of ontological priority, violates the principle of perspective in being unconditioned and absolute and is incompatible with the moving spirit of Whitehead's perspectivism.[15]

All forms of ontological priority have a dominant function—one that is especially paramount in Whitehead's cosmology: to provide for a unified world amidst a rich and complex array of categories, beings, and principles. We recall the richness of Whitehead's categories, especially the eight categories of existence. All are genuine modes of existence; each is perfectly real. The world is filled with many diverse but related things. All are to be interpreted in terms of the eight categories of existence. And by the principle of coherence, these categories involve each other.

By the principle of perspective, being is always from a point of view and qualified. The eight categories of existence are qualified in one sense by the presence of the others, but there is a far stronger qualification required that Whitehead does not develop. To be an actuality or a possibility is also qualified and functional: actual entities are actualities in one role and potentialities in another; eternal objects have individual essences and relational essences and are both actual determinants and potential forms of determination. Actualities and possibilities are not distinct *kinds* of beings but different functions played by the same beings in different perspectives. Possibilities are not unconditioned, nor are actualities. From such a perspectival point of view, there cannot be ontological priority, for what is prior in one sense is secondary or derivative in another. As a consequence, perspectival being is inexhaustible.[16] This inexhaustibility is the central corollary of the principle of perspective which is entirely incompatible with the cosmological principle and ultimate realities. Whitehead recognizes inexhaustibility, but not its incompatibility with cosmology. "The complexity of nature is inexhaustible" (PR 106). Perspectival inexhaustibility is not just incompleteness and transcendence, but the complementarity of determinateness and indeterminateness in every condition and being. Cosmology and ontological priority are unconditioned in certain absolute respects.

The final test of doctrines of ontological priority is the particular mode of being they take to be fundamental. Yet no such selection can be justified or intelligible. The ontological principle has a variety of analogues, but it is basically arbitrary. Actual entities could not exist without eternal objects. Therefore, it is correct to say that all existence depends on eternal objects, and they are essential to all definiteness. Why, then, are they abstract? Because they are *for* actualities. This is no explanation. Actual entities are equally *for* the ingression of eternal objects.[17]

Eternal objects are not active and are not subjects. But they are individuals with individual essences. Subjectivity is no explanation; it is a criterion for making a distinction that has no legitimacy. The conjunction of individual and relational essences in eternal objects is either ultimate and unintelligible or it is perspectival, making them equally perspectival and real, if not prehensive, subjects. Like actual entities, eternal objects are profoundly perspectival in that they transcend their relations while being constituted by them.

> No eternal object in any finite realization can exhibit the full potentialities of its nature. It has an individual essence—whereby it is the same eternal object on diverse occasions, and it has a relational essence whereby it has an infinitude of modes of entry into realization. (Whitehead 1963, p. 299)

Eternal objects can be regarded as abstract only in virtue of the onto-logical principle with its cosmological implications. The *total* related-ness of eternal objects is both unnecessary and unintelligible with respect to the determinateness of each eternal object, its individual essence, which is effectively an exclusive sphere of relations among other forms of determination.[18]

The bias is clear: Whitehead takes the succession of events to be primary and fundamental and the basis from which everything else is derived. This is incompatible with his emphasis on timeless forms, but that is not crucial. The issue is whether history and causal succession comprise the ultimate basis of things. The issue is also whether there is a supreme viewpoint or perspective on the entire world—in Whitehead's case, defined by the ontological principle. The alternative is to deny ontological primacy. No single system can comprise the world. There is no supreme or absolute perspective on any mode of being, but in-exhaustibly many and irreducibly diverse perspectives, each constituted by its relations and conditioned by other perspectives, but also irreduc-ibly unique in its perspectival focus. In the complexity of things, processes are sometimes of paramount importance, sometimes not. Importance and primacy are perspectivally determined; there can be no unqualified primacy or importance from an absolute or total point of view.

The arbitrariness of a doctrine of ontological priority is the result of the conviction, based on the cosmological principle, that there is an ultimate, absolute, and most complete conception of the universe. In that ultimate conception, the passage of events appears to be of fundamental and unqualified importance. But if we deny all ultimate conceptions, due to the inexhaustible complexity of things and based on the principle of perspective, we must regard causal order as but one of many different types of order. And not all perspectives or types of order can be con-joined in a unified system. Such a conjunction would be a violation of the principle of perspective.

Notes to Chapter 8

1. I call this relationship between actual entities and eternal objects "complementary," for that is what I take it to be in Whitehead's theory, freed from the arbitrariness of the ontological principle and grounded more thoroughly on the principle of perspective. Nevertheless, some commentators, by radically overemphasizing the importance of eternal objects, have found Whitehead to be inconsistent.

> The character of eternal objects is such as to enable them, alone among all the elements of Whitehead's universe, to exist in and through themselves while other types of existence are in some sense derivative from theirs. (Pols 1967, p. 158)

> Despite all his insistence on the principle of coherence, which holds that none of the conceptions of a philosophy is fully meaningful without its relations to all the others, he does in fact accord eternal objects—his version of Platonic Forms—more of the traditional marks of substantiality than he does other ingredients of his system. . . . the ontological principle . . . plays a less important role in his philosophy than his explicit references to it would lead us to believe. (Pols 1967, p. 159)

2. There is nothing in reality over and above potentiality except definiteness." (Hartshorne 1972, p. 34)

3. It is worth noting Hartshorne's proposed solution to this difficulty. (Hartshorne 1972, p. 34) (See above, note 10, p. 56)

4. Compare Leclerc:

> The ontological principle . . . is the affirmation, first, that some entities are "actual," i.e., fully existent entities—or that at least one entity is "actual"; and secondly, that actual entities "form the ground from which all other types of existence are derivative and abstracted." (1958, p. 24)

Leclerc does not recognize the limitations of such an ontological principle: that generality is restricted by ontological primacy. "Whitehead could define metaphysics as the study of the completely general or generic features or characteristics of actual entities, the study of actual entities *qua* actual entities" (Leclerc 1958, p. 33). "The ideas in question, because they are the conceptions of the generic features of actual entities, must be *completely general*" (Leclerc 1958, p. 34). Generality over *all actual entities*, which are a restricted category of existence, ontologically primary or not, is not generality over all modes of existence, over all beings, including eternal objects and nexūs. Determinateness, definiteness, individuality, and relatedness are properties that pertain to all being, even in Whitehead's theory, though he does not develop their general characteristics.

5. Compare Leclerc:

> What Whitehead has done is to put "act" in the place of the Aristotelian "prime matter." It must be explicitly understood that Whitehead has not *ascribed* activity to matter; matter cannot act—on this Whitehead and Aristotle are in complete agree-

ment. But whereas Aristotle saw no alternative in that case but to ascribe act to form, Whitehead abolishes "matter" entirely, and in its place puts "act" or "activity," pure creative activity. That is to say, Whitehead replaces the Aristotelian category of "prime matter" by the category of "creativity." (1961, p. 178)

6. According to Leclerc, "An *actual* entity is an *acting* entity; that is to say, it is "acting," "agency" which constitutes *existence* in the "full" sense (Leclerc 1958, p. 70).

7. See in particular, Everett Hall's "Of What Use are Whitehead's Eternal Objects?":

It is natural to wonder whether "eternal objects" play any role which could not be legitimately taken over by actual occasions. . . . eternal objects are made to account for identity, permanence, universality, abstractness, and potentiality. (Hall 1963, p. 102)

Since we now learn that identity, permanence, universality, abstractness, and possibility are all definable in terms of occasions, we cannot avoid wondering whether eternal objects have not virtually become so much useless baggage. (Hall 1963, p. 105)

8. The question of the necessity of eternal objects was posed as long ago as 1930 by Everett Hall (see note 7 above). It is clear that possibilities are essential in Whitehead's theory to allow for an open future and for novelty. Hall does not explain how these may be derived from actual entities alone, nor does he even recognize their importance. Nevertheless, as Hartshorne notes, unconditioned and unchanging eternal objects are deeply problematical.

Independence of temporal context may be relative as well as absolute. . . . "essences" may perfectly well emerge in the universe, not merely in the world of actuality but in the total universe of actuality and possibility. . . . if red is an emergent in the universe, then before this emergence it was neither true nor false that red was red—or anything else. (Hartshorne 1972, p. 32)

9. Wittgenstein's arguments against private languages, in *Philosophical Investigations* (1958), are effective arguments against pure forms of determinateness.

10. Leclerc offers a defense of eternity:

The forms as that which constitute the "what" and "how" of things are necessarily eternal. That is, that the forms as such should be capable of change, of flux, is impossible. To be the form of changing things, form must itself be exempt from change, from flux. For it is in the forms themselves that we have to understand change; and therefore that the forms themselves should be capable of change is absurd, a contradiction. (1964, p. 129)

11. "I would like to maintain the emphasis that platonic mathematical structures do not change, as affirmed by Whitehead and Augustine, but relax the requirement that no new potentials or structures be added to the realm of eternal objects" (Granville Henry, 1973, p. 12). Such a view is somewhat similar to mine, but is drastically limited, for Henry does not recognize that mathematical

structures may not change in *some* respects but certainly do change in others—their ingressions and applications. There is no absolute distinction in a perspectival theory between what changes and what does not: change is always in certain respects and not in others.

12. "A doctrine that new eternal objects are created from time to time could be incorporated into Whitehead's thought without necessitating a wholesale revision of his system" (Shahan 1950, p. 123).

13. It also resolves the problem Cobb poses as a consequence of the timelessness of God:

> God's aim at universal intensity of satisfaction determines a specific aim at the appropriate satisfaction of each individual occasion. But it is very difficult to imagine how these individual aims can be wholly timeless and yet become relevantly effective at particular moments of time. (Cobb 1965, p. 180)

See also Wells's argument that eternity is incompatible with a process theory, that Whitehead's logical theory is incompatible with his theory of events.

> With his recognition that nature is process, he can make no sense of rational meaning unless there are eternalities in nature, entities which do not change but are just what they are, and which are not in the process of becoming something else at the same time. His assumption is that unless a thing has a tautological relation to itself, unless it can be said that it is itself and not at the same time not itself, there can be no possibility of rendering a rational account of nature. It is this assumption which forces him to divorce objects from process. (1950, p. 12)

Wells criticizes Whitehead for not being Hegelian enough: "Identity involves internal opposition, rather than its exclusion" (1950, p. 111). I suggest that the principle of perspective, even in its limited form in Whitehead's theory, carries the duality of opposition and multiplicity essential to process without Hegel's commitment to historicism and temporality. Wells is correct that to make *process* primary, a dialectical theory is necessary. (See Vlastos's similar position, note 2, p. 21.) But perspectivity is a more general notion than process and needs no dialectical element to save it from regress.

14. Calling the aspect of Whitehead's system that strives for the definition of what is most concrete, real, fundamental, or ultimate, "Trend II," Justus Buchler states:

> The main question is whether Trend II weakens the structure to which it contributes; whether it casts a shadow of crude myth upon a remarkably intricate tissue of distinctions and generalizations; whether it spawns a formidable strain of arbitrariness in a system above all designed to avoid arbitrariness. (1969, p. 591)

Buchler's argument is summarized in the following passages:

> If we ask why pure possibilities (eternal objects) should be secondary and actual entities primary, when it is repeatedly stated that neither of these two kinds of being is conceivable apart from the other; what it means for one actuality to be "more"

concrete or "less" concrete than another actuality; why any kind of unity or oneness is "more" of a unity, a truer oneness than any other; why individuals are "more real" than societies, why they "make up the sole reality of the universe," when nonindividual actualities have been discriminated just as decisively; what it means to be a "completely real thing"—we find no answers. (1969, p. 592)

Witness the statement that "in separation from actual entities there is nothing, merely nonentity." One could ruminate over the precise force of the phrase "in separation from," and then render it as "except in relation to." But the important observation to make is that, in spite of the emphasis intended, the Whiteheadian scheme permits us to say with equal validity: in separation from eternal objects there is nothing, merely nonentity. (1969, p. 596)

My feeling is that if Trend I had gained the ascendancy, with its more relentless scrutiny of discriminanda, its independence of ultimate rankings and destinies, there would have emerged a structure equally majestic, freer from disparity and gratuitousness, and more subtle in its exhibitive dimension. (1969, p. 601)

The issue Buchler raises is of great importance in terms of the principle of perspective.

15. Note in this connection Leclerc's reply to Buchler, which effectively concedes the arbitrariness of ontological priority while denying that there is an incompatibility between what Buchler calls Trends I and II.

Whitehead has definitely recognized that when the distinction is made into types of entities the problem requires to be faced not merely as to how they are related to each other, but how they are related in respect of "being."
The outcome of Whitehead's reflection on this problem was to bring him into essential agreement with Aristotle in his solution to this problem. This is that the different senses of "being" are not on a parity, that the various senses ultimately have reference to one sense as basic. (Leclerc 1971, p. 57)

The criterion of primary reality is agency or power.

The Aristotelean doctrine is that there is one type of entity or being which "acts" in this sense of itself initiating and carrying out the "work," the "doing," and "moving," by its own inherent power. Whitehead shares this position with Aristotle. (1971, p. 57)

Yet there is no *reason* for assigning actual entities absolute primacy over eternal objects and even propositions, when the former could not be without the other modes. Even more important, from the standpoint of perspective, that something is an actual entity, in Whitehead's theory, is absolute and unconditioned, not a function, and this too is arbitrary: a character of being that has no relations outside itself. Rather, that an actual entity is an actual entity, is an actuality rather than a potentiality (for the future), must be a function of its relations to other entities, actual and potential.

16. See my "The Inexhaustibility of Nature," (1973, pp. 251–53); *Transition to an Ordinal Metaphysics* (1980); *Philosophical Mysteries* (1981).

17. See Pols:

> While eternal objects are transcendent in the sense that one of them may ingress in many actual entities, they are . . . meant precisely for that role of ingression. They do not lead another life of which their ingression in actuality is but a reminder. They are possibilities, but only by being forms of definiteness *of* actual entities. (1967, p. 7)

18. The remarks by several commentators that the relational and individual essences of eternal objects are totalistic and effectively nonperspectival are even more unintelligible than Whitehead's own formulations. See, here, Sherburne's words (above, note 14, pp. 166–167). Compare Whitehead's own words:

> The relational essence of each "Etern. Obj." involves its (potential) interconnections with all other eternal objects. The traditional doctrine of the absolute isolation of universals is as great a (tacit) error, as the isolation of primary substances. . . . The *absolute* abstraction of eternal objects from each other is an analogous error. (Whitehead 1963, p. 199)

CHAPTER NINE

GOD

The primordial created fact is the unconditioned conceptual valuation of the entire multiplicity of eternal objects. This is the "primordial nature" of God. By reason of this complete valuation, the objectification of God in each derivate actual entity results in a graduation of the relevance of eternal objects to the concrescent phases of that derivative occasion. There will be additional ground of relevance for select eternal objects by reason of their ingression into derivate actual entities belonging to the actual world of the concrescent occasion in question. But whether or no this be the case, there is always the definite relevance derived from God. (PR 31)

So Whitehead begins the first elaboration of his categoreal scheme. God is central to his metaphysical system, due in part to genuine religious conviction, but far more important, it seems to me, as embodiment of the principle which closes the scheme of metaphysical explanation. Such closure is incompatible with the principle of perspective with respect to both the primordial and consequent natures of God: the one because it is unconditioned, the other because it is complete and all-inclusive. God is the supreme embodiment of the cosmological principle, and one of the weakest elements of Whitehead's system where that principle is regarded as questionable, one of the most attractive elements where cosmology and metaphysics are effectively equated. Nevertheless, although God is unique in certain fundamental respects in Whitehead's system, and represents a uniquely inclusive and cosmological perspective on all other perspectives, he does not, in Whitehead's view, violate the other metaphysical principles in order to bring the system into completion. "God is not to be treated as an exception to all metaphysical principles, invoked to save their collapse. He is their chief exemplification" (PR 343). Whether God is an exception to Whitehead's fundamental principles is of major importance in evaluating his theory.

God is clearly incompatible with some of the central features of the principle of perspective—though by no means all, since he is perspectival in fundamental ways—but is certainly a dominant expression of the principle of experience.

Before examining these matters more closely, I will consider God in his primordial and consequent natures and discuss his complex role in Whitehead's system. In particular, I will examine the claim that a metaphysical system requires a principle of completion. The question is whether what God represents categorially is necessary to metaphysical understanding and, if necessary, whether it can be represented in any other way.[1]

The Primordial Nature of God

God's primordial nature is "the primordial created fact," and is "the unconditioned conceptual valuation of the entire multiplicity of eternal objects." It is *primordial* because it is first in every becoming and entirely unconditioned: no other mode of being determines it. "The given course of history presupposes his primordial nature, but his primordial nature does not presuppose it" (PR 44). The totality indicated here, the *entire* multiplicity of eternal objects, with the unconditioned nature of God's conceptual valuation, are all expressions of a cosmological perspective. God is *first* in the universe, in his primordial nature, in that all definiteness is a result of his unconditioned and free gradation among eternal objects.[2] The principle of perspective is nevertheless preserved in the profound insight that even God's primordial nature is selective and restrictive, imposing a unique order upon eternal objects, thereby upon actualities. The totalistic nature of the selection, its eternal, unchanging nature, its independence from individual events, all are violations of the principle of perspective.[3]

In *Science and the Modern World*, Whitehead carefully defines the function of God in terms of his primordial nature: occasions "require that the course of events should have developed amid an antecedent limitation composed of conditions, particularizations, and standards of value" (SMW 249). He goes on to explain that God represents a "ground for limitation," and that this principle of limitation is the ultimate principle, which has no explanation, and upon which all explanation rests. "God is the ultimate limitation, and His existence is the ultimate irrationality" (SMW 240). "No reason can be given for just that limitation which it stands in His nature to impose. . . . No reason can be given for the nature of God, because that nature is the ground of rationality" (SMW 249–50). The world, understood in the deepest sense, nevertheless possesses an ultimate irrationality. All explanation must cease at some point. What is required is a formal representation of this ultimate arbitrariness, represented in Whitehead's system by the primordial nature of God.

> What is metaphysically indeterminate has nevertheless to be categorically determinate. We have come to the limit of rationality. For there is a categorical limitation which does not spring from any metaphysical reason. There is a metaphysical need for a principle of determination, but there can be no metaphysical reason for what is determined. (SMW 250)[4]

God's primordial nature is primordial and unconditioned in being *that which has no explanation beyond itself*, and represents categorially that there is an ultimate.

The difficulty is not that there are unresolvable questions, limits, even mysteries. It is the monolithic completion Whitehead seems to think is required. There is no justification for the view that there is a single principle of concretion, one ultimate metaphysical reason, or one ultimate irrationality.[5] Self-causation is equally inexplicable. It is a rationalistic bias that everything is unintelligible but an ultimate irrationality, a bias rooted in the cosmological principle and incompatible with the principle of perspective. The latter principle, with its inexhaustible plurality, makes every being mysterious in some respects, not as *beyond* analysis and explanation, but as *inexhaustible* by any particular analysis or explanation. The emergent novelty, the unique identity, of every perspective is analyzable as much as possible by constituents and relations—but never exhaustively analyzable; for all constituents are from the unique and novel point of view of the perspective they constitute. This is the essential meaning of the doctrine of prehension, and it is strong enough to make cosmological principles unnecessary, on the one hand, and unintelligible, on the other. If the world is viewed as irreducibly many, indefinitely complex, inexhaustibly perspectival, then there are no *ultimate* principles. More accurately, everything is based on principles beyond which intelligibility cannot be realized. Conversely, however, everything is indefinitely analyzable. This complementarity of analyzability and inexhaustibility, identity and multiplicity, determinateness and indeterminateness, is inherent in the principle of perspective. Limitations and exclusions pervade reality. These limitations simultaneously and inseparably constitute intelligibility and circumscribe it. In this sense, the selectivity of perspectives is commonplace and provides no ultimate ground for the world.

I have discussed many of these matters in connection with the timelessness of eternal objects. The unconditioned nature of eternal objects is expressed recurrently by Whitehead, in their individual essences in *Science and the Modern World* (corresponding to a mere multiplicity in *Process and Reality*) and in the unconditioned nature of the primordial nature of God. From the standpoint of actual occasions, God imposes an unconditioned limitation on events entirely independent of their decisions. Only God's consequent nature is a function of the becomings of actual occasions. Whitehead must then add to the self-causation of every occasion the unconditioned decision in the primordial nature of God and the conditioned self-determination inherent in the consequent nature of God. God thus embodies two ultimate principles of determination. I have suggested that a simpler and far more plausible view would be to make God's entire nature conditioned by actual events, so that both his primordial and his consequent natures would be a consequence of his prehensions of actual occasions, supplemented by his cosmic satisfaction.[6] The advantages of this modification are that God would then embody only one mode of self-causation, like every other actual entity; that even his primordial nature would be conditioned and temporal in fundamental ways; and that, along with other conceptual envisagements, each such envisagement would be a particular perspective upon the wealth of eternal objects. This suggestion preserves the cosmological principle in the totality of God's conceptual envisagement and in his prehensive satisfaction of all occasions, but it enhances the importance of the principle of perspective in relation to God. I consider even this large a concession to the cosmological principle unjustifiable and will discuss its limitations in relation to the consequent nature of God. Nevertheless, the suggestion does resolve many of the difficulties produced by the unconditioned nature of eternal objects.

The primordial nature of God is the basis of God's immanence in all actual occasions. God is immanent in three related senses. One is his determination of what is relevant to every event. The second is his yearning for the future.

> God's immanence in the world in respect to his primordial nature is an urge towards the future based upon an appetite in the present. Appetition is at once the conceptual valuation of an immediate physical feeling combined with the urge towards realization of the datum conceptually prehended. (PR 32)

This appetition and yearning are expressions of the principle of experience in relation to God. Like the prehensions of every other experient entity, God's prehensions are teleological. His primordial nature is not a passive entertainment of conceptual forms, merely contemplated, but an active urge for their realization in actuality.

If we say that God's primordial nature is "vision," we suggest a maimed view of the subjective form, divesting it of yearning after concrete fact—no particular facts, but after *some* actuality, There is deficiency in God's primordial nature which the term "vision" obscures. (PR 33)

This yearning after *some*, but no *particular*, actualities is another rejection of conditions, for only some range of possibilities can be treated as an end. In addition, yearning would be unnecessary from the standpoint of the principle of perspective. Whitehead's conception of the unconditioned valuation of eternal objects in God's primordial nature requires a principle of transition from possibility to actuality, realized through a yearning based on the principle of experience. Where conceptual envisagement is regarded as thoroughly conditioned by actuality, no such transition is required. Actual events in the aggregate determine their own possibilities for their own future.

The third form of immanence is that "God is the principle of concretion; namely, he is that actual entity from which each temporal concrescence receives that initial aim from which its self-causation starts" (PR 244). Whitehead tells us that "the initial stage of the aim is rooted in the nature of God" (PR 244) and that "God and the actual world jointly constitute the character of the creativity for the initial phase of the novel concrescence" (PR 245). A question for examination is whether this function of the primordial nature of God is something in addition to the functions already described, or whether it is included in his conceptual valuation of the multiplicity of eternal objects.[7]

In what sense does God provide the initial stage of the subjective aim? And if he does so, does it eliminate self-causation? I argued in chapter 3 that self-causation is fundamental in Whitehead's theory. There are, then, two specific senses in which God may be thought to be "the principle of concretion": (1) He provides the aim, in synthesis with what is given, as one of a range of relevant possibilities. This function is precisely that of the primordial nature of God. It is what allows Whitehead to state that "the initial stage of the aim is rooted in the nature of God" (PR 244). The subjective aim is a determinate possibility (or range of possibilities) made relevant by the order imposed by the primordial nature of God.[8] (2) God provides the urge inherent in the world to move from one actuality to the next. Without God, the satisfaction realized in a concrescence might be terminated and the future never come to pass.

This last interpretation is supported by the deficient character of the primordial nature of God. In being "deficient in actuality," God's primordial nature requires something more for his completion—realization in concrete actuality. But God's consequent nature is never finished; thus it imposes a continual creativity upon the universe. In "yearning after concrete fact," God provides the impulse toward the initial stages of every concrescence.

I have noted how this function of God may be thought to resolve a difficulty taken to prevail in the transition within an actual entity from being a subject to being an object for subsequent occasions.[9] My view is that the actual entity viewed as superject makes this function of God entirely unnecessary. Moreover, the dependence of actual occasions on God for the basis of the principle of relativity—that to be is to be relevant to other becomings—entirely undercuts the perspectivity of perished occasions. They cease to be perspectival except through God, and the entire past becomes irrelevant to the future except through God. I claim that, to the contrary, based on the principles of perspective and relativity, the transition from subject to object is necessary to the fulfillment of an actual entity as a superject. Every event establishes the conditions for its supersession and must be superseded if it is to be fulfilled. The being of an actual occasion is two-dimensional, a direct expression of the complementary nature of perspective.

> God and the actual world jointly constitute the character of the creativity for the initial phase of the novel concrescence. The subject, thus constituted, is the autonomous master of its own concrescence into subject-superject. It passes from a subjective aim in concrescence into a superject with objective immortality. (PR 245)

The past is comprised of perished occasions functioning objectively in later concrescences. The urge toward further creativity is embodied in the principle that each occasion seeks a satisfaction with a double function—for its own feeling and for the future occasions that prehend it. God is not necessary to provide the transition from the past to the future, only to provide determinants for that transition. If we take the perspectives of actual entities seriously, we must take seriously as well their self-determining nature, in their own becoming and thereafter, as superjects, for the future. God's yearning for the future is an essential component of his being an experiencing actual entity requiring physical feeling for completion. Nevertheless, this yearning cannot be thought to be so efficacious for other entities as to eliminate their own relevance for the future.[10]

It is worth considering again the fact that eternal objects, apart from the primordial nature of God, comprise a multiplicity, not an order.[11] In *Process and Reality*, Whitehead seems to wish to avoid the conception of a *realm* of forms antecedent to and independent of actuality. Eternal objects are merely a multiplicity without God, and God is incomplete without the actual world he prehends in his consequent nature. Yet we may wonder just what eternal objects might be, apart from their relations. In their sheer multiplicity, they apparently possess individual, but not relational, essences. If so, they do so without being actual or self-caused. Worst of all, they violate the principle that nothing is wholly in itself, apart from constitutive relations. The separation of the individual from relational essences for eternal objects is a repetition of the Bradleyan problem of relations, which Whitehead resolves for actual entities by the theory of prehensions. Perspective is essential to identity amidst relations. The abstractness and purity of eternal objects does not resolve this problem, but only emphasizes their exceptional nature. Perspectivity must be as essential to eternal objects as it is to actual entities, if they are to have both individuality and relationality, and if the two are to be conjoined.

Perhaps we should not separate the multiplicity of eternal objects from their valuation. Here, the individual as well as the relational essences of eternal objects would be jointly constituted—both of them a function of events. Here, every eternal object would be a double function of relations—to other eternal objects and actual entities—and individuality, intelligible only on some version of the principle of perspective. A particular eternal object can have an individual essence, an identity, only in virtue of its unique functions amidst a multiplicity of relations. Here the function of God becomes largely irrelevant except for defining a totality among all eternal objects, a function closely allied with his unconditioned primordial nature. To take eternal objects seriously as perspectival modes of being is to make the function of God in Whitehead's theory far less plausible.

The Consequent Nature of God

God's consequent nature is "the weaving of God's physical feelings upon his primordial concepts" (PR 345). In his primordial nature, he is "deficient in actuality," since he possesses only conceptual feelings and lacks the completion provided by a subjective aim. It is in his consequent nature that God is completed as an actual entity, in the integration of his physical feelings of the actual world with the conceptual feelings of his primordial nature.

> One side of God's nature is constituted by his conceptual experience. This experience is the primordial fact in the world, limited by no actuality which it presupposes. It is therefore infinite, devoid of all negative prehensions. This side of his nature is free, complete, primordial, eternal, actually deficient, and unconscious. The other side originates with physical experience derived from the temporal world, and then acquires integration with the primordial side. It is determined, incomplete, consequent, "everlasting," fully actual, and conscious. His necessary goodness expresses the determination of his consequent nature. (PR 345)

God's primordial nature plays an important categorial role in Whitehead's theory, though it is fraught with difficulties. I have made several suggestions for modifying it in accordance with the principle of perspective, while maintaining the relevance of forms of definiteness required for creativity. However, from the standpoint of actual occasions, God's consequent nature is entailed only by the ontological principle, which requires that he be an actual entity. Nevertheless, it is through this consequent nature that Whitehead accommodates most of the notions found in traditional religious thought. He claims that our intuition of the primordial nature of God is far more pervasive than our religious intuitions. "They lie at a far lower level of experience than do the religious emotions" (PR 207). Our religious intuitions are directed at God's consequent nature. I will briefly consider some of the striking traits Whitehead attributes to the consequent nature of God.

Consciousness. "The consequent nature of God is conscious" (PR 345). Consciousness in Whitehead's theory is the subjective form of the affirmation-negation contrast (PR 243). "It is the contrast between '*in fact*' and '*might be*,' in respect to particular instances in *this* actual world" (PR 267). The primordial nature of God is constituted by conceptual feelings of what might be—the entire wealth of possibility in ordered gradations of relevance. His consequent nature is comprised of his physical feelings of actual occasions as they become in the world. But God is an actual entity, and all actual entities satisfy the conditions of subjective unity and subjective harmony—that is, the integration of all elements of concrescence in a satisfaction. There is no final satisfaction for God, but that does not relieve him of the categoreal obligation to integrate the various elements of his experience. Otherwise they could not be unified in his experience nor constitute the world.

Therefore, God's consequent nature must include an integration of the entire wealth of possibility with his physical prehension of everything that actually occurs. This generates a contrast between what is and what might be, and must be the object of a conscious feeling. The consequent nature of God is conscious because it involves a contrast of a complexity that can only be found in consciousness.[12]

Here the obtrusiveness of God's encompassment of the world is severe, for if God is conscious, then the world is unified not only in its interactions, involvements, and categories, but even in thought. Not only is there a comprehensive point of view, but it is a conscious point of view. Whitehead continues the classic cosmological mission to make the world a complete object for God's thought. The major difficulty of his position is the traditional one that a consciousness without significant perspectival limitations is no consciousness at all. The totality of prehensions assigned to God makes focal attention meaningless. In other words, by the principle of perspective, God's consciousness must be from a particular point of view, and there is no qualified point of view assignable to God, for he is both everywhere and nowhere, unconditioned.

By the principle of experience, God is a prehensive entity. Yet he violates the principle of perspective, that experience and relation always be from a particular, qualified point of view. God is not located in space and time, has no place in relation to the succession of becomings or the regions of the extensive continuum. That there should be a consciousness without perspectival limitation and exclusion is but a manifestation of the general problem of the cosmological principle in relation to God: too many of God's features are unconditioned.

Wisdom. God's consequent nature and his subjective aim are called by Whitehead "wise." By this he means a sense of "rightness," things as they belong together and harmonize, rather than in their fitful discordancies and passing irrelevancies.

> The wisdom of subjective aim prehends every actuality for what it can be in such a perfected system—its sufferings, its sorrows, its failures, its triumphs, its immediacies of joy—woven by rightness of feeling into the

harmony of the universal feeling, which is always immediate, always many, always one, always with novel advance, moving onward and never perishing. (PR 346)

The consequent nature of God is the physical prehension of what is or has been, contrasted with what might be. It is the feeling of what has made its influence felt in the course of events. Whitehead speaks of "the *perfection* of God's subjective aim" (PR 345). This is no human sense of perfection, but one in which everything that occurs belongs. "There is no loss, no obstruction" (PR 346). There is no dismissal of irrelevancies or meaningless eventualities. In human experience, we find the imperfection of errors needing correction, steps taken in vain, elements that are incompatible with our ideals. In God, everything belongs, a step in the realization of his subjective aim. Thus, his aim is perfect, wise, and everlasting.

> The consequent nature of God is his judgment on the world. He saves the world as it passes into the immediacy of his own life. It is the judgment of a tenderness which loses nothing that can be saved. It is also the judgment of a wisdom which uses what in the temporal world is mere wreckage. (PR 346)

The perfection of God here is cosmological, unconditioned, and incompatible with the principle of perspective. The difficulty with the perfection of God is not his supremacy but the cosmological assumption that the properties derived from a multiplicity of perspectives can be extended to an absolute, all-inclusive perspective. I have suggested that consciousness may be a function of particularity of perspective, of limitation. The contrast of what is with what might be can be meaningful only from a particular point of view—and God has no such point of view. Equivalently, there is no total and unconditioned possibility, what might be, with which all of actuality is contrasted. Possibility as well as actuality are conditioned determinations. Analogously, wisdom is relative to selection and exclusion. The ideas of *no* loss, *no* obstruction, of saving *everything* that can be saved, are unconditioned, nonperspectival. Saving and loss are always from a point of view.

Patience. "The universe," Whitehead says,

> includes a threefold creative act composed of (i) the one infinite conceptual realization, (ii) the multiple solidarity of free physical realizations in the temporal world, (iii) the ultimate unity of the multiplicity of actual fact with the primordial conceptual fact. If we conceive the first term and the last term in their unity over against the intermediate multiple freedom of

physical realizations in the temporal world, we conceive of the patience of
God, tenderly saving the turmoil of the intermediate world by the
completion of his own nature. (PR 346)

The finite and ongoing world is a place of turmoil and resistance, of
struggles and destruction. But in the union of his primordial nature in
its timeless valuation with the continual and never-ending contrast
between what is and what might be, God surveys the world patiently and
tenderly. Here, the multiplicity of occasions is relegated to a merely
intermediate state, fulfilled in the completion of God's aesthetic experience. God "is the poet of the world, with tender patience leading it by
his vision of truth, beauty, and goodness" (PR 346). The requirement
that the poet have a point of view, that he poetize from a standpoint
different from every other, based on limitation and exclusion, is incompatible with the perfections and incomparabilities assigned to God.
If God is a poet, he achieves a perspective on the world that is typically
his own, with its own limitations, and that can be contrasted with what
there is from other standpoints.

Everlastingness. Every occasion is *objectively immortal*, a condition
for every future, a potential for every becoming. No occasions are lost in
the course of the development of the world, since the future depends on
them. They may diminish to negligible relevance, but they cannot
altogether vanish.[13] The future bears the mark of the efficacy of the past.
This is the meaning of the principle of relativity. The past is totally
relevant to the future, and every occasion plays a relevant role for every
subsequent event. I have noted the cosmological elements of Whitehead's
principle of relativity, and suggested that a far weaker principle of
relativity, based entirely on the principle of perspective, would be more
effective theoretically and far more congruent with the testimony of
experience—that to be is to be in some perspective, relevant to some
other beings. In particular, past occasions are relevant to some future
occasions, but not all. Some events of the past diminish to irrelevance for
the future, by selection and exclusion. No justification can be given for
the requirement that every occasion prehend *every* past occasion.
Causation does not require this, nor does our sense of the past. There
must be a past relevant to the present. It need not be all-inclusive.
Cosmology here takes precedence over perspectivity, and objective
immortality is at stake.

Yet even so cosmological a conception as objective immortality is
insufficient to satisfy Whitehead's cosmological intuitions. "Objective
immortality within the temporal world does not solve the problem set by

the penetration of the finer religious intuition. 'Everlastingness' has been lost; and 'everlastingness' is the content of that vision upon which the finer religions are built—the 'many' absorbed everlastingly in the final unity" (PR 347). Objective immortality is the enduring relevance of past occasions to later occasions. But it lacks completion in the solidarity of the world. Some elements of past events become irrelevant, if not the events themselves. God's consequent nature is required to bring occasions' experiences into one all-inclusive experience. Even so, God's experience must be selective and limited, if it is to be experience at all.[14] Yet the consequent nature of God constitutes a vision of the entire universe from what seems to be a comprehensive point of view. All occasions in the universe, with all their feelings, are elements in the unity of feeling which is the consequent nature of God.

Thus, God recurrently represents the basis for the unity of the world. In its most extreme cosmological form, the immanence of the consequent nature of God in all occasions seems to suggest a unification that transcends all the principles of Whitehead's theory.

> The principle of universal relativity is not to be stopped at the consequent nature of God. This nature itself passes into the temporal world according to its gradation of relevance to the various concrescent occasions. . . . The perfected actuality passes back into the temporal world, and qualifies this world so that each temporal actuality includes it as an immediate fact of relevant experience. For the kingdom of heaven is with us today. . . . What is done in the world is transformed into a reality in heaven, and the reality in heaven passes back into the world. By reason of this reciprocal relation, the love in the world passes into the love in heaven, and floods back again into the world. In this sense, God is the great companion—the fellow-sufferer who understands. (PR 350–51)

If Whitehead means that each occasion prehends this consequent nature *directly and objectively*, his position is incompatible with the principle of subjective unification, since until God has been completed, he cannot be prehended objectively.[15] I cannot see how Whitehead could justify the relevance of the consequent nature of God to occasions except as an anticipated fulfillment, a love *to be realized*, continuously and proleptically, but never actually immanent in any actual occasion.

In any case, the moving principle is cosmological. Whatever is lacking from the world of events, insofar as they comprise one world, is provided by God. The religious intuition predominates over metaphysical considerations. The cosmological principle predominates over the principle of perspective. Cosmology predominates over inexhaustibility. The multiplicity of individual occasions is transformed into partial, imperfect perspectives upon their surroundings, diminished in comparison with the supreme and absolute perspective of God. There can be no supreme perspective, no unqualified perspective, that does not undermine the legitimacy of every other point of view, making it merely a distorted part of the whole.

Whitehead summarizes his discussion of the consequent nature of God in six antitheses, which summarize God's relationship to the world. These represent two fundamental principles: God and the world are one in that each requires the other; God is the completion of the world in providing its final unification. The antitheses represent the great reconciliation of the cosmological principle with the principle of perspective, the mating of inexhaustible plurality with the unity of the world. Whitehead accepts the testimony of religious intuition that the world can be the object of a vision, that it comprises a unity and an order; in short, the world entails God, but God also requires the world.

> Opposed elements stand to each other in mutual requirement. In their unity, they inhibit or contrast. God and the World stand to each other in this opposed requirement. God is the infinite ground of all mentality, the unity of vision seeking physical multiplicity. The World is the multiplicity of finites, actuality seeking a perfected unity. Neither God, nor the World, reaches static completion. Both are in the grip of the ultimate metaphysical ground, the creative advance into novelty. Either of them, God and the World, is the instrument of novelty for the other. (PR 348–49)

The two together comprise one world. Nevertheless, the reconciliation is achieved by stringent limitations upon the legitimacy and authority of individual perspectives. The need the world has for God is supreme, unconditioned, and calls into question the authenticity of all other perspectives.

The Cosmological Status of God

Whitehead claims that "God is not to be treated as an exception to all metaphysical principles, invoked to save their collapse. He is their chief exemplification" (PR 343). Yet God is certainly exceptional in some important respects—particularly, in being an actual entity that does not perish. Moreover, for occasions, physical prehensions are logically prior to conceptual feelings; the reverse is true for God. "For God the conceptual is prior to the physical, for the World the physical poles are prior to the conceptual poles" (PR 348). "God differs from other actual entities in the fact that Hume's principle, of the derivative character of conceptual feelings, does not hold for him" (PR 87). It may be worth studying in detail what Whitehead means by saying that God is no exception. The fundamental metaphysical principles of his system are his forty-six categories. We may consider each of them briefly with respect to God.

Categories of Existence: God is an actual entity, though not an actual occasion.

Categories of Explanation: (i) God becomes in his consequent nature. He does not perish, but perishing is not mentioned in the category. (ii) God is a unification of many possibilities in his consequent nature. (iii) Irrelevant. (iv) God's primordial nature is the fundamental ground of potentiality for every becoming. (v) God differs from other actual entities in having an all-inclusive actual world. Nevertheless, his actual world differs from every other. God's all-inclusiveness is cosmological, and is incompatible with the principle of perspective. As important as this issue is, however, it is not immediately relevant, since the totality of occasions comprising the actual world for God is unique for him. (vi) As true for God as for any other actual entity. (vii) Irrelevant. (viii) The two poles of actuality—subjective and objective—are relevant to God in his two natures. (ix) God's being is his becoming only for his consequent nature, but certainly there. (x)–(xvii) Irrelevant. (xviii) The ontological principle is the basis of God's existence. (xix) God is an actual entity. (xx) God illustrates definiteness, both in the multiplicity of his primordial nature and in what is felt in his consequent nature. He belongs as its complement to the nexus which is the entire world. (xxi)–(xxiii) Certainly God has significance for himself, since he provides the universe with its subjective aim toward intensity. God is self-creative via the universe, by contributing some determinateness to the multiplicity of occasions, though not diminishing their freedom. (xxiv) As applicable to God as to any other actual entity. (xxv)–(xxvii) Here there may be a difficulty, for there is no final phase of God's becoming, therefore no complete "satisfaction." The question here that requires an answer is whether the categories that are applicable to the satisfaction of actual entities are also applicable to God, or whether his eternal becoming is an exception to the categories. Postponing this question for a moment, we may consider the remaining principles.

Categoreal Obligations: (i) *Subjective Unity*. All of God's feelings are compatible as are the feelings in any other actual entity. God views the world from a comprehensive perspective, and from that point of view, the world comprises a whole through time. To deny this category in relation to God is to deny the solidarity of the entire universe through succession. (ii) *Objective Identity.* As true for God as for any actual entity. (iii) *Objective Diversity.* As true for God as for any actual entity. (iv) *Conceptual Valuation.* Satisfied by God's consequent nature. (v) *Conceptual Reversion.* Does not technically apply to God. His primordial nature includes all possibility and is incompatible with supplementation. Nevertheless, the important function of the category remains applicable. More is possible in experience than is inherited from the past. (vi) *Transmutation.* May be regarded as a form of confusion—the prehension of a multiplicity or nexus of actualities as one, rather than many. In God there is the complete preservation of the identities of each occasion in a multiplicity. But also, God must prehend in his consequent nature the contrast between each individual member of a nexus and the nexus as a whole. This category applies to God, provided that nexūs are a genuine mode of existence. (vii)–(viii) *Subjective Harmony* and *Subjective Intensity.* Both of these categories apply to the final stages of concrescence. But there are no final stages for God. Nevertheless, God's subjective aim predetermines the ongoing nature of his prehensions. His aim is directed toward intensification and complexity. If the world is one world, all feelings of it in God's consequent nature can be harmonized and balanced aesthetically. The difficulty is whether God's single act of becoming is consonant with the multiple acts of becoming that comprise the actual world, where the former does not *succeed* the latter. (ix) *Freedom and Determination.* God's freedom is not that of occasions. They are free in choosing their becoming subsequent to the reception of data from other entities. The consequent nature of God is essentially a passive vision without supplementation or exclusion. But the primordial nature of God is a free and unconditioned valuation of all possibility. I have criticized this notion of God's freedom, suggesting modifications to make it consonant with the self-determination of actual occasions.

From this summary, it is clear that God generally satisfies all of the explicit conditions necessary to actual entities but one—that of perishing with its concomitant unity and completeness. The obligations are held to apply even in the context of an experience that is never completed, based on the unification, harmonization, and intensification of all feelings in one all-inclusive experience. There is here a tension between the completeness imposed by the cosmological principle and the deficiency in God's experience imposed by his incompleteness at any time. The consequent nature of God must be a unified synthesis of the multiplicity of his physical prehensions according to the categories of subjective unity, subjective harmony, and subjective intensity. His incompleteness and lack of final satisfaction are problematic only where perishing is taken to be a fundamental metaphysical principle. Whitehead, it seems to me, offers a case for God's being an exception in this respect only.

If there are difficulties—and I have argued that there are many—they lie not at the level of the categories in Whitehead's theory, which include God as one of their major determinants, but at the level of the principles that establish the categories. I have formulated four such principles, which I take to embody the fundamental insights on which Whitehead's theory is based. The major conflict—which is only weakly resolved by the principle of experience—is that between the cosmological principle and the principle of perspective. Can a multiplicity of perspectives be reconciled in one supreme vision of the universe? [16] The violation by God of the principle of experience, attaining no satisfaction, completing no experience, but nevertheless harmonizing and reconciling all occasions' experiences together in one comprehensive experience, is cosmological. The violation by God of the principle of perspective, excluding no occasions and no eternal objects, in his unifying experience, is also cosmological. Experience and perspective are principles of limitation; God transcends limits synthetically and absolutely, in his totalistic experience, physical and conceptual. Yet Whitehead above all other metaphysicians understands that God's experience does not relegate other experiences to mere partiality, other perspectives to mere finitude, for his experience and perspectivity are subordinate in important ways to the experiences and perspectives of actual occasions. This tension, between cosmology and perspective, totality and limitation, absolutes and conditions, is the predominant element of Whitehead's theory of God.

The cosmological principle is that whatever happens, whatever has happened, transpires in one universe and can be understood or felt in a unified way. Without God, this claim has no metaphysical foundation. It requires a foundation if we are to avoid the anti-cosmological implications of the principle of perspective. Each actual occasion prehends the universe from a selective standpoint that involves exclusion. All the various standpoints and actual worlds must comprise one all-inclusive world. This can be true only if there is a comprehensive standpoint within which they are all unified. This standpoint is provided by God.

Whether this conception of the cosmological principle can be reconciled with an inexhaustibility of perspectives depends on how perspectivity is understood. The reconciliation depends in effect on a supreme perspective in relation to which all other perspectives are limited, as if exclusion and limitation belonged only to finite, and not infinite, perspectives. Yet even actual occasions in Whitehead's theory are infinite in many ways: they prehend the entire past, the entire multiplicity of eternal objects, and so forth. It is not finitude that is relevant here, but exclusion and limitation. God must be limited because all perspectives are limited; and if any perspective is unlimited, all are thrown into jeopardy. I have argued that even the principle of relativity must be qualified, and that no serious consequences would follow from such limitation that was not based on the arbitrariness of the cosmological principle.

In the final chapter I will sketch two ways of modifying Whitehead's system to make the principle of perspective predominant. One will preserve the relevance of God, in concession to the religious intuition, but minimize the cosmological assumptions. The other will entirely eliminate the closure upon perspectives imposed by God. Both, I will argue, can serve Whitehead's major purposes if they can be separated from his cosmological requirements.

Notes to Chapter 9

1. In this connection, see Wells:

> Whitehead is impelled to bifurcate nature into events as process and objects as permanences primarily because he accepts the traditional meaning of rationality. This division of nature into dynamic process and static objects implies and requires a metaphysics which will bring them into one system of relations. The dynamic process becomes the "consequent nature of God," and the static objects become the "primordial nature of God." The former is the "dynamic history," the latter is the "static vision," and the two together approach the Absolute Idealism of Hegel in which the world is the dynamic self-development of the static idea which was already there in the beginning. (1950, p. 11)

Wells takes the role of God in Whitehead's system to be incompatible with his process theory, a result of his incomplete conception of process. Wells simply overstates the point at issue and misrepresents both Hegel and Whitehead in fundamental ways.

> Whitehead's preconceived identification of rationality and method with self-identity, leads him to a dualistic philosophy of nature. Primarily, nature is process. It is this fact which has most impressed him. But in order to deal with process, he finds that he has to eliminate it. (Wells 1950, p. 68)

I trace these difficulties to the cosmological principle.

2. Compare Thompson:

> The subjective aim of God differs in several fundamental respects from that of other actual entities. For one thing, it is unbounded. It does not arise from any actual world. Furthermore, God's subjective aim includes the entire realm of possibilities. Since God's aim, like that of all actual entities, is at an intensity of realization, we can say that it is infinite and inexhaustible. (1971, p. 80)

Inexhaustibility here, without conditions and limitations, becomes absolute, swamping the self-decisions of individual occasions. There is very little freedom available for an occasion in Thompson's view except that of sin.

> The initial aim derived from God . . . involves a determinate unification of all actual entities and moreover the envisagement of the ideal possibility relative to these actual entities. . . . The initial datum of an occasion establishes a categoreal limit of what may be admitted in the way of a lure for feeling, but that what is in fact admitted to feeling up to and including this ideal limit, is determined by the actual entity in process of concrescence. God lures each actual entity toward the perfection possible for it, but each occasion "is finally responsible for the decision by which any lure for feeling is admitted to efficiency." (Thompson 1971, p. 96)

3. The importance of God in Whitehead's system depends on the relative importance assigned to cosmological unity and to religious insights.

> If you start to use its [the philosophy of organism's] fundamental categories—creativity, actual entities, and eternal objects—in the manner prescribed by Whitehead's categoreal scheme, you cannot avoid introducing an actual entity which from eternity to eternity holds the entire multiplicity of eternal objects in its conceptual experience. And once you have this primordial nature of God, the completeness of the system in its own terms necessitates some doctrine of God's consequent nature. (Lowe 1966, p. 102)

There is, however, the alternative of emphasizing the principle of perspective at the expense of both the cosmological principle and the principle of experience, leading, I suggest, to a more adequate and plausible theory without the arbitrary closure provided by God. Two such theories—both with a conception of God, but without his systematic culmination—will be discussed in the final chapter.

4. These passages, from *Science and the Modern World*, are not matched in *Process and Reality* in their direct expression of ultimate limits. Yet I find nothing in Whitehead's later work that is explicitly incompatible with this cosmological emphasis.

5. A remarkably strong version of the cosmological arguments presumably to be found in Whitehead's theory is formulated by Thompson (see above, note 11, p. 57). Thompson converts the ontological principle into a very strong cosmological argument:

> This order inherent in the course of the world is not self-explanatory because it is not itself an actuality. It is not explained by reference to eternal objects or creativity. And it is not explained by the actual occasion upon which it is imposed. There must be some

further principle to explain why this sort of order is inherent in the actual course of things. (Thompson 1971, p. 33)

Why is it a metaphysical feature of the actual world that causal efficacy is qualified in such a way as to enhance the exclusiveness of the occasions within the general order of logical necessity and extensive continuity? . . . The fact that an order of particularity inheres in the actual world requires there to be another principle of limitation. (Thompson 1971, p. 37)

6. Hartshorne appears to agree with me on this suggestion.

Independence of temporal context may be relative as well as absolute. . . . "essences" may perfectly well emerge in the universe, not merely in the world of actuality but in the total universe of actuality and possibility. . . . if red is an emergent in the universe, then before this emergence it was neither true nor false that red was red—or anything else. (Hartshorne 1972, p. 32)

See also:

God might be thought of, not as an actual entity, but as a "route" of actual entities, . . . Whitehead certainly does say that he is an actual entity. (Emmet 1966, p. xxxiii)

7. Compare Thompson:

Providing the initial aim for occasions is a function which has to be performed, which can be performed only by God, and without the performance of which there might be no actual world at all. In this specific sense, Whitehead's metaphysics seems to suggest that God is creator of the world. (1971, p. 127)

8. Only this understanding of God's role in providing the initial subjective aim as one among a multiplicity of lures for feeling can resolve the threats of determinism, on the one hand, and the unintelligibility of propositional lures which are not felt, on the other. Thus, when we emphasize the *modifications* of subjective aim, we must, I suggest, interpret this to mean a choice of final aim among a range of alternative aims. The initial aim is indeterminate in relation to the final aim and the occasion's decision, but not otherwise.

During the successive phases of the occasion's self-actualization, as it compares and harmonizes the data it has received from the world, it also modifies and adapts its subjective aim. (Cobb 1965, p. 96)

Creativity does

not appear to be the source of any (active) power to bring about the modification of subjective aim, so that this modification must seem to come about *ex nihilo*, or to result from the character of determinate components. (Pols 1967, p. 142)

Only the interpretation I am proposing seems to me to resolve the problem posited by Pols. (It does not resolve the problem of the arbitrariness of self-causation.)

Vagueness and ideality with specific alternatives define an unintelligible relationship between the initial and final aim, and make the role of God far too strong in relation to individual events.

> In its initial phase the concrescing actual occasion already possesses, in a sense, a unity, an indivisible togetherness, as a result of its subjective aim. But this unity provided by the subjective aim is an ideal unity, not a concrete unity of feeling. (Sherburne 1961, p. 46)

Other confusions based on an inadequate sense of alternative possibilities in relation to the initial aim from which the final aim emerges can be found in Christian:

> to maintain the principle of creativity, the datum of the initial aim must be something objective to God as well as to the concrescence. . . . this is to say precisely that the datum of the initial aim must be a pure potential, indeterminate as to its realization. . . .
> God does not create eternal objects any more than he creates actual occasions—and for the same reason, namely the principle of creativity. There must be room in every concrescence for the self-creativity of the actual entity, however faint in intensity. (Christian 1959, p. 216)

> we are tempted to think of the occasion as selecting or picking out the datum of its initial aim from among the possibilities envisaged by God. The determination would be made by the novel concrescence itself. But this cannot be the case. . . . it would not make sense, on Whitehead's principles, to say that the concrescence has any *real* alternatives to the possibility which becomes the datum of its initial aim. (Christian 1959, p. 307)

> The initial aim is vague in the sense that the relations of its data to other possibilities and to the physical data are not completely determinate. . . . The concrescence aims at "that sort of thing." (Christian 1959, p. 315)

9. See discussion in chapter 2, pp. 32–33. Christian's difficulty with the transition from past to future in perished occasions is closely related to his view of an occasion's initial aim.

10. The cosmological elements of God's functions approach determinism very closely and have frequently been misunderstood as abolishing individual freedom.

> The most disquietive thing about Whitehead's theology . . . is neither more nor less than the abnegation of human freedom. There is much *talk* of freedom—of waves of creation bearing unpredictability on their crests—but it turns out that this creative advance is not a human adventure. It is God's adventure. (Jordan, 1968, p. 173)

The principle of perspective is completely neglected by such interpretations.

11. This is a difficult topic in connection with *Process and Reality*, for Whitehead neither asserts nor denies that eternal objects have reality or essences apart from God's primordial ordering among them. The very vagueness of Whitehead's view on this matter is the subject in question.

12. I must confess that there is nothing in my argument to support the view that God is continually conscious. I think it far more plausible that God cannot succeed in integrating the relevant contrasts until his experience is complete, thereby either attaining consciousness only in the end (which will never come), or equivalently, never raising the relevant integration to consciousness.

13. It follows that God is not necessary to immortality, only to everlastingness. Yet many commentators overemphasize God's contribution to immortality, thereby in my opinion, inflating the importance of God in Whitehead's system. "We are already immortal ... *every* occasion in the life of *every* temporal creature has this immortality in God and then in the temporal world" (Lowe 1966, p. 106). Such inflation is based on religious more than philosophical considerations.

"To God only belongs immortality.": this New Testament phrase may be taken to describe Whitehead's position.... But this means that a *kind* of immortality is bestowed on all that is thus received into God. Whitehead calls this "objective immortality." He would appear to have been ambiguous about what we might style "the individual's survival of the death of the body." Professor Hartshorne, Whitehead's distinguished contemporary expositor, rejects survival of persons after death. Yet there is nothing *in the system* to make belief in this incredible as an "act of faith." (Pittenger 1969, pp. 37–38)

Immortality of the person—of social togetherness—is a further arbitrary condition imposed on Whitehead's metaphysical system, a condition even God could not perform without a more particular immanence in human personal affairs than metaphysical principles allow. The principle of perspective, with its emphasis on conditions and limitations, suggests that personal immortality can be sustained only on the basis of a *personal* God—a stronger condition than Whitehead affords. In addition, however, the principle of relativity is cosmological in its totality and arbitrariness, with or without God.

14. Limitation is essential to perspective and, by the principle of perspective, a determinate condition of being. It would appear as such to carry no value in itself. Yet the awareness of limitation is frequently made the foundation of the religious intuition, leading directly to God's absolute perfection.

Whitehead's is a much more radical eschatology than is to be found in any contemporary existentialist system. Whitehead's concept of man is imbued with greater poignancy and tragedy. The crucial fact is not that, soon or late, death will put an end to an individual's achievements; it is rather that no present achievement is fully open to conscious enjoyment.... an actual entity is closed to the conscious experience of its own satisfaction. (Hall 1973, p. 107)

15. See also Wilcox's argument that such immanence is incompatible with the theory of relativity.

Can a temporal theist accept relativity physics? ... The result of which seems to be that God could prehend nothing until he prehended everything. God would have to take the world process all in at a gulp.... This implies, in turn, the falsity of

Whitehead's claim that "the perfected actuality passes back into the temporal world, and qualifies the world," because the world must be totally complete before there can be any perfected actuality in God. (Wilcox 1961, p. 298)

The solution is to let God prehend a given occasion only along with all its contemporaries, not with members of its duration alone. This makes the concept of a unison of becoming a bit difficult, from God's point of view. The fundamental problem, however, is the immanence of God. In this connection, see Paul Fitzgerald (1972, pp. 251–6), though he does not deal with the question of immanence.

16. I should not overlook the difficulty of the reconciliation of the two natures of God—a reconciliation that could easily be accomplished by emphasizing the principle of perspective, but only by sacrificing the cosmological functions and totality of God's vision.

The objection to Whitehead's formulation, then, is that too often he deals with the two natures as if they were genuinely separable. Further, he frequently writes as though God were simply the addition of these natures. (Cobb 1965, p. 178)

CHAPTER TEN
SUMMARY AND EVALUATION

I have discussed a number of important aspects of Whitehead's theory as developed in *Process and Reality* from the standpoint of the principle of perspective. This principle—that to be is to be in perspective—is, I have argued, central to Whitehead's thought and a major factor in his permanent contribution to metaphysics. I have also criticized his theory in a number of ways, but primarily to the extent that the principle of perspective is incompatible with the principle of experience—that actuality is experience, and the cosmological principle—that the universe is unified and complete. Given the number and diversity of criticisms, it would be reasonable to assume that my general view is antithetic to Whitehead's, and that I am generally unsympathetic to his achievements.

Such a conclusion would be a severe misunderstanding of my position. To the contrary, I have explored Whitehead's theory in detail to indicate what I take to be its major and enduring contribution, an achievement which I believe further metaphysical understanding must accept and build upon. This contribution, I have suggested, is embodied primarily in the principle of perspective. It follows that this principle must be brought to prominence in relation to the other, equally general principles definitive of Whitehead's theory. I will sketch two ways in which such prominence can be achieved. The first makes as few modifications of Whitehead's theory as are consonant with the general enterprise of preserving God and the extensive continuum largely as Whitehead defines them, and closely in accord with his religious intuitions. The second is a far more sweeping "objective perspectivism" in which perspectivity is made the foundation of the theory, affecting how we regard all relations, constituents, qualifications, and the universe as a whole. Even here, however, I will keep the general outlines of Whitehead's theory.[1]

Before developing these sketches, however, it may be valuable to recapitulate the major criticisms developed up to this point, largely in the order in which they have been presented (neglecting repetitions), to evaluate which of them can be met with minor changes in Whitehead's theory and which require significant reformulations.

1. Whitehead's discussion of perception, especially in the context of epistemological issues, often confuses *perception* and *prehension*. Part of this confusion reflects an inadequate and misguided attempt to conjoin metaphysical with epistemological issues—prehension as relation with perception as testimony. Complicating this issue is Whitehead's mechanical principle of analysis which leads him to *pure* modes of perception, even in human experience. The confusion here is based on too crude an application of the principles of experience and analysis, but can be avoided by emphasizing the differences between low-level prehensions and higher-level perceptions. This difficulty exhibits important tendencies in Whitehead's thought, but it can be resolved without fundamental changes.

2. Self-causation is ultimately arbitrary and unintelligible. This is a major limitation of Whitehead's theory, especially conjoined with his division of actual entities into stages, as if self-causation might be localizable in a particular stage. Actual entities are indivisible in their uniqueness of perspective, and this uniqueness is inseparable from their prehensions. I have suggested that the principle of perspective contains within it a wider and more thorough ground of novelty and uniqueness, emphasizing the full complementarity of determinateness and indeterminateness. When this complementarity is complete, however, the principle of experience is no longer necessary or plausible.

3. By the pervasiveness of the principle of experience, occasions in the lowest-level grade of inorganic occasions prehend and feel with subjective forms. The principle of experience postulates a *private* dimension of becoming in events whose privacy has no criterion. The principle of perspective can carry the weight of uniqueness and constitutive relation without requiring subjective forms in every molecule, rock, and stone. Prehension is a perspectival notion more than it is a subjectivistic notion. This universal subjectivity is an important implausibility in Whitehead's theory, but requires primarily a sharper distinction between lower-level prehension—perspectivity, and higher-level feeling —experience.

4. Occasions both are and are not divisible into stages and prehensions. The difficulty is a consequence of Whitehead's mechanical view of analysis, but it is also a product of the weakness of experience and subjec-

tivity as unifying grounds. The solution is to let entities be perspectives, divisible in some respects and indivisible in others, while divisibility and indivisibility are complementarily interrelated and correspond to relatedness and identity.

5. Propositions have a double function, as real possibilities and as components of judgment. These two functions are in some ways incompatible and Whitehead does not satisfactorily reconcile them. The difficulty is complicated by the cosmological principle and the principle of objective immortality, which make a proposition, once relevant, forever relevant. The solution is to separate real possibilities, which become and may perish from the standpoint of certain actual entities, from propositions as expressions of facts, which remain attached to these facts and their constituents, and which are relevant in precisely the same terms in which the facts are relevant. In my view, facts are perspectival, relative to judgment. Nevertheless, both of these types of propositions express a type of relevance that is not a direct function of prehension. Perspectivity, here, is clearly wider than experience.

6. Some kinds of judgment are incorrigible, in Whitehead's theory, being derived directly from rudimentary forms of prehension. This is closely related to the difficulty in criticism 1 above, and can be resolved by emphasizing the indivisibility of human experience, thereby emphasizing both symbolic reference and reversion in human judgment. Whitehead's metaphysical realism does not and should not entail epistemological realism or any type of incorrigibility. Perspectivity of judgment makes incorrigibility meaningless.

7. By the cosmological principle, Whitehead conceives of the universe as unified, a totality. There is a cosmic order grounded in the principle of relativity, the extensive continuum, and God. This is a major element in Whitehead's theory, but it is incompatible with the pluralism of the principle of perspective.

8. The reality and generality of extensive relations that underlie all occasions, past, present, and future, is implausible, possibly altogether beyond confirmation. I have argued that the extensive continuum is a fusion of extensive possibilities in the primordial nature of God with conditions relevant to any and all actual worlds. The latter relation is necessary to avoid incompatibility between the abstractness of the extensive continuum and the requirement of the ontological principle that every mode of being be relevant to some experience. The question is whether any particular relations—extensive relations in particular—may be relevant to *all* occasions, through *all* cosmic epochs. The greatest generality we seem to be able to achieve at this level of analysis

would appear to be throughout a cosmic epoch. The totality of extensive relations Whitehead demands is cosmological, not perspectival.

9. The primordial nature of God is unqualified. The consequent nature of God is unrestricted, though qualified. Both are incompatible with the principle of perspective in its stronger forms. Eternal objects must be qualified by their ingressions; all prehensions of actualities must be selective and exclusive.

10. Whitehead's theory of a unison of becoming can be made compatible with the theory of relativity, but is not consonant with its rejection of absolute simultaneity. However, the unison of becoming is required by Whitehead's atomism and the self-causation of actual entities. The solution is to make perspective inclusive of more than indivisible atoms and to make divisibility itself perspectival.

11. Actual entities are the ultimate and final realities, although eternal objects and the extensive continuum are equally necessary to the system. Ontological priority is arbitrary and indefensible. It is a consequence of the cosmological principle, and forces us to reject that principle.

Of the above difficulties, 1, 4, 5, and 6 are minor difficulties that can be resolved without major changes in Whitehead's theory, though not without weakening the force of the principle of experience and emphasizing perspectivity in lower-level occasions. Difficulties 2, 3, 8, and 10 are more fundamental, a consequence of the atomistic prehensiveness central to Whitehead's theory. Here, a more general theory of perspective leads to fairly significant modifications of his theory. Difficulties 7, 9, and 11 are a direct consequence of the cosmological principle; they can be met only by abandoning that principle, along with the unity of the world, in favor of the principle of perspective.

It would be appropriate at this point to sketch the consequences of emphasizing the principle of perspective at the expense of both the cosmological principle and the principle of experience. I will offer two such sketches, one with the fewest possible changes in Whitehead's theory, to preserve congruence with his own work as well as the theological and religious convictions that his present-day followers seem to hold. The second is more radical, for it manifests the principle of perspective without structural concessions to Whitehead's theory. In both cases, however, the debt to Whitehead is immense. I am not so much replacing his theory by a different one as sketching the range of certain concepts and principles in his system that I believe to be essential to any significant metaphysical theory.

A Modest Perspectivism. By the principle of perspective, we must abandon the ontological principle, the purity of eternal objects, and the totality inherent in the extensive continuum, the principle of relativity, and the primordial and consequent natures of God. We may postulate that actual occasions are atomic perspectives, in this case, to retain congruence with Whitehead's theory. Occasions are therefore constituted by their relations to other occasions—typically in the past—and also by their relations to eternal objects, to God, and to every other kind of entity. The principle of relativity here is that every being is potential for *some* becoming, emphasizing process, but qualifying totality according to the principle of perspective. Conversely, every being is a relational composite constituted by other beings. Every being is in perspective; every being is a perspective. Both of these relationships are required by the principle of perspective. The two together express the principle of perspective and include its selectivity, exclusiveness, and qualification. The two together are needed to express the two poles of perspective: relation and identity.[2] These are complementary and inseparable, jointly constitutive of perspectival being. To be, here, is to be *in* perspective, from some point of view, and to be *a* perspective, definitive of a point of view. In fact, perspectivity entails inexhaustible points of view.

An actual occasion, here, is constituted by its perspectival relations, from its point of view, to some occasions of the past. The principle of experience can be relaxed so that the perspectivity of relation is sufficient for prehension, without other features of subjectivity. Every occasion is divisible by its constituents—as every perspective is divisible by relations. But the divisibility is itself perspectival, from a point of view, and does not eliminate or replace the unity of a perspective, from its point of view. It is also divisible into its forms of determinateness, universals qualifying it. But these are neither eternal nor unconditioned; they are themselves constituted by ingressions into occasions. In relation to the past, then, an occasion is a selective perspective on past occasions, constituted by them, but a point of view on them, therefore transcending any causal givenness. As a consequence, objective immortality (where it obtains) is not a necessary condition of causation, but a property of at best some occasions and a function of the future as well as the past. Actual entities are units of perspective in having an identity. They are divisible but also indivisible, in different respects, complementarily related.

Actual entities are divisible extensively, if there is a spatiotemporal extensive continuum. Yet spatial divisibility of an occasion of becoming does not exhaust its becoming, for this is a qualified divisibility, relative only to space. Spatial whole-part relations are only a species of a far wider genus of constitutive relations—including prehensions for example. Temporal divisibility is even clearer: relative to discriminated successive moments, an act of becoming can be divided—but both its point of view and its constituents, other than those locatable temporally, are irrelevant to such division. By the principle of perspective, divisibility is always qualified, not absolute, and manifests only some of the constituents of a perspective. Thus, an occasion would be *in time* relative to temporally locatable constituents and *out of time* relative to nontemporally locatable constituents—aims and forms, for example. An aim is located where it is realized but also, quite differently, where it functions as a lure. Some formal determinants of an extended object qualify it grossly, but not by division.

The social-environmental paradigm of perspective is fundamental. An occasion is an intersection of an inexhaustible multiplicity of overlapping societies and environments. Each society is itself a perspective, comprised of occasions but also contributing to their character. Each society, however, inhabits an indefinite number and variety of environments, each of which contributes some determination to it, and, by the principle of perspective, there is no total or all-inclusive environment. It follows that the multiplicity of factors contributing to an occasion—from the past, forms of definiteness, and social environments—aggregates to no sum *outside* the occasion that may determine its nature, but uniquely contributes to it because it is the unique perspective it is. Everything is determined to the extent and in the ways it is determined: but determination is always complemented by indetermination—the unique point of view of the individual perspective as it is constituted. Every occasion transcends its modes of determination, not by arbitrary self-causation, but by the inexhaustibility of determining conditions.

Eternal objects—or formal determinants—are neither pure nor eternal. Rather, they are perspectival, for they have both individual and relational essences. The relational essence is a function both of other formal determinants and of ingressions into occasions. Such determinants as intelligence, rationality, beauty, and even straightness change with changing conditions. They are *open-ended*, a function of social orders. Individual formal determinants are comprised of their relations to other forms and to actual occasions, involving both relation and exclusion, changing with changing conditions at least in some respects. And there is no complete and totalistic system of formal determinants, for new determinants emerge with changing conditions. These can always be traced back to, analyzed in terms of, other formal determinants and past occasions. But such analysis is valid only from a particular point of view, in certain respects. Every perspective—including each formal determinant in both its individual and relational essence—is analyzable and relational, but also unique and singular. The distinction between formal determinants and propositions is eliminated: all possibilities are real possibilities, qualified by different subjects.

The extensive continuum, here, cannot be a ground for all occasions, for there is no total ground, extensive or otherwise. Extension, then is a general condition for the togetherness of certain becomings—valid only where they are together, from some point of view. There may be no spatial or temporal continuum locating events of the remote past (more than thirty billion years ago) in relation to contemporary events. There may be no spatial continuum locating remote events in distant galaxies in relation to events on the planet earth, even if the two galaxies are in spatial relations. Here, extension is an essential condition for contemporary and future togetherness in becoming, derived from the social conditions of togetherness of past occasions, but it is neither all-inclusive nor independent of events and their particular social relations.[3]

A human being, along with other higher organisms, is a society or complex of nexūs and societies. But societies are themselves perspectives and are not less real than occasions. The analysis of a person into occasions is not the ultimate analysis but only one among other modes of analysis that are relevant to complex organisms. At this point the principle of perspective permits us to escape from the unfortunate consequences of Whitehead's derivative theory of social order, where human beings are less ultimate and final than their constituents in an apparently unqualified and absolute sense. Human consciousness, morality, and responsibility require that human beings be full and individual perspectives even if they are also divisible into successive occasions, under one mode of analysis, and into their environmental determinants, under another.

Human experience is higher experience here. Human perception is analyzable into perspectival relations, to the past and by extension, but it is so remarkable and complex a mode of relation that all forms of purity and incorrigibility are typically irrelevant. Experience is a complex and sophisticated process in which a variety of atomic constituents participate. It is always from a point of view—in fact, inexhaustibly diverse points of view. Experience, here, is no paradigm for prehension, but is rather constituted as a complex perspective by a welter of other perspectives. Perspectivity is the more general notion.

Finally, God is not a comprehensive and all-inclusive perspective or actual entity here. There can be no such entity. There can be no primordial nature to the extent that it is unqualified and all-inclusive. There can be no consequent nature to the extent that it is all-encompassing. God, here, must be entirely *with* emerging occasions, a consequence of their own acts of becoming. It follows that God is not in one sense *necessary* to occasions, for they constitute themselves perspectivally by prehension and relation. No cosmological argument for God can be sustained in a thoroughly perspectival theory. Rather, God is a ideal expression of natural order, a togetherness of occasions in becoming, realized through their becoming.[4] Neither an occasion nor an entity, God is a social and pervasive mode of relatedness, expressive of those conditions emergent in the course of natural events and relevant for the future. But there is no total union of occasions or of forms of determinateness. The latter are modified by ingression and change through time; the former admit only of very general, but still qualified, modes of union. As a consequence, there are either many Gods, each changing through time and manifesting a general meeting of past and future in becoming, or there is a general but amorphous order in the universe that is emergent from the past and ideal for the future, but determinative of events only through occasions. This God is closer to Hegel's than Whitehead's, but without total and absolute inclusiveness.[5] God is simply an ideal comprehensiveness located in particular, actual conditions and a promise for the future—but a multifarious, inexhaustible promise because of the inexhaustibility of individual perspectives. God is *with*, or *consequent upon*, occasions to the extent that both formal and prospective order are conditioned by events. God is *for*, or *immanent* in, occasions only to the extent that the social order he manifests is a condition of occasions necessary to their locations and for the future. But God is derived from occasions in both of these senses, independent in neither his conceptual nor his physical nature.[6] Here we may say that God's body *is* a pervasive society of actual occasions—but not all-pervasive—while his conceptual envisagement *is* the promise of the future resident in those occasions, thereby a promise for his body that may be realized through further becoming. God is inseparable from natural events, but is nevertheless an incomplete manifestation of their order. All perspectives and orders, including God, are selective and qualified, exclusive and restrictive. Metaphysics and religion here offer not so much an affirmation of divine order as its realization through mankind. Human consciousness, in its potentialities as well as its achievements, is divine, here, in its kinship with God realized by science, philosophy, and religion, a kinship that presupposes limits upon the inclusiveness of divinity in natural events. God, here, is the transcendent promise of order for the future, produced by past events and fulfilled by future events, conditioned by our bravest attempts at defining order achievable through directed efforts at fulfillment.

A Thoroughgoing Perspectivism. The second theory I will sketch resembles Whitehead's in a less obvious or superficial way. A complete rejection of the cosmological and ontological principles and the principle of experience means that acts of becoming or drops of experience have no absolute primacy. Whatever is is perspectival: in perspective and possessor of a unique point of view. Properties and qualities are as perspectival as events and activities, comprised of constituents in relation from a unique point of view. The most obvious constitutive relations of a universal trait—for example, the number two—are other traits and principles of relation: other numbers and arithmetic relations. But properties are also functions of their ingressions or instantiations. The number 2 is modified, not only by applications that define the number system applicable to them, but by particular instances, pairs of objects, to the extent that such applications are also perspectival, from the point of view of the relevant property. Pairs manifest the scope or range of the number 2, while the successor relation defines the arithmetic properties of the number 2 in conjunction with the number 1. Part of the nature of a being is given by what it constitutes, what it applies to—pairs and conjunctions in this particular case.

The dissimilarity of such a theory to Whitehead's should not be exaggerated. The principle of perspective is, I have argued, central to Whitehead's theory, and should be considered as a potential for a metaphysical system independent of the principles with which it is in tension in Whitehead's theory. The functionality of Whitehead's understanding of being is exhibited in the double existence of occasions as subjects and superjects, as actual and potential; in the corresponding double existence of eternal objects, as forms of definiteness and as possibilities; in the double function of propositions and prehensions; and in the functional analysis of universals and particulars, so that actual entities are particulars as individuals and universals in recurrent objectifications, and eternal objects are universals in ingression and particulars in their individual essences. All these exhibit a fundamental corollary of the principle of perspective: being is perspectival, conditioned, and functional. What a being *is* is given by what it *does*, how it functions relative to other beings.

Thus, all the modes of existence in Whitehead's theory—especially actual entities, eternal objects, nexūs, and prehensions—are perspectives: constitutive of other beings and constituted by other beings. Even a multiplicity is a perspective, or it would be nothing at all. A mere disjunction is still *a* disjunction. Its identity must be based on some mode of singularity or unitariness. No perspectives are more fundamental than others. There is no all-inclusive or total perspective, for it would then be unconditioned in that respect. There is no unqualified perspective, no perspective simple in all respects and without relation to other perspectives.

The unique characteristics of such metaphysical perspectives manifest the complementarity of unity and multiplicity, determinateness and indeterminateness, that is essential to the concept of perspective. Every perspective is unitary in some respects but plural as well in its ramifications from other perspectives. Every perspective is located and locating. Every perspective is constituted by other beings and constitutes other beings. Every perspective is also typical in certain ways, relative to certain standards or patterns, and atypical, variant, in other ways. Finally, every perspective is actual in certain respects, relative to relevant alternatives, and possible in other respects, where alternatives are relevant. And alternatives are always relevant, in any perspective—at least in certain ways—as a consequence of the diversity of different perspectives, intersecting in inexhaustibly diverse ways, where no total, all-inclusive perspective is established or even intelligible. Every intersection of perspectives engenders alternatives for some of their constituents, alternatives produced by coincidence and openness to other perspectives. There is novelty and uniqueness, indeterminateness and incompleteness, relative to every perspective as a result of its selectivity and restrictions. Every limit, every boundary of a perspective makes it determinate in certain respects but also indeterminate in certain respects, and the converse.[7]

To be, here, is to be qualified and functional: to be *a* perspective and to be *in* perspective are functional, qualified, and perspectival distinctions, not unqualified distinctions of kind. The distinction in Whitehead's theory between occasions and eternal objects, for example, is absolute and unconditioned: one entity can be of one kind only. His perspectivity and functionalism are here limited by his cosmological and ontological principles. But a thoroughgoing perspectivism entails that every mode of being, every qualification, is itself qualified. These qualifications, I repeat, manifest *both* determinateness and indeterminateness. Skepticism, which overemphasizes the latter, is illegitimate. To the contrary, the argument that indeterminateness entails skepticism is always itself determinately conditioned, effectively undermining itself. Whitehead's argument for induction is effectively generalized: to be able to ask questions is to postulate determinations that make certain answers possible—but not in all respects. In any case, the inexhaustibility inherent in perspectivity entails that something is always a function of wider and narrower perspectives in which it is located. These constitute its determinateness but, simultaneously and complementarily, constitute its openness and indeterminateness.

Whitehead's cosmology is, from this wider perspectival point of view, a highly restricted and limited metaphysics. The principle of perspective establishes all modes of being as equally perspectival and conditioned, only some of which are events, located in events (very large numbers are not, for example), or spatiotemporal and extended in a homogeneous continuum (the time of music and the space of certain paintings). The succession of events, here, is not a fundamental element of the universe, in all respects and unqualifiedly, but a particular mode of order, defined by selection and exclusion. Extension here is a condition for succession, involving both space and time, but not a condition for certain numbers and elements of some works of art, except from a particular point of view. The past is relevant only in certain respects to any present, for some events are lost forever, their relevance dissipated into past events. God here is indeed a perspective (or many perspectives) on human and natural events, but all-too-human and of limited relevance. God, here, it seems to me, is less a metaphysical than a local condition, a manifestation of a yearning for comprehensive order that is doomed to failure amidst the inexhaustible multiplicity of perspectives. Nevertheless, even inexhaustibility has another face, an impetus toward inclusion and comprehension that is manifested and attained by human beings in their most rational and spiritual activities, testimony to possibilities of inclusiveness and generality greater than any previously attained.

This thoroughly perspectival theory—I have called it "ordinal," the notion of "order" generically replacing the notion of perspective—may appear too different from Whitehead's to be considered in the context of an examination of his theory. I will pursue it no further. Nevertheless, it manifests what I have argued is the most powerful and effective principle in his theory: the principle of perspective. But that principle is weakened and confused in his theory by the cosmological principle and the principle of experience. The latter principle is a relic of Kant gone astray, a capitulation to the assumption that only mind can constitute a ground of unity and order. The former is an arbitrary assumption that has always led philosophy astray. The cosmological principle is, I believe, the source of the greatest errors in the history of thought, but also of the most sublime and creative works of the human spirit. The ordinal or perspectival theory I have sketched here cannot attain the sublime vision of God that cosmology affords, but it replaces it with far richer possibilities of achievement for the human imagination: to constitute novel modes of order and inclusiveness, not merely to mirror or re-enact them. We honor Whitehead's achievement for its grandeur and imagination, its plausibility and its sublimity, not merely for its accuracy.

Notes to Chapter 10

1. A thoroughly perspectival metaphysical theory can be found in Justus Buchler's *Metaphysics of Natural Complexes* (1966) and in my *Transition to an Ordinal Metaphysics* (1980).

2. See Cobb:

> Just because we humans can transcend ourselves, we can and must recognize the extreme finitude of all our experiences, all our judgments, all our thoughts. Every criterion we establish to evaluate our claims to truth must be recognized as itself involved in the finitude it strives to transcend. From this situation there is no escape. We must learn to live, to think, and to love in the context of this ultimate insecurity of uncertainty. (1965, p. 275)

This limitation, and the consequent element of transcendence, is inherent in all perspectives, not limited to human beings, and inclusive of God. Perspectivity is incompatible with absolutes and demands qualification. Yet only the absolute perfection of God and the world need be sacrificed to the pervasiveness of limitation and point of view.

See here also:

> Whatever the idea of God may mean or fail to mean, it cannot mean a being whose mere existence would be exclusive in any respect. . . . There can be no such thing as the possibility of the ultimate creator; there can only be his necessary reality, prior to all contingent alternatives. (Hartshorne 1961, p. 113)

3. An interesting discussion of Whitehead's system that bears some resemblance to the theory sketched here can be found in Milič Čapek:

> In the dynamic Universe—or rather "multiverse"—in which individual causal lines, partially separated by the gaps of causal independence, are being continuously prolonged in the direction of the future, the concept of the absolutely coherent universe—coherent either in a temporal or spatial dimension—loses its meaning. . . . Reality is neither an undifferentiated and completed whole nor is it a bundle of

externally related entities; it is a polyphonous process, never complete, never entirely one and never entirely many. (Čapek 1964, pp. 99–100)

4. Shahan offers a reformulation of the nature of God somewhat similar to the one developed here, though without complete acknowledgment of the principle of perspective.

> God, in this conception, represents that element in experience which is associated with the striving for an ideal.
> This conception of God as exhibited in Whitehead's thought fits in with all the other process concepts. (Shahan 1950, p. 129)

5. It is also close in certain respects to the positions of Hartshorne and Cobb with respect to God, that God is a society or a living person. (Hartshorne 1972, p. 166; Cobb 1965, pp. 188–92) It is also worth noting Cobb's understanding of the limitations of God's perspective. "There is prima facie support for the doctrine that God, like all actual occasions, has a standpoint. Since that standpoint could not be such as to favor one part of the universe against others, it must be all-inclusive" (1965, p. 195). The argument is invalid but it does express the ideal of inclusiveness that I take to be definitive of the divine order as it functions in human experience.

6. The dependence of God, in both his primordial and his consequent natures, upon actual events is after all not so far from Cobb's view that "if, as I hold, God can function as principle of limitation only by entertaining a specific aim for each becoming occasion, that aim must take account of the actual situation in the world" (Cobb 1965, p. 189).

7. For a complete account of this theory, see my *Transition to an Ordinal Metaphysics* (1980). The technical categories corresponding to the properties of perspectives listed are order-constituent, integrity-scope, prevalence-deviance, and actuality-possibility. For an examination of some of the consequences of this theory for philosophy and rationality, see the final chapter of *Transition* and my *Philosophical Mysteries* (1981).

WORKS CITED

Alston, William. 1951. "Whitehead's denial of simple location." *Journal of Philosophy* 48 (8 November).

———. 1952. "Internal relatedness and pluralism in Whitehead." *Review of Metaphysics* 5 (June).

Ballard, Edward G. 1961. "Kant and Whitehead, and the philosophy of mathematics." *Tulane Studies in Philosophy* 10.

Blyth, John W. 1941. *Whitehead's Theory of Knowledge*. Providence: Brown University Press.

Bradley, F. H. 1946. *Appearance and Reality*. London: Oxford University Press.

Brinkley, Alan B. 1961. "Whitehead on symbolic reference." *Tulane Studies in Philosophy* 10.

Buchler, Justus. 1966. *Metaphysics of Natural Complexes*. New York: Columbia University Press.

———. 1969. "On a strain of arbitrariness in Whitehead's system." *Journal of Philosophy* 66 (2 October).

Čapek, Milič. 1964. "Simple location and fragmentation of reality." In *Process and Divinity: The Hartshorne Festschrift*, ed. W. L. Reese and E. Freeman. LaSalle: Open Court.

Chappell, Vere C. 1963. "Organic categories in Whitehead." In *Alfred North Whitehead: Essays on His Philosophy*, ed. George Kline. Englewood Cliffs, N. J.: Prentice-Hall.

Christian, William A. 1959. *An Interpretation of Whitehead's Metaphysics*. New Haven: Yale University Press.

———. 1963. "Whitehead's explanation of the past." In *Alfred North Whitehead: Essays on His Philosophy*, ed. George Kline. Englewood Cliffs, N. J.: Prentice-Hall.

Cobb, John B., Jr. 1965. *A Christian Natural Theology*. Philadelphia: Westminster Press.

———. 1971. "The 'Whitehead without God' debate: The critique." *Process Studies* 1 (summer).

Cobb, John B., Jr. and Donald W. Sherburne. 1972. "Regional inclusion and the extensive continuum." *Process Studies* 2 (winter).

Dewey, John. 1929. *Experience and Nature*. 2nd ed. LaSalle: Open Court.

———. 1937. "Whitehead's philosophy." *Philosophical Review* 46.

Edwards, Rem B. 1975. "The human self: An actual entity or a society? *Process Studies* 5 (fall).

Emmet, Dorothy. 1966. *Whitehead's Philosophy of Organism*. 2nd ed. New York: St. Martin's Press.

Fancher, Robert. 1971. "Of time, the self, and Rem Edwards." *Process Studies* 7 (spring).

Fitzgerald, Paul. 1972. "Relativity physics and the god of process philosophy." *Process Studies* 2 (winter).

Ford, Lewis S. 1971. "Genetic and coordinate division correlated." *Process Studies* 1.

Gentry, George. 1944. "The subject in Whitehead's philosophy." *Philosophy of Science* 11.

———. 1946. "Eternal objects and the philosophy of organism." *Philosophy of Science* 13.

Grünbaum, Adolf. 1963. *Philosophical Problems of Space and Time*. New York: Knopf.

———. 1953. "Whitehead's method of extensive abstraction." *British Journal for the Philosophy of Science* 4 (November).

———. 1962. "Whitehead's philosophy of science." *Philosophical Review* 71.

Gutting, Gary. 1971. "Metaphysics and induction." *Process Studies* 1 (fall).

Hall, David L. 1973. *The Civilization of Experience. A Whiteheadian Theory of Culture*. New York: Fordham University Press.

Hall, Everett W. 1963. "Of what use are Whitehead's eternal objects?" In *Alfred North Whitehead: Essays on His Philosophy*, ed. George Kline. Englewood Cliffs, N. J.: Prentice-Hall.

Hartshorne, Charles. 1972. *Whitehead's Philosophy*. Lincoln: University of Nebraska Press.

———. 1961. "Metaphysics and the modality of existential judgments." In *The Relevance of Whitehead*, ed. Ivor Leclerc. London: George Allen and Unwin.

Henry, Granville C., Jr., 1973. "Nonstandard mathematics and a doctrine of god." *Process Studies* 3 (spring).

James, Robison B. 1972. "Is Whitehead's 'actual entity' a contradiction in terms?" *Process Studies* 2 (summer).

James, William. 1912. *Essays in Radical Empiricism*. New York: Longmans, Green.

Johnson, Charles Michael. 1976. "On prehending the past." *Process Studies* 6 (winter).

Jordan, Martin. 1968. *New Shapes of Reality*. London: George Allen and Unwin.

Kirkpatrick, Frank G. 1973. "Subjective becoming: An unwarranted abstraction?" *Process Studies* 3 (spring).

Kraus, Elizabeth M. 1979. *The Metaphysics of Experience*. New York: Fordham University Press.

Lango, John W. 1972. *Whitehead's Ontology*. Albany: State University of New York Press.

Lawrence, Nathaniel. 1956. *Whitehead's Philosophical Development*. Berkeley: University of California Press.

―――. 1954. "Single location, simple location, and misplaced concreteness." *Review of Metaphysics* 7.

―――. 1961. "Time, value, and the self." In *The Relevance of Whitehead*, ed. Ivor Leclerc. London: George Allen and Unwin.

Leclerc, Ivor. 1958. *Whitehead's Metaphysics*. Bloomington: Indiana University Press.

―――. 1961. "Form and actuality." In *The Relevance of Whitehead*, ed. Ivor Leclerc. London: George Allen and Unwin.

―――. 1963. "Whitehead and the problem of extension." In *Alfred North Whitehead: Essays on His Philosophy*, ed. George Kline. Englewood Cliffs, N. J.: Prentice-Hall.

―――. 1964. "Whitehead and the theory of form." In *Process and Divinity: The Hartshorne Festschrift*, ed. W. L. Reese and E. Freeman. LaSalle: Open Court.

―――. 1971. "A rejoinder to Justus Buchler." *Process Studies* 1 (spring).

Lee, Harold N. 1961. "Causal efficacy and continuity in Whitehead's philosophy." *Tulane Studies in Philosophy* 10.

Levi, Albert William. 1964. "Bergson or Whitehead?" In *Process and Divinity: The Hartshorne Festschrift*, ed. W. L. Reese and E. Freeman. LaSalle: Open Court.

Lovejoy, Arthur A. 1930. *The Revolt against Dualism*. New York: Norton.

Lowe, Victor. 1966. *Understanding Whitehead*. Baltimore: Johns Hopkins University Press.

Lowe, Victor. 1961. "The approach to metaphysics." In *The Relevance of Whitehead*, ed. Ivor Leclerc. London: George Allen and Unwin.

Lowry, Ann P. 1971. "Whitehead on the nature of mathematical truth." *Process Studies* 1 (summer).

Mays, Wolf. 1959. *The Philosophy of Whitehead*. London: George Allen and Unwin.

―――. 1977. *Whitehead's Philosophy of Science and Metaphysics*. The Hague: Martinus Nijhoff.

McGilvary, Evander Bradley, 1959. *Toward a Perspective Realism*. LaSalle: Open Court.

Mead, George Herbert. 1959. "The objective reality of perspectives." In *The Philosophy of the Present*, ed. Arthur A. Murphy. LaSalle: Open Court.

Miller, David L. 1936. "Purpose, design, and physical relativity." *Philosophy of Science* 3.

―――. 1946. "Whitehead's extensive continuum." *Philosophy of Science* 13.

Murphy, Arthur A. 1927a. "Objective relativism in Dewey and Whitehead." *Philosophical Review* 36.

―――. 1927b. "The anti-Copernican revolution." *Journal of Philosophy* 26 (23 May).

————. 1928. "What is an event?" *Philosophical Review* 37.

Neville, Robert C. 1980. *Creativity and God.* New York: Seabury.

Nobo, Jorge Luis. 1974. "Whitehead's principle of process." *Process Studies* 4 (winter).

Norman, Ralph V., Jr. 1963. "Whitehead and 'mathematicism.'" In *Alfred North Whitehead: Essays on His Philosophy,* ed. George Kline. Englewood Cliffs, N. J.: Prentice-Hall.

Northrop, Filmer S. C. 1951. "Whitehead's philosophy of science," In *The Philosophy of Alfred North Whitehead,* ed. Paul A. Schilpp. New York: Tudor.

O'Keefe, Thomas A. 1951. "Empiricism and applied mathematics in the natural philosophy of Whitehead." *Modern Schoolman* 28 (May).

Palter, Robert M. 1960. *Whitehead's Philosophy of Science.* Chicago: University of Chicago Press.

————. 1963. "The place of mathematics in Whitehead's philosophy." In *Alfred North Whitehead: Essays on His Philosophy,* ed. George Kline. Englewood Cliffs, N. J.: Prentice-Hall.

Palter, Robert M. 1964. "Science and its history in the philosophy of Whitehead." In *Process and Divinity: The Hartshorne Festschrift,* ed. W. L. Reese and E. Freeman, LaSalle: Open Court.

Pittenger, Norman. 1969. *Alfred North Whitehead.* Richmond: John Knox.

Plamondon, Ann L. 1979. *Whitehead's Organic Philosophy of Science.* Albany: State University of New York Press.

————. 1973. "Metaphysics and 'valid induction.'" *Process Studies* 3 (summer).

Pols, Edward. 1967. *Whitehead's Metaphysics: A Critical Examination of Process and Reality.* Carbondale and Edwardsville: Southern Illinois University Press.

Reck, Andrew J. 1958. "Substance, process, and nature." *Journal of Philosophy* 55.

Reese, W. L. and E. Freeman, eds. 1964. *Process and Divinity: The Hartshorne Festschrift.* LaSalle: Open Court.

Ross, Stephen David. 1980. *Transition to an Ordinal Metaphysics.* Albany: State University of New York Press.

————. 1981. *Philosophical Mysteries.* Albany: State University of New York Press.

————. 1973. "The inexhaustibility of nature." *Journal of Value Inquiry* 7 (winter).

Rotenstreich, Nathan. 1952. "On Whitehead's theory of propositions." *Review of Metaphysics* 5 (March).

Schmidt, Paul F. 1967. *Perception and Cosmology in Whitehead's Philosophy.* New Brunswick: Rutgers University Press.

Seaman, Francis. 1955. "Whitehead and relativity." *Philosophy of Science* 22 (July).

Shahan, Ewing P. 1950. *Whitehead's Theory of Experience.* New York: King's Crown Press.

Sherburne, Donald W. 1961. *A Whiteheadian Aesthetic*. New Haven: Yale University Press.

———. 1971a. "Whitehead without God." In *Process Philosophy and Christian Faith*, ed. D. Brown, R. James, and G. Reeves. Indianapolis: Bobbs-Merrill.

———. 1971b. "The 'Whitehead without God' debate: A rejoinder." *Process Studies* 1 (summer).

Thompson, Kenneth F., Jr. 1971. *Whitehead's Philosophy of Religion*. The Hague: Mouton.

Urban, Wilbur M. 1938. "Elements of unintelligibility in Whitehead's metaphysics." *Journal of Philosophy* 35 (10 November).

Vlastos, Gregory. 1963. "Organic categories in Whitehead." In *Alfred North Whitehead: Essays on His Philosophy*, ed. George Kline. Englewood Cliffs, N. J.: Prentice-Hall.

Wallack, F. Bradford. 1980. *The Epochal Nature of Process in Whitehead's Metaphysics*. Albany: State University of New York Press.

Wells, Harry K. 1950. *Process and Unreality*. New York: King's Crown Press.

Whitehead, Alfred North. 1922. *Principle of Relativity*. Cambridge: Cambridge University Press.

———. 1925. *Science and the Modern World*. New York: Macmillan.

———. 1955. *Adventures of Ideas*. New York: Mentor.

———. 1958. *Modes of Thought*. New York: Capricorn.

———. 1964. *The Concept of Nature*. Cambridge: Cambridge University Press.

———. 1978. *Process and Reality*, ed. D. R. Griffin and D. W. Sherburne. Corrected ed. New York: Free Press.

———. 1937. "Remarks." *Philosophical Review* 46.

———. 1951a. "Immortality." In *The Philosophy of Alfred North Whitehead*, ed. Paul A. Schilpp. New York: Tudor.

———. 1951b. "Mathematics and the good." In *The Philosophy of Alfred North Whitehead*, ed. Paul A.Schilpp. New York: Tudor.

———. 1963. "Whitehead to Hartshorne 2 January 1936." In *Alfred North Whitehead: Essays on His Philosophy*, ed. George Kline. Englewood Cliffs, N. J.: Prentice-Hall.

Whittemore, Robert C. 1961. "The metaphysics of Whitehead's feelings." *Tulane Studies in Philosophy* 10.

Wilcox, John T. 1961. "A question from physics for certain theists." *Journal of Religion* 41 (October).

Williams, Daniel Day. 1964. "How does God act?: An essay in Whitehead's metaphysics." In *Process and Divinity: The Hartshorne Festschrift*, ed. W. L. Reese and E. Freeman. LaSalle: Open Court.

Wittgenstein, Ludwig. 1958. *Philosophical Investigations*. Oxford: Blackwell.

INDEX

DATE DUE